Time, Temporality and Legal Judgment

This book challenges the correspondence theory of judicial fact construction – that legal rules resemble and subsume facts 'out there' – and instead provides an account of judicial fact construction through legally produced times- or adjudicative temporalities- that structure legal subject and event formation in legal judgement.

Drawing on Bergsonian and Gadamerian theories of time, this book details how certain adjudicative temporalities can produce fully willed and autonomous subjects through 'time framed' legal events – in effect, the paradigmatic liberal legal subject – or how alternative adjudicative temporalities may structure legal subjects that are situated and constituted by social structures. The consequences of this novel account of legal judgement are fourfold. The first is that judicial fact construction is not exclusively determined by the legal rule(s) but by adjudication's production of temporalities. The second is that the selection between different adjudicative temporalities is generally indeterminate, though influenced by wider social structures. As will be argued, social structures, framed as a particular type of past produced by certain adjudicative temporalities, may either be incorporated in the rendering of the legal event or elided. The third is that, with the book's focus on criminal law, different deployments of adjudicative temporalities effect responsibility ascription. Finally, it is argued that the demystification of time as that which structures event and subject formation reveals another way in which to uncover the politics of legal judgement and the potential for its transformative potential, through either its inclusion or its elision of social structures in adjudication's determination of facts.

This book will be of interest to students and scholars in the field of legal judgement, legal theory and jurisprudence.

Tanzil Chowdhury is a Lecturer (Assistant Professor) in Public Law and Co-Director of the Centre for Law and Society in a Global Context at Queen Mary, University of London.

Time, Temporality and Legal Judgment

Tanzil Chowdhury

Routledge
Taylor & Francis Group
a GlassHouse Book

First published 2020
by Routledge
2 Park Square, Milton Park, Abingdon, Oxon OX14 4RN

and by Routledge
52 Vanderbilt Avenue, New York, NY 10017

Routledge is an imprint of the Taylor & Francis Group, an informa business

British Library Cataloguing-in-Publication Data
A catalogue record for this book is available from the British Library

Library of Congress Cataloging-in-Publication Data
A catalog record has been requested for this book

ISBN: 978-1-138-32450-3 (hbk)
ISBN: 978-0-367-51789-2 (pbk)
ISBN: 978-0-429-45083-9 (ebk)

Typeset in Times New Roman
by codeMantra

As with everything, this is for amar Amma ar Abba.

Contents

Acknowledgements

This book has been some years in the making as it was met with fierce resistance in its writing, almost exclusively from myself. It was my intention to write my first monograph on something entirely different, but friends and colleagues of mine had other ideas, for which I am grateful. I would like, therefore, to thank all those that encouraged me to write this book. That includes the Hakeem Yusuf, Jamie Woodcock, and a whole host of others that I can only apologise to for not remembering and mentioning by name.

I'd also like to thank friends for their comments, including Kojo Koram, Kathryn McNeilly, Renisa Mawani, Isobel Roele, Emily Grabham, Kate Malleson and Lizzie Barmes for working through drafts of each chapter. I'd also like to extend my gratitude to my School of Law at Queen Mary, University of London, including both my academic and professional support staff colleagues. Thanks to the Faculty of Law at Hong Kong University (HKU) for allowing me to visit as a researcher, where I wrote substantial parts of the book (despite the incredible events that were taking place there at the time). I'd also like to thank Kay Lalor for the conversations we had with one another, way back when I was a doctoral candidate. I would also like to thank the publishers and the editors at Routledge for their support and diligence with the drafts, in particular Colin, Nicola, the two reviewers of my proposal, the commissioning committee and the copy editors, including Assunta.

Thanks also to God and to my family and extended family (especially my dear friends, who have been so supportive and the important whatsapp ecologies they have produced – 'Badminton Bolsheviks', 'Alle Einsteigen', 'The Fire Now', 'O La Cubano', 'Rosa May Fan Club' and many more. Special thanks to Kamran, Nabeela and Isaac for keeping me company during my visiting post at HKU; and also Tom Cowan (who promised to mention me in the acknowledgements of his book if I did the same- but also for spending many hours in the library with me while I worked on this monograph). I'd also like to thank the inspirational people in the book that I write about, particularly in Chapter 5. Kiranjit's case was one that caught my attention in the second year of my undergraduate degree at law school and one that has stayed with me ever since.

Finally, to those who dedicate their life to struggle, often at great expense to themselves. They are worthy of our unconditional respect and admiration, and I continue to be humbled by their work.

Preface

The reasons a group of activists were acquitted of causing up to £180,000 of damage in an arms factory in 2011 is a question of how courts produce 'pasts and futures' or *adjudicative temporalities* in their determination of facts. This book challenges the correspondence theory of judicial fact construction – that legal rules resemble and subsume facts 'out there' – and instead provides an account of fact construction through legally produced times or *adjudicative temporalities* that structure legal subject and event formation in legal judgement. Drawing on Bergsonian and Gadamerian theories of time, this book details how certain adjudicative temporalities can produce fully willed and autonomous subjects through 'time framed' legal events – in effect, the paradigmatic liberal legal subject – or how alternative adjudicative temporalities may structure legal subjects that are situated and constituted by social structures. The consequences of this novel account of legal judgement are fourfold. The first is to argue that judicial fact construction is not exclusively determined by legal rules but by 'adjudicative temporalities'. The second is that the selection between different adjudicative temporalities is generally indeterminate, though influenced by wider social structures. As will be argued, social structures, framed as a particular type of past produced by certain adjudicative temporalities, may either be incorporated in the rendering of the legal event or elided. The third is that, with the book's focus on criminal law, different deployments of adjudicative temporalities effect responsibility ascription. Finally, it is argued that through the demystification of time as that which structures event and subject formation, the book reveals another way in which to uncover the politics of legal judgement and the potential for its transformative potential, through either its inclusion or its elision of social structures in adjudication's determination of facts.

Introduction

> We can only understand the present by continually referring to and studying the past: when any one of the intricate phenomena of our daily life puzzles us; when there arise religious problems, political problems, race problems, we must always remember that while their solution lies here in the present, their cause and their explanation lie in the past.[1]
>
> The imprint of history marks all of our days. We know it and yet we carry on, willing ourselves out of the dead weight of those who went before...Is it possible to escape the horrors of the history that spit us out into social relations dripping with pre-determination of events that have already happened?...Or is the ugliness of today its own special creation?[2]

This book begins with the story of a South Asian woman, Kiranjit Ahluwalia, a former law student from Chak Kalal, a small village located in the Punjab State of India. She moved to the UK in 1979, amidst Conservative Party rule and Thatcher's acceleration of the 'neoliberal revolution', dismantling a society she claimed did not exist.[3] Ahluwalia, arriving in a country still routed in postcolonial melancholia, gained public attention through a protracted legal and political struggle against her violently abusive husband whom she had killed. Her case was well known both within and without legal circles, prompting substantial media interest; a film[4]; and the support of the Southall Black Sisters (SBS),[5] a South Asian women's anti-fascist collective who provided support throughout her litigation. Her case both provokes and illustrates the argument of this monograph.

The case of *R v. Ahluwalia*[6] is familiar to many in presaging the reception of Battered Woman Syndrome[7] as a then new ground for diminished responsibility in charges of homicide. After initially being convicted of murder, momentum behind the case garnered widespread support with the help of the SBS who, sharing Ahluwalia's rage that there had been a huge miscarriage of justice, supported her campaign to appeal the decision. Looking at the facts of the trial hearing, one abstraction of what happened presented a non-descript woman pouring petrol onto her sleeping husband

and setting him alight, causing injuries from which he later died. The judge in the appeal, however, Lord Taylor CJ, opted for an alternative summation of the facts, describing Ahluwalia as a victim of sustained domestic violence and, through this, implied that her history compromised her volition. In this rendering of the legal event and the legal subject, the latter as a situated person rather than an abstracted individual, the ascription of responsibility was reconfigured. In the trial court, the fragmentation and elision of Ahluwalia's experience of sustained, domestic violence, and the bounded focus on the killing of her husband, produced a legal subject as agential, responsible and guilty of murder. In the appeal, inclusion of a history, or what I call a particular *type of past*, produced a constituted legal subject, the recognition of which brought with it exculpatory possibilities.[8] In consequence, Ahluwalia's responsibility was mitigated and she was charged with manslaughter, the prison sentence for which she had served. She walked out of court a free woman to a throng of supporters and well-wishers.

To put it another way, the legal event in the appellate proceedings began not when Ahluwalia poured petrol on her husband but earlier. With this enrichment of the legal event, through the recognition of a less proximate although more enduring past, there emerged complexity, difference, singularity, contingency and a concreteness, all of which altered the attribution of responsibility. Ahluwalia ceased to be an abstracted legal subject who, for the purposes of the trial court, only appeared when she poured petrol on her husband. Instead, through a 'temporal stretching of the legal subject',[9] she was rendered in the appeal as a person who was constituted by a sustained history of violence.

Importantly too, the appellate judge *appeared*[10] to have discretion in structuring the legal event and legal subject either as entirely separate from and independent of the history of violence (as the trial judge had) or as necessarily connected to and constituted by it (as the appellate judge appeared to do). One rendering of the facts therefore produced a fully agential subject of law, making a victim of sustained domestic violence a murderer, while the other, rather than acquiescing in overarching structures that often erase or acquiesce in violence against women, produced a constituted subject of law that complicated the picture of a fully willed legal actor. History, or temporality, as I argue in this book, appeared to determine what facts were deemed relevant in the case – *not the legal rule* – and, in turn, Kiranjit Ahluwalia's guilt. The main argument I develop in what follows is that differences in the factual rendering in adjudication (here, between the trial and the appellate court) can be explained, not through the application of the legal rule but through the deployment of different legally produced temporalities – what I later refer to as adjudicative temporalities – upon which event and subject formation are structured. Relatedly, as this appears to be a seemingly indeterminate and therefore political process, it is through temporality that power, specifically juridical power, is articulated, rendering subjectivities such that victims of domestic violence can be considered fully agential individuals or where they are recognised as constituted and situated subjects of law.

Judicial fact construction is a largely overlooked element in theories of adjudication,[11] and the connection between temporalities and fact construction in law has scarcely been discussed.[12] Where these issues have been addressed, a sustained theoretical exposition of the temporalities that presuppose fact construction in adjudication has not been elaborated. These are the omissions that my book seeks to address, taking the initial focus[13] of Emily Grabham's forensic work on temporal mechanisms as 'shaping behaviours, subjectivities, and institutional action'[14] as my starting point. Legally produced temporalities determine judicial facts – not legal rules – and this can effect determinations of criminal responsibility. The focus of this book will primarily be in the areas of criminal law and criminal responsibility, though the claims of this book are not necessarily limited to this field. In what follows, therefore, I investigate how contemporary law sees those whom it judges[15] and build my argument that this is through time and temporalities that are actively produced by adjudication rather than the legal rule.

The association between temporality and factual construction may more broadly be drawn from phenomenological, sociological and anthropological forays. In Kant's rendering of the transcendental consciousness in *Critique of Pure Reason*,[16] he argued that time (along with space) was an *a priori* feature of the intellect that allowed the subject to make sense of data to produce phenomena. Heidegger's 'originary temporality', in developing *Critique*, underwrote Kant's transcendental consciousness, whereby Heidegger located the question of being in temporality.[17] Sociologists and anthropologists like Durkheim[18] and Geertz[19] have been key in challenging the hegemonic visages of scientific, Platonic-inspired conceptions of time. In particular, Barbara Adam argues that 'any new perspective on the world entails a reconceptualization of the temporal relations involved'.[20] This project creatively engages these claims – that time frames consciousness – in arguing that temporality structures judicial factual construction.

Investigation of the relationship between adjudicative temporalities and judicial factual construction also invites explanation and deconstruction of the seemingly indeterminate[21] nature of adjudicative temporalities. My book argues that adjudicative temporalities are deeply political, not least because they are largely undertheorised and thus can be a means by which judges act politically. If we return to the case of *Ahluwalia*, the judicial techniques that led to the facts being rendered as either fragmentary or necessarily interconnected was not due to the correlation of the legal rule with the facts 'out there'. Rather it consisted in judges making choices between, I argue, competing and contested adjudicative temporalities. These changing 'time frames' have elsewhere been described as an 'arational choice',[22] the exercise of judicial whim that provides judges with a power to weave together or cleave apart *ex post* facticity in adjudication. One type of adjudicative temporality, for example, may display features of spatiality[23] that enable the separability and detachment of a proximate past from a more remote one – pouring petrol on one's husband as distinct from experiencing sustained domestic violence. Another type of adjudicative temporality may display qualities of interconnectedness,[24] which Henri Bergson calls *durée* – that the pouring of petrol on another is linked to being a victim of their persistent gendered violence. One could push this even further and argue that structures of violence[25] or 'planned misery'[26] form other types of pasts which adjudication can either ignore or attempt to incorporate in its rendering of the facts. In *Ahluwalia*, the discretion of judges can either reproduce oppressive gendered social structures by ignoring histories of violence and producing subjects of law who are fully agential and responsible for the deaths of their partners, or it can open up possibilities for structural change by making histories of violence visible when determining facts in adjudication and rendering subjects of law who are more fully situated in their social reality.

Overall the book therefore does two things. The first is to contribute to a dynamic field within critical socio-legal scholarship that seeks to de-naturalise[27] time, especially time *in* criminal law rather than time or temporality conceived as 'a natural phenomenon, unfolding effortlessly and inconspicuously as the backdrop to social and political life'.[28] The purpose is, as Grabham and Beynon-Jones write, to examine 'the making of time through a focus on law'.[29] The second is to provide an account of the temporalities produced by criminal legal judgement, which I term *adjudicative temporalities*, and to show how these structure the formation of legal subjects and events in criminal law rather than legal rules. Adjudicative temporalities refer to the way that law produces different types of pasts and futures and thus facts in legal judgement. I demonstrate that adjudicative temporalities enable legal judgement to either visibilise or elide social structures in its determination of facts and show how this determines criminal responsibility. The account I develop further distinguishes different types of legal judgement according to how they produce adjudicative temporalities and, given my focus on criminal law,[30] the effect this has on responsibility ascription. Given the general absence in theories of adjudication of any problematising of time, the book contributes to answering larger questions about: indeterminacy and the politics of legal judgement; the reproduction of structural violence through legal judgement; and, critically, how specific adjudicative temporalities may create openings for radical social change by visibilising structures of violence.

Rule and fact scepticism

The biggest challenge this book offers it to decentre legal rules. Indeed, don't legal rules and principles determine relevant judicial facts? What might emerge as fatal, or at least inhibitory, to my general claim that fact construction is structured by adjudicative temporalities are our intuitions of correspondence-type theories of legal rules and fact. We see or read these everywhere, in that laws often state explicitly which facts they correspond to, whether it proscribes X or prescribes Y. Indeed, 'facts asserted by sentences correspond to facts-in-the-world'.[31] It is, as Raz calls it, the classical role of the judge in which they identify 'the law, determines the facts, and applies the law to the facts'.[32] Radin's statement on the rule of law, for example, 'is to think that somehow the applications to particulars are already present in the rule itself'.[33] Such a statement would leave little room for a claim espousing the correlative relation between adjudicative temporality and judicial facts that are central to this book. However, I attempt to argue a rejection of a 'rule-centric' approach to adjudication that rules determine facts. Instead, I draw from, though I am not necessarily committed to,[34] the rule- and fact-sceptic orientations of both Legal Realism (LR) and Critical Legal Studies (CLS). While LR has become a hypernym for several, and at times conflicting, strands of legal thought,[35] both it and CLS's confrontations with legal formalism[36] offer an opening which this book pries open. Fundamentally, this book, like LR and CLS, contests the causal relation between legal rules and the decisions of judicial authorities and the ways and varying degrees to which legal judgement is political.

LR rule-scepticism[37] argued that there were interpretive indeterminacies in applying precedent as either 'strict' or 'loose' modes. Other articulations of LR attempted to decipher the certainty of judicial decisions based on the underlying factual scenarios. Precedents therefore are not categorised by rules but 'situation types'.[38] Frank Jerome's fact scepticism describes the ambiguity of factual determinations in trial courts as 'extensive guessing'.[39] Jerome's schema for how courts operate, where R is the legal rule, F is the facts and D is the decision, is as follows[40]:

$$R \times F = D$$

All things being equal, according to Jerome, if you know both R and F with some degree of certainty, the decision D will be equally determinate. Once there is some level of unknowability of either, a lawyer's ability to advise her client as to the prospective decision D is compromised.

There are three important insights that Jerome makes which are pertinent to this book. The first is that he attributes the indeterminacy of facts (F) to the vagaries of human memory, the institutional pressures of providing accurate testimony in court, the spectre of perjurers, biases, the inability of the courts to spot such discrepancies, the judge's subjectivities and the upper courts' general inability to contest facts. Indeed, Lord Bingham has described such a process as unregulated.[41] This means that facts are indeterminate and not based on their strict correspondence with rules. This book argues that the indeterminacy of F facts stems not just from the judicial fact-finding process and its limits thereof, but that of competing and contested adjudicative temporalities which actively produce different renderings of the legal subject and events.

Second, Jerome argues that the *operationalisation* of *R* is contingent on *F*. Change *F*, and the applicability of *R* changes (and consequently *D*).[42] As has been mentioned and will later become clear, the application of Rules *R* is not indicative of the construction of Facts *F* in adjudication. Additionally however, the *form* of *R* is in part contingent on *F*.[43] This foregrounds an earlier CLS debate around the 'formal realizability' of legal norms and their deployment by judges as either rules or standards.[44] The argument goes that legal norms can be deployed as either rigid rule forms or as standards that allow for discretion in their application. Elsewhere, this realisability of legal norms has been described as *sensed* or *senseless*.[45] In this articulation, 'sensed legal rules' anticipate the facts which they apply to, whereas 'senseless legal rules' elevate the fact situation, which then determines how a legal rule is applied, opening up the possibility for a creative-type of adjudication, particularly in response to so-called 'hard cases'. The relationship between adjudicative temporality and legal form will therefore also be central to this book.

The third and final insight that Jerome provides relates to *F* facts, specifically what he refers to as the 'background of social and economic facts' and their inclusion in the trial court's determination of what happened.[46] The book argues that these 'background facts' are the expression of particular adjudicative temporalities which are typically elided in conventional forms of legal judgement. Things we may consider like socio-economic context racial or gendered structures of violence may constitute these background facts.

Similarly CLS scholars, applying Wittgenstein's reflections on language, rules and indeterminacy,[47] level their charges against the silent contradictions of legal liberalism in three pairs of rhetorical arguments: a simultaneous commitment to (i) rigid rules and situation-sensitive standards, (ii) subjective and objective moral truths and (iii) free will and determinist discourses in legal thought and practice.[48] The 'generality' of the juridical form, in attempting to anticipate multiple factual situations mean that adjudication has to go 'beyond' correspondence theories in its judicial factual determinations.[49] Indeed, 'rules are by their definition general'.[50] The important departure point that both LR and CLS provide therefore is the decentring of the rule (though to varying degrees) in adjudication.

We can further strengthen both the decentring of the rule and the shortcomings of the correspondence theory in adjudication in the following ways. The correspondence theory is known elsewhere as the 'subsumptive fallacy'.[51] Alexandre Lefebvre writes that the subsumptive fallacy rejects the representation of objects external to the rule and instead constructs the object as a representation from within the rule. In other words, 'conduct is not apprehended in and of itself but only insofar as it has been represented through rules'.[52] However, this appears to provide an inadequate account of how judicial fact determination works in adjudication. We can demonstrate how the *same* legal rules can produce different factual determinations. The old provocation defence in the case of *R v. Ahluwalia*[53] can be contrasted with its deployment in *R v. Baillie (John Dickie)*.[54] In determining what facts satisfied, or gave content to, the first limb of the defence – *sudden and temporary loss of self-control*[55] – the courts adopted contrastingly narrow and broad time frames, respectively. In the initial hearing of *Ahluwalia*, despite having suffered horrendous domestic violence over several years, the courts were unwilling to entertain a lapse of time between the most recent bout of violence from her husband ('the provocation') and the conduct. The appellant unsuccessfully argued for a 'slow burn' approach as a justification for the lapse of time, which would have necessarily required the adoption of a broad time frame in the structuring of the legal event. Lord Taylor CJ stated that 'the defence is concerned with the actions of an individual who is not, *at the moment* when he or she acts violently, master of his or her own mind'.[56] Conversely, in the *Baillie* case, a man, who, upon hearing that his son had been threatened by a drug dealer, set off for the drug dealer's house, was able to successfully argue to the courts that a lapse of time – adopting a broader time frame – amounted to a sudden and temporary loss of self-control. To quote Lord Henry J, 'the judge[57] clearly expressed the view that in her judgment this was not a case of provocation because any sudden or temporary loss of self-control must have ceased by the time of the fatal act... it seems to us that that approach is too austere an approach'.[58] Through a comparative reading of these two cases, one can infer, at the very least, inadequacies with the simple correspondence theory of law and fact. If rules do not determine facts in legal judgement, I argue that adjudicative temporalities, of whatever features and textures, conditioned how the legal event and subject was structured in both of these cases.

What this book does, therefore, is argue that judicial fact construction is largely independent of the rule and is structured by adjudicative temporalities, that is, different types of juridically produced pasts and futures. As with *Ahluwalia*, juridically produced temporalities were the difference between the trial judgement's legal event, which began from the time she formulated the intent to kill her husband, and the appeal judgement's legal event, which began from her protracted history of violence. One may discern between these differences as being symptomatic of opposing types of legal judgement, which are further distinguished by the adjudicative temporalities that they produce.

Abstract and concrete legal judgement

If adjudicative temporalities do structure judicial fact construction – through its creation of different types of pasts and futures – and the form of legal rules, and we can distinguish between different types of legal judgement on the basis of their temporalities, what are these different forms of judgement? I attempt to describe two antipodal types of legal judgement and distinguish them by their adjudicative temporalities. I describe them as antipodal rather than binary in an attempt to imagine a spectrum such that legal decisions may *tend* towards either end rather than be an example of either/or. The paramount claim is that adjudicative temporalities are the difference between the different ends of the adjudicative spectrum, diverging in their renderings of the legal subject, legal event, their constructions of the past and future and their subsequent decision. One can then annotate Jerome's formulation as such:

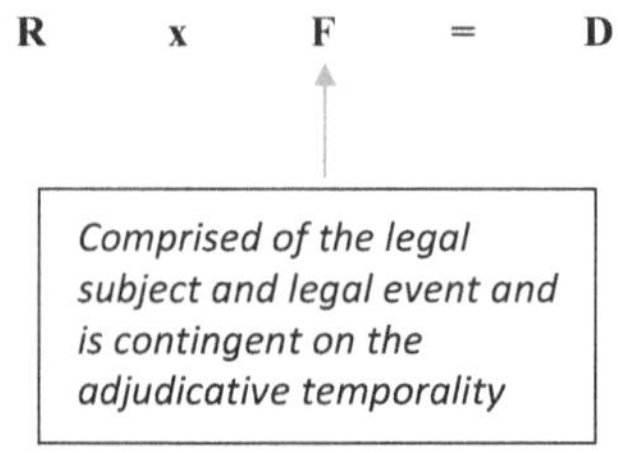

I want to describe these counter points of the adjudicative spectrum, drawing on the work of others,[59] as *abstract* and *concrete*. It will be their adjudicative temporalities that capture the differences in these counterpoints of legal judgement. If these antipodes are defined by different adjudicative temporalities, it means that they will construct their pasts and futures, and thus their facts of a case, in different ways.

Abstract legal judgement (ALJ) 'judges us (i) not in all our particularity but as identical abstract beings; (ii) by reference to general and objective standards equally applicable to all such beings; (iii) the application of these standards being mitigated only by a limited range of exculpatory claims'.[60] Conjuring up this term, William Lucy identifies ALJ as morally problematic for the reason that all natural persons are reduced to formally equal legal subjects, exercising reason that is 'the principal means by which the law treats those before it as abstract beings rather than as the beings they actually are'.[61] ALJ constructs the legal subject as having 'the same in terms of those capacities, cognitive and physical, which enable humans to comply with achievable and intelligible legal standards'.[62] This is what he calls *presumptive identity*[63] and what I later refer to as the liberal legal subject of ALJ, such that it generally elides pre-exiting physical or mental ailments or the socio-economic ecology and situatedness of the litigant. Alan Norrie's elucidation of legal subjectivity in criminal law doctrine develops this characterisation of liberal legal subjectivity further:

> In place of real individuals belonging to particular social classes, possessing the infinite differences that constitute individuality, the reformers proposed an ideal individual living in an ideal world. 'Economic

> man' or 'juridical man' were abstractions from real people emphasising one side of human life- the ability to reason and calculate- at the expense of every social circumstances that actually brings individuals to reason and calculate in particular ways.[64]

Further, Lucy characterises ALJ by the *uniformity component*[65] in which legal rules, because they are insensible to particularities of the legal subject, are applied uniformly – what is known as isonomy.[66] To use an example, rules criminalising begging may apply equally to the homeless and the CEO of Amazon (even though the rule is unlikely to impair the latter). Lucy goes on to state that though there are numerous divergences from ALJ, 'more or less pure versions are found in most current legal systems' and that they are 'a more pronounced feature of liberal or bourgeois legal systems'.[67]

Concrete legal judgement (CLJ), however, is 'tempered not just with mercy but also by knowledge: not only of the conduct in question and its context, but knowledge of our character...in all our particularity...we are not strangers but intimates, with a history'.[68] Here, we observe not a transcending of circumstances and history, but an embeddedness in it. Indeed, it is these very circumstances that also structure the legal event.

I argue that the uniformity component and presumptive identity (later the liberal legal subject) in ALJ is the product of the adjudicative temporalities that produce them. Contrastingly, CLJ, productive of other temporalities, constructs different legal subjects and events, and produces different forms of legal rules (what we may liken to as standards[69] or senseless rules[70] as above). In other words, the attempt of this book will be to explain the variations of these different types of legal judgements with reference to the temporalities that structure them.

Adjudication's production of multiple pasts and futures

So far I've said that adjudicative temporalities refer to different types of juridically produced pasts and futures. What exactly does that mean? Lon Fuller writes that laws proper movement is forward in time, given that they guide our future conduct.[71] But then, how do we account for adjudication? In adjudication, 'timeless' legal norms come into a seemingly time-bounded world. So though in principle, laws are normative *ex ante*, no written legal order can do without *ex post* adjustments.[72] However, Renisa Mawani writes that these types of claims tend to exteriorise time as something distinct from law, as an atemporal normative system which operates *within* time, constructed as clock or calendrical time, in the backdrop.[73] Hence, why we get Fuller's claim of the future-oriented-ness of legal normativity and the retroactivity of adjudication. I am not concerned with how laws relate to or operate alongside clock or calendrical time – indeed I later question that very possibility[74] – but rather with how law, and specifically adjudication, actively *produces* time and how they produce their own pasts and futures.

To speak of adjudicative temporalities, given it is *ex post factum*, is to speak of variations of past-inquiry. To quote Frank Jerome once again on the role of the judge in fact-finding:

> Since actual facts of a case do not walk into court, but happened outside the court-room, and always in the past, the task of the trial court is to reconstruct the past from what are at best second-hand reports of the facts. Thus the trial court acts as a historian, its job being much the same as a historian's.[75]

Rosemary Coombe describes the determination of facts in adjudication as an interpretive act of 'what happened'[76] or, as Crowe and Lee write, a 'project of retrieval'.[77] Part of describing adjudicative temporalities therefore requires a detailing of *past construction* in adjudication and the *multiple pasts*[78] which structure event and subject formation. Indeed, this is something that William Lucy intimates towards when discussing what is omitted in ALJ's production of presumptive identity – a certain type of past. This poses several questions not just about how adjudicative temporalities produce certain types of pasts but about how they may enable the *elision* of certain types of pasts. Indeed, for *Ahluwalia* the absence of a certain past – the history of violence of her husband against her – was productive. In this process of abstraction, I want to answer the question what enables the elision and invisibilisation of certain types of past ('irrelevant' or 'immaterial facts'). What types of adjudicative temporalities lend to selection or 'framing in- or out' of facts? What adjudicative temporalities produce legal subjects that are situated in pasts as inexorable conditions, causes and effects? Then there is a normative question: which, if any, of these types of past are desirable?

But adjudicative temporalities, despite their necessary *ex post* proximity to the legal event, also construct futures. Kathryn McNeilly[79] is particularly instructive in this regard. In her rendering of international human rights law as a transformative project committed to radical social change, she argues for a conception of rights that are 'untimely'. This involves a 'leap into the future without adequate preparation in the present'.[80] It is worth quoting her at length to fully explain what she means by untimely futures:

> Untimeliness thought in this way requires abandoning commitment to linearity, progression and predictability in understanding international human rights. In contrast, this area of law must be apprehended as operating via a conception of the future that does not necessarily follow progressively from the past or present, that is unknown and out of control of the present, and that better foregrounds the continual elaboration of the new. Reconsidered as untimely concepts, international

> human rights are always orientated towards the future. A futural focus is one which has indeed been imagined by existing work re-evaluating rights...However, untimeliness embeds a particular futurity at the heart of rights: the future they offer is not knowable – outlined in relevant declarations, treaties and other instruments – nor progressively following from the present. In contrast, it is one that cannot be known in advance. While this contains significant risk and uncertainty, it also enhances the possibility for international human rights law to be used for radical social change – defined as a transformation of social structures facilitating inequality on grounds such as race, gender and class – through stimulating radical democratic debate on current relations of living which embraces new and alternative directions for social life.[81]

McNeilly's intervention is especially illuminating in its departure from Modernity's linear and connected temporality of past, present and future. Adjudicative temporalities that produce untimely futures that rupture the hegemony and prophecy of the present open up the possibility for transformative futures – something I argue is produced by CLJ, a less conventional and under-utilised form of legal judgement. ALJ, however, produces knowable or constructed futures. While this may sound overly conceptual and abstract, we can observe this concretely in the principles of certainty and stability, both of which are deemed central to legal orders. For example, if one thinks about formalism's commitment to knowable rules that presupposes a causal relation between said legal rule(s) and a *future* legal decision, then legal formalism is underscored by a determinism that produces knowable futures that promote certainty and stability. Thus a future which is knowable is consistent with the rigid application of a past rule. What McNeilly is arguing for, however, are untimely futures: a type of open-ended, radically oriented, legal pragmatism that belies the lineal teleology of legal orders that are saturated with certainty, predictability and knowability.

So, by adjudicative temporalities we mean the juridically produced pasts (interconnected or separable it seems) and futures (knowable or untimely) in adjudication. I will therefore spend the rest of this book writing about how these juridically produced pasts and futures construct different legal subjectivies and events, and consequently determine ascription of responsibility in criminal law.

The politics of adjudicative temporality

Once I have argued that adjudicative temporalities, rather than legal rules, determine judicial fact construction, I also want to examine how this conceals the politics of legal judgement. We may borrow from Steve Smith and John Baylis' observations on theory. They expound the salience of theory for it is theory that 'decide which of the millions of possible facts to look at',[82] it is 'a simplifying device that allows you to decide which facts matter and which do not'.[83] Susan Marks, following on from Smith and Baylis, in her critique of ideology links the determination of the 'facts which matter' through which 'asymmetrical power relations are constituted and reproduced- and, potentially, transformed.'[84] We may understand adjudication as a theory for understanding the world of facts around it. Different conceptions of adjudicative temporalities, this book argues, determine which facts count as facts and reveal the potentialities of transformation in such types of determination. The first conceit, as I have already discussed, is to claim that rules decide facts in legal cases. The second conceit is that, if one accepts that temporalities determine this, this is an apolitical process. I shall now turn to this point.

The politics of temporality has a rich vintage. However, it first requires one to disentangle time from its common designation and understanding as 'regular, eternal, container time',[85] which appears as 'a natural phenomenon, unfolding effortlessly and inconspicuously as the backdrop to social and political life'.[86] Its production, contingency, malleability by people, institutions and by social structures therefore, becomes apparent. Central to sociological and anthropological interventions to temporality have been to examine how *constructed* time has been central to social ordering[87] as well as the political machinations of this ordering – even with seemingly naturalised constructions of linear time. Indeed, Carol Greenhouse, whose work has been central to the exploration of legal temporalities, argues how linear time tends to naturalise events and structures by rendering them part of an irreversible, logical progression from past to present.[88]

The historical formation of linear temporalities also appears to be conterminous with empire, capitalism and modernity. The discourses surrounding the colonial encounter of the 'New World' projected 'a science of other men in other Time' or what Johannes Fabian referred to as *allochronic discourse*.[89] The so-called 'natives', were considered, as Chakrabarty argues, out-of-time, positioning Europe as the 'site of first occurrence and the colonies as oriented "not yet"'.[90] This discursive work had material effects, enabling the allochronic discourse to rationalise colonial settler and extractive interventions. Much like colonial spatialities which rendered inhabited land as *terra nullis* or 'waste', typically for not satisfying the Lockean principle of mixing a particular type of productive labour with land, indigenous or autochthonous temporalities were displaced by the temporal linearity of imperial-capitalist modernity and its concomitant progress and advance. Indeed, 'linearity can be violently excluding of those who do not or cannot fit within the historico-developmental project'.[91] In Keenan's work on the Torrens land registry system in 1800s South Australia for example, the 'mirror and curtain' principle denied indigenous 'un-registered' claims to the land by 'drawing a curtain' against histories of local ownership and habitation. Thus the registry system 'produces an overarching time of repetitive new beginnings, a series of staccato-like slices of time in the land that are detached from the past and oriented only toward a limited and memory-free colonial future'.[92] Though speaking in the context of symphysiotomy survivors, but relevant for Keenan's original insights, Máiréad Enright states that 'homogeneity enables a radical break with the past- there are no important stragglers'.[93]

Even 'clock-time', building on the Aristotelean abstraction of time as a measurement of change,[94] was, as E P Thompson argues, co-constitutive of industrial capitalism. He states that 'the small instrument (watch) which regulated the new rhythms of industrial life was at the same time one of the more urgent new needs which industrial capitalism called forth to energize its advance'.[95] Carol Greenhouse explains how 'the vulnerability of political institutions to legitimacy crises of different kinds' are premised on the temporalities they produce.[96] Political discourse is fundamentally structured by the temporalities essential to it. Grabham summarises this well by writing how 'time in social and political theory help us to understand how changing temporal orientations- apparently uncertain worlds and futures, new configurations of labour time, horizons of speculation- authorize multiple shades and tactics of intervention'.[97] Even if we think about dominating theories of moral theory, they attempt to control futures (such as consequentialism) or derive their legitimacy from a 'timeless realm' (such as deontological musings of morality).[98] Time is also central to the delineation of rights, argues Rosalyn Higgins,[99] while Grabham writes that 'right regimes are…often conceived and implemented through temporal mechanisms that rely, at least, on a "before" and an "after"'.[100] Time and temporality are contingent, contestable, fiercely political and central to forms of governance and governmentality.

In this book, I set out to argue that legal judgement operates along a spectrum, ranging from ALJ to CLJ, both of which are defined by the different adjudicative temporalities that inform them. Throughout this book, I write about how these temporalities enable judges and courts with discretion to either reproduce or disrupt social structures, produced (or not) in adjudication as certain types of pasts, in judicial fact construction. If the claims of the book are correct, then the determination of which adjudicative temporalities are deployed by judges will be central to the rendering of subjects and events and the resultant ascription of responsibility. More generally, particular adjudicative temporalities may either reproduce social structures of violence through there active elision or, as McNeilly has argued, enable the 'transformation of social structures facilitating inequality on grounds such as race, gender and class'[101] through the juridical production of certain types of pasts and futures that visibilise and incorporate these. Further, adjudicative temporalities are deeply political, not least because they are largely undertheorised and arguably conceal the way judges decide the fact of a case (through the rules), but because of their mystification, they allow judges to do politics through another means, especially important given that legal interpretation takes place in a field of pain and death.[102]

Adjudicative temporality's key claims

There are three contributions that I attempt to make to the emergent field of law and time: (i) adjudicative temporalities structure subject and event formation through its production of pasts and futures – not legal rules, (ii) different adjudicative temporalities condition the form of the rule and responsibility ascription, and (iii) adjudicative temporalities may either reproduce social structures or be a site of transformative potential through the disruption of these social structures.

The first of the claims, drawing on the rule and fact scepticism of LR and CLS, rejects the rule-centric, correspondence theory of adjudication. This is in light of the generality of legal norms – their ambivalent nature as either hard-rules or general standards – and the inability of correspondence or subsumptive theories in providing adequate accounts of how adjudication determines relevant points of fact in trial hearings (recall *Baillie* and *Ahluwalia*). In this book, I will provide a detailed account of how adjudicative temporalities structure judicial fact construction. As a project of retrieval which is necessarily positioned *ex post factum*, the book details the types of pasts that are constructed through different adjudicative temporalities. I will explain how certain temporalities produce certain types of pasts that are separable, such that certain facts are considered immaterial and are central to producing the presumptive identity typical of ALJ, an abstracted, deracinated subject of law – the paradigmatic liberal legal subject. Indeed, this will be one of the central contributions of the book, that is to say subjectivity, and here legal subjectivity is engendered through temporality. Other temporalities will produce pasts that construct legal subjectivities that are situated, contingent and constituted by social structures.

The second claim is that adjudicative temporalities, in their production of the legal event, also condition legal responsibility ascription. In *Ahluwalia*, I observed how a 'temporal stretching of the subject' mitigated her legal responsibility. What this also means, however, if we refer back to Jerome's equation, is that rule *R* is also reformulated through adjudicative temporalities. This draws on both Duncan Kennedy's 'formal realizability' thesis and what Alexander Lefebvre has referred to as sensed or senseless rules.[103] *Sensed* legal rules correlate to Lucy's characterisation of ALJ's uniformity component. When a rule is sensed, it treats the facts so as to abstract them in such a way as if they were merely representations of the rule or as preordained fact situations which they anticipate. Legal rules therefore subsume new factual situations as if they were already inhered in the legal rule or legal concept. Here, we observe that the legal form is co-constitutive of the types of pasts and futures that particular adjudicative temporalities produce.

The third and final claim of the book examines the possibility of CLJ as being a site for radical social change. Drawing on McNeilly's untimely futures and the multiple types of pasts that are produced by CLJ'S adjudicative time, CLJ may enable an adjudication that attempts, albeit within limits,[104] to address systemic or structural violence.[105]

Outline and methodological limitations

Legal rules don't determine facts in adjudication, temporality does – and adjudication produces temporalities. In the opening chapter, therefore, I argue how temporalities are produced by legal institutions and through juridical techniques. Part of this discussion requires contesting some of the claims in the law-time scholarship that treat them as distinct. Of course, this is essential before we proceed for the reason that this book presupposes that law produces time, and does not exist in time. As I've argued that adjudication can produce different types of pasts and futures, the following chapter then develops theories of past and future, drawing on the writings of Bergson and Gadamer. It is in this exposition that I equip myself with the theoretical tools to discuss and describe the different adjudicative temporalities in ALJ and CLJ. The following two chapters therefore detail the temporalities of the different ends of the legal decision-making spectrum – ALJ and CLJ. The penultimate chapter then looks at how we might reread judicial fact construction in key criminal law cases as examples of adjudicative temporalities and what that re-reading looks like. Finally, the book ends with some concluding remarks that identify the challenges to convention legal judgement as well as a legal judgement that attempts to be transformative.

There are certain methodological limitations that are important to address, particularly as one of the central claims of the book is to argue that adjudicative temporalities condition judicial fact determination (subject and event formation) through its production of pasts and futures. Given the focus on *criminal law* cases in this book, the key limitation is that *triers of fact* in the UK are typically determined by trial courts (either by a judge or jury) and are not officially reported. While court transcripts can sometimes be obtained for some trial hearings, they do not hold the same rigour in their reportage as official law reports, and when they are, they are often produced at great expense. In law reporting for appellate hearings, certainly in more contemporary reporting, the relevant or 'material' facts of the case, which are deemed settled, will always be contained in the headnote of a law report along with the relevant legal principle. There may be a slightly more detailed summary of the facts in what is sometimes known as the 'facts paragraph', which will also contain the procedural history of the case.[106] Appeals to the higher court can sometimes report detailed summations of the facts, but appeals tend to focus on points of law. More often, the facts are brief and do not match the detail of the proceedings in the trial hearing. In particular, as will be apparent particularly in the final chapter of this book, the kinds of facts which are associated with transformative legal judgement are more readily discussed in trial hearings. Further, no attempt is made nor can be made to replicate fact-finding in any appellate hearing. Lewison LJ in *Fage* wrote that 'in making his decisions the trial judge will have regard to the whole of the sea of evidence presented to him, whereas an appellate court will only be island hopping'.[107]

It is generally assumed, therefore, that judicial facts in the trial courts are settled and cannot be disturbed in any appeal hearings. Thus there is generally no right to appeal on points of fact in appellate jurisdictions. In the case of *Hamid v. Khalid Co-Operative Insurance Society General Insurance Ltd*,[108] the appellate judges were invited to consider whether the trial judge was wrong to find that a road traffic accident had occurred in the circumstances alleged by the claimant.[109] Drawing from previous case law,[110] Henderson LJ re-iterated that appellate courts should not interfere with the trial judge's conclusions on primary facts unless it was satisfied that the trial judge was 'plainly wrong', that is, a decision which no reasonable judge could have reached (as opposed to the appellate judges reasonably arriving at a different conclusion). Quoting Lord Reed in *Henderson*:

> It follows that, in the absence of some other identifiable error, such as (without attempting an exhaustive account) a material error of law, or the making of a critical finding of fact which has no basis in the evidence, or a demonstrable misunderstanding of relevant evidence, or a demonstrable failure to consider relevant evidence, an appellate court will interfere with the findings of fact made by a trial judge only if it is satisfied that his decision cannot reasonably be explained or justified.[111]

Judicial guidance also states that appellate courts should not review findings of fact unless compelled to do so.[112] It may seem arresting to the thesis of this book that a *detailed* summation of the facts are not typically reported, nor details as to how those facts are arrived at. Further, many cases are not appealed. This means that the very category of court cases, those which adjudicate on fact, appear to be extinguished from this exegesis. This book will attempt to, in part, circumvent this problem through the following ways. It will, of course, refer to the headnotes in judgements (especially with detailed exposition of the facts of a case), but also transcripts of judicial summings up.

As I will hopefully demonstrate in Chapter 5, examining the cases to determine their adjudicative temporalities will require an adventurous and prudential reading. Such types of reading has been attempted elsewhere. Karin Van Marle probes into whether *delay* as a temporal strategy provides a partial solution to law's general inability to accept multiple truths and meanings[113] or, to translate this to the scope of this work, whether delay can counter the abstracting tendencies that produce presumptive identities in ALJ. Lefebvre refers to this as 'attentive judgement', which affords primacy to the facts (and thus the specific temporalities which underwrite them) and to the complexity, difference and singularity that this brings with it.[114] Lefebvre, drawing from the work of Deleuze's Encounter and Problem, provides an irradiating explanation that counters the subsumption of facts to rules,[115] which the book will also examine. We may once again bring in Jerome's formulation to annotate the nature and variation of legal rules.

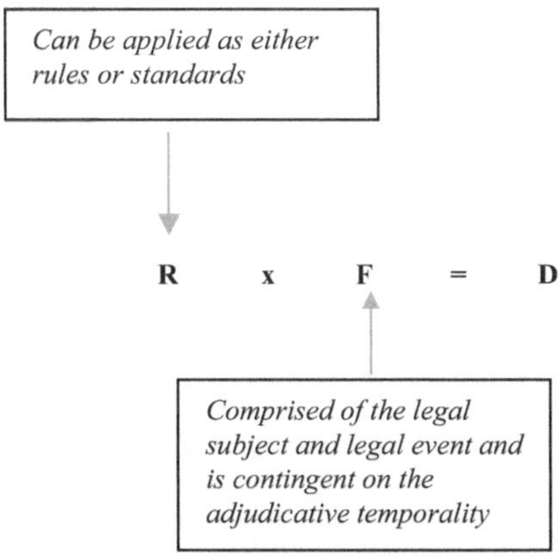

Adjudicative temporalities, therefore, deal not just with construction of pasts, but also futures, the integrity of rules and the concomitant techniques used to produce and construct these temporal dimensions. The ways in which these writers determine these temporally constructed forms of legal judgement is through a forensic reading of the facts. The combination of chapters 2–4 will illustrate how we can read the case law to ascertain its temporalities.

As I've mentioned before, the focus of many of the cases are drawn primarily from criminal law (as the *Ahluwalia* example illustrates). The book attempts to be as broad as possible but is primarily more interested in problematising temporality in judicial fact construction so that any future research, should it use this book as a point of departure, may explore these claims in other areas of law. The benefit of an exclusive focus on the criminal law also limits the possibility of other variables that may sway judicial fact construction and judicial technique (e.g. civil law claims involve two natural persons, whereas we need only focus on one set of legal subjects in criminal proceedings). It is important therefore to bear this in mind when considering the central thesis in this book and how this may operate differentially in other fields of law. Indeed, it is humbly accepted that how these claims manifest in different fields may radically differ.

Notes

1 W E B Du Bois, 'The Beginnings of Slavery' (1905) 2 Voice of the Negro 104.
2 Gargi Bhattarcharya, *Rethinking Racial Capitalism: Questions of Reproduction and Survival* (Rowman and Littlefirled International 2018) 71.
3 Stuart Hall, 'The Neo-Liberal Revolution' (2011) 25,6 Cultural Studies 705–728.
4 *Provoked* starring Aishwarya Rai and Robbie Coltrane (2006).
5 Southall Black Sisters <http://www.southallblacksisters.org.uk/> accessed 15 April 2019.
6 [1993] 96 Cr. App. R. 31.
7 Lenore E. Walker, *The Battered Woman* (Harper and Row 1979); See also Aileen McColgan, 'In Defence of Battered Women Who Kill' (1993) 13,4 Oxford Journal of Legal Studies 508–529.
8 As William Lucy notes, there are 'far fewer exculpatory claims [that] are currently legally recognised that would be if defendants were judged by reference to all the details of their context and particular attributes'. See also William Lucy, *Law's Judgement* (Bloomsbury 2017) 7.
9 James Boyle, 'Is Subjectivity Possible? The Postmodern Subject in Legal Theory' (1991) 62 University of Colorado Review 522.
10 As is later discussed, this 'choice' of adjudicative temporalities and the subsequent construction of subjectivity and event formation is influenced by structural factors that have conventionally not been receptive to reading women litigants/defendants in the way the books argues. In other words, there are structural factors relevant to the temporal choices of the judges here which might be alluded to.
11 Emmet Flood, 'Factual Construction and Judgment in Constitutional Adjudication' (1991) 100,6 Yale Law Journal 1795; See also Duncan Kennedy 'Freedom and Constraint in Adjudication: A Critical Phenomenology' (1986) 36 Journal of Legal Education 518–562.
12 See also Mark Kelman, 'Interpretive Construction in the Substantive Criminal Law' (1981) 33,4 Stanford Law Review 591; Kevät Nousiainen, 'Time of Law, Time of Experience' in Jes Bjarup and Mogens Blegvad (eds), *Time, Law and Society: Edited Proceedings of a Nordic Symposium at Sandbjerg Gods* (Franz Steiner Verlag 1994) 23; Alan Norrie, *Crime, Reason and History: A Critical Introduction to Criminal Law* (CUP 2011) 137–140.
13 Emily Grabham, *Brewing Legal Times: Things, Forms and the Enactment of Law* (University of Toronto Press 2016) 8–12; See also Emily Grabham, 'Governing Permanence: Trans Subjects, Time, and The Gender Recognition Act' (2010) 19,1 Social and Legal Studies 108.
14 Emily Grabham, *Brewing Legal Times: Things, Forms and the Enactment of Law* (University of Toronto Press 2016) 9.
15 William Lucy, *Law's Judgement* (Bloomsbury 2017) 3.
16 Immanuel Kant, *Critique of Pure Reason* (Paul Guyer and Allen W. Wood eds. & trs, CUP1998) 163.
17 Martin Heidegger, *Kant and the Problem of Metaphysics* (Richard Taft trs, Indiana University Press 1997).
18 Emile Durkheim, *The Elementary Forms of Religious Life* (Karen Fields trs, NYU Press 1995) 9–11.
19 Clifford Geertz, *Person, Time and Conduct in Bali. The Social Nature of Thought* (Yale University Press 1966).
20 Barbara Adam, *Time* (Polity Press 2004) 22.
21 Again, as n 10 above, the ability to choose between different adjudicative times (and this rendering of facts) are not entirely autonomous but can be dictated by

social structures. For example, legal systems situated against a backdrop of patriarchal violence will opt for adjudicative temporalities that produce agential subjects of law in domestic violence cases that render such subjects of law fully responsible.

22 Mark Kelman, 'Interpretive Construction in the Substantive Criminal Law' (1981) 33,4 Stanford Law Review 594.

23 See Chapter 2.

24 See Chapter 2.

25 Johan Galtung, 'Violence, Peace, and Peace Research' (1969) 6,3 Journal of Peace Research 167–191.

26 Noami Klein, *The Shock Doctrine: The Rise of Disaster Capitalism* (Henry Holt and Company 2010) 117, 155, 301, 344, 352; See also Susan Marks, 'Human Rights and Root Causes' (2011) 74,1 Modern Law Review 57–78; Alan Norrie, *Crime, Reason and History: A Critical Introduction to Criminal Law* (CUP 2011) 137–140.

27 Emily Grabham and Siân Beynon-Jones (eds), *Law and Time* (Routledge 2019) 1–28; More generally, see Emile Durkheim, *The Elementary Forms of Religious Life* (Karen Fields trs. NYU Press 1995).

28 Renisa Mawani, 'Law as Temporality: Colonial Politics and Indian Settlers' (2014) 4 University of California Irvine Law Review 71.

29 Emily Grabham and Siân Beynon-Jones (eds), *Law and Time* (Routledge 2018) 2.

30 The focus of this book will be on criminal law doctrine. However, it is hoped that this book opens up possibilities for examining adjudicative temporalities in other fields of legal inquiry.

31 Jules Coleman, 'Truth and Objectivity in Law' (1995) 1,1 Legal Theory 39.

32 Joseph Raz, *The Authority of Law: Essays on Law and Morality* (OUP 1979) 182.

33 Margaret Radin, 'Reconsidering the Rule of Law' (1989) 69 Boston University Law Review 781.

34 This will become more apparent in Chapters 4 and 5 as well as the Concluding Remarks. Briefly however, ALR is said to have developed within the milieu of Franklin D Roosevelt's New Deal, committed to the recovery of the economy, relief for the poor and unemployed and reform of the financial system (the so-called 3 Rs). It has been typically argued that 'realist jurisprudence was New Deal jurisprudence'. See also Neil Duxbury, *Patterns of American Jurisprudence* (OUP 2001) 149–158.

35 Brian Leiter, 'Legal Realism and Legal Positivism Reconsidered' (2001) 111,2 Ethics 278–301.

36 Frederick Schauer, 'Formalism' (1988) 97,4 Yale Law Journal 534.

37 Karl Llewellyn, *The Bramble Bush: On Our Law and Its Study* (OUP 2008 (Originally published in 1930)).

38 Herman Oliphant, 'A Return to Stare Decisis' (1928) 14 American Bar Association 159–160.

39 Frank Jerome, *Courts on Trial* (Princeton University Press 1949) 16.

40 Frank Jerome, *Courts on Trial* (Princeton University Press 1949) 14.

41 Tom Bingham, *The Business of Judging: Selected Essays and Speeches* (OUP 2011) 3.

42 This relates to the degree of formal realisability of legal norms which Duncan Kennedy describes. See also 'Form and Substance in Private Law Adjudication' (1976) 89 Harvard Law Review 1685, 1687–1688.

43 There is something that says this in Jeromes 3rd chapter. Frank Jerome, *Courts on Trial* (Princeton University Press 1949) 15–17.

44 See also Duncan Kennedy D, 'Form and Substance in Private Law Adjudication' (1976) 89 Harvard Law Review 1685, 1687–1688.

45 Alexandre Lefebvre, *The Image of Law: Deleuze, Bergson, Spinoza* (Stanford University Press 2008).
46 Frank Jerome, *Courts on Trial* (Princeton University Press 1949) 32, 190–222.
47 Saul Kripke, *Wittgenstein on Rules and Private Language: An Elementary Exposition* (Harvard University Press 1982).
48 Mark Kelman, *A Guide to Critical Legal Studies* (Harvard University Press 1987) Chapters 1–3.
49 See also Simon Deakin, 'Juridical Ontology: The Evolution of Legal Form' (2015) 40,1 Historical Social Research 170–184.
50 Fredrick Schauer, 'Formalism' (1988) 97,4 Yale Law Journal 534.
51 Alexandre Lefebvre, *The Image of Law: Deleuze, Bergson, Spinoza* (Stanford University Press 2008) 12.
52 Alexandre Lefebvre, *The Image of Law: Deleuze, Bergson, Spinoza* (Stanford University Press 2008) 13.
53 [1993] 96 Cr. App. R. 31.
54 [1995] 2 Cr. App. R.
55 *R v Duffy* [1949] 1 AER 932.
56 [1993] 96 Cr. App. R. 31 [138] emphasis added.
57 Referring to the trial judge.
58 [1995] 2 Cr. App. R [37].
59 William Lucy, 'Abstraction and Equality' (2006) 62,1 Current Legal Problems; See also William Lucy, *Law's Judgement* (Hart 2017) 22–70.
60 William Lucy, 'Abstraction and Equality' (2006) 62,1 Current Legal Problems 23.
61 William Lucy, 'Abstraction and Equality' (2006) 62,1 Current Legal Problems 25.
62 William Lucy, *Law's Judgement* (Bloomsbury 2017) 4.
63 William Lucy, *Law's Judgement* (Bloomsbury 2017) 4.
64 Allan Norrie, *Crime, Reason and History: A Critical Introduction to Criminal Law* (CUP 2011) 21.
65 William Lucy, 'Abstraction and Equality' (2006) 62,1 Current Legal Problems 26.
66 William Lucy, *Law's Judgement* (Bloomsbury 2017) 4.
67 William Lucy, *Law's Judgement* (Bloomsbury 2017) 5–6.
68 William Lucy, 'Abstraction and Equality' (2006) 62,1 Current Legal Problems 22.
69 Pierre Schlag, 'Rules and Standards' (1985) 33 University of California Law Review 379.
70 Alexandre Lefebvre, *The Image of Law: Deleuze, Bergson, Spinoza* (Stanford University Press 2008) 102.
71 Lon Fuller, *The Morality of Law* (Yale University Press 1969) 53; the exception to this of course would be retroactive laws.
72 Christopher Hutton, 'Meaning, Time and the Law: Ex Post and Ex Ante Perspectives' (2009) 22 International Journal of the Semiotics in Law 279.
73 Renisa Mawani, 'Law as Temporality: Colonial Politics and Indian Settlers' (2014) 4 University of California Irvine Law Review 70.
74 See Chapter 1.
75 Frank Jerome, *Courts on Trial* (Princeton University Press 1949) 37.
76 Rosemary Coombe, 'Same as It Ever Was: Rethinking the Politics of Legal Interpretation' (1989) 34 McGill Law Journal 615.
77 Jonathan Crowe and Constance Youngwon Lee, 'Law as Memory' (2015) 26,3 Law and Critique 251–266.
78 Tanzil Chowdhury, 'Temporality and Criminal Law Adjudication's Multiple Pasts' (2017) 38 Liverpool Law Review 187–206.
79 Kathryn McNeilly, 'Are Rights Out of Time? International Human Rights Law, Temporality, and Radical Social Change' (2018) Social and Legal Studies 2.

80 Elizabeth Grosz, 'The Untimeliness of Feminist Theory' (2010) 18,1 Nordic Journal of Feminist and Gender Research 49.
81 Kathryn McNeilly, 'Are Rights Out of Time? International Human Rights Law, Temporality, and Radical Social Change' (2018) Social and Legal Studies 2–3.
82 Steve Smith and John Bayliss (ed.), The Globalization of World Politics (OUP 1997) 3.
83 Steve Smith and John Bayliss (ed.), The Globalization of World Politics (OUP 1997) 3.
84 Susan Marks, The Riddle of all Constitutions: International Law, Democracy, and the Critique of Ideology (OUP 2000) 121.
85 Emily Grabham and Siân Beynon-Jones (eds), *Law and Time* (Routledge 2018) 2.
86 Renisa Mawani, 'Law as Temporality: Colonial Politics and Indian Settlers' (2014) 4 University of California Irvine Law Review 70.
87 Carol Greenhouse, *A Moment's Notice: Time Politics across Culture* (Cornell University Press 1996); David Engel, 'Law, Time and Community' (1987) 21,4 Law and Society Review 605.
88 Carol Greenhouse, *A Moment's Notice: Time Politics across Culture* (Cornell University Press 1996).
89 Johannes Fabian, *Time and the Other: How Anthropology Makes Its Object* (Columbia University Press 1983).
90 Dipesh Chakrabarty, *Provincializing Europe: Postcolonial Thought and Historical Difference* (Princeton University Press 2000) 9.
91 Emily Grabham and Siân Beynon-Jones (eds), *Law and Time* (Routledge 2018) 4.
92 Sarah Keenan, 'Smoke, Curtains and Mirrors: The Production of Race through Time and Title Registration' (2017) 28 Law and Critique 97–87.
93 Máiréad Enright, "No. I Won't Go Back:' National Time, Trauma and Legacies of Symphysiotomy in Ireland' in Emily Grabham and Siân Beynon-Jones (eds), *Law and Time* (Routledge 2018) 48.
94 Aristotle, 'Time' in Richard M Gale (ed), *The Philosophy of Time: A Collection of Essays* (Harvester Press 1978) 9–23.
95 E P Thompson, 'Time, Work-Discipline, and Industrial Capitalism' (1967) 38 Past & Present 56–97.
96 Carol Greenhouse, *A Moment's Notice: Time Politics across Culture* (Cornell University Press 1996) 15.
97 Emily Grabham, *Brewing Legal Times: Things, Forms and the Enactment of Law* (University of Toronto Press 2016) 7.
98 Myrtle Korenbaum, in the preface to Georges Gurvitch, *The Spectrum of zSocial Time* (D. Reidel Publishing Company 1964) xxii.
99 Rosalyn Higgins, 'Time and Law: International Perspectives on an Old Problem' (1997) 46,3 International and Comparative Law Quarterly 501.
100 Emily Grabham, 'Governing Permanence: Trans Subjects, Time, and the Gender Recognition Act' (2010) 19,1 Social and Legal Studies 108.
101 Kathryn McNeilly, 'Are Rights Out of Time? International Human Rights Law, Temporality, and Radical Social Change' (2018) Social and Legal Studies 2–3.
102 Robert Cover, 'Violence and the Word' (1986) 85,8 Yale Law Journal 1601.
103 Alexandre Lefebvre, *The Image of Law: Deleuze, Bergson, Spinoza* (Stanford University Press 2008) 102; Duncan Kennedy, 'Form and Substance in Private Law Adjudication' (1976) 89 Harvard Law Review 1685 1687–1688.
104 On the limits of human rights law to address 'state-mediated structural injustice' See also Virginia Mantouvalou, 'Welfare-to-Work, Structural Injustice and Human Rights' (2020) MLR 1–26.

105 Johan Galtung, 'Violence, Peace, and Peace Research' (1969) 6,3 Journal of Peace Research 167–191.
106 For a brief overview on facts in law reporting, see also ICLR 'What Is a Law Report?' <https://www.iclr.co.uk/blog/archive/what-is-a-law-report/> accessed 17 June 2019.
107 *Fage UK Ltd v Chobani UK Ltd* [2014] EWCA Civ 5 [114].
108 [2017] EWCA Civ 201.
109 [2017] EWCA Civ 201 [1].
110 These were initially stated in *McGraddie v. McGraddie* [2013] UKSC 58 and Henderson v Foxworth Investments Ltd [2014] UKSC 41.
111 [2014] UKSC 41 [67].
112 *Fage UK Ltd v Chobani UK Ltd* [2014] EWCA Civ 5 [114–115].
113 Karin Van Marle, 'Law's Time, Particularity and Slowness' (2003) 19 South African Journal on Human Rights 239.
114 Alexandre Lefebvre, *The Image of Law: Deleuze, Bergson, Spinoza* (Stanford University Press 2008) 167.
115 Alexandre Lefebvre, *The Image of Law: Deleuze, Bergson, Spinoza* (Stanford University Press 2008).

Chapter 1

The polytemporalities of law

Introduction

In order to locate the contributions of this book – that adjudicative temporalities shape judicial fact construction through their production of pasts and futures rather than legal rules – and to thus make sense of cases like *Ahluwalia* as being shaped and formed by temporalities, this chapter seeks to survey some of the recent work on law and time. In doing so, I have two principal aims in this chapter: to elucidate both the contingency of time and temporality and to then describe the ways in which legal actors, institutions and structures actively produce time. Indeed, the book can only proceed by upending the idea of time as a naturalised, metaphysical entity, through confronting the discussions of law and time as distinct entities, and drawing from a literature that argues time is a juridical form. This chapter attempts to synthesis, systematise then problematize the literature around law and time.

Arguably, the seeds of a 'Western Modernity' are said to have been planted in the fields of Athens; and along with this, time's exteriorisation. Thus 'Legal Temporalities' or the 'making of time through a focus on law',[1] at first, perhaps provokes bewilderment. This is in part due to the naturalisation of Platonic notions of temporality which largely envisage time as a phenomenon that is linear; progressive; invariable; irreversible; and, perhaps most importantly, a 'container' in which 'things and events' (including law and adjudication) take place. It exists in the realm of the metaphysical against which things or the change of things are measured.

This book, however, locates itself in a literature that disrupts this abstraction. Carol Greenhouse argues how this rendering of time as linear, progressive, invariable, irreversible and container-like is actually contingent, basing this upon social claims of order and legitimacy. Greenhouse locates the origins of its linearity among biblical narratives of genesis, original sin and redemption, subsequently adopted by scientific ideas of progress and then 'embedded in specific state practices – bureaucratic administration, taxation and the regulation of economic life, and through a variety of executive, legislative, and judicial powers'.[2] Indeed, 'what passes for the natural rationality of linear time is, in fact, a set of cultural claims about the efficacy of law and specific technologies of social ordering'.[3] Such configurations have also been central to imperial machinations, providing 'the authority of a universal, secular, and singular Western time' that 'has underwritten global histories of capitalism, what counts as politics, as well as prevailing conceptions of the modern political subject'.[4] The container metaphor derives from *substantivalist* conceptualisations of time, born in Plato but bred in Newton[5] that largely theorised time as a universal invariant, independent of the events that take place 'in it'. However, central to this chapter and the book is how 'objective conceptions of time and space are necessarily created through material practices and processes which serve to reproduce social life'.[6]

One might, more broadly, translate these productions of Platonist time as symptomatic of Modernity. Indeed, in recent years, approaches to understanding Modernity describe it as a 'kind of temporality...of modern science, in which mathematically expressed laws apply uniformly across time and space'.[7] Its naturalised transcendence, Bruno Latour writes, is an attempt by Modernity to recreate a split between nature and culture when in fact it is a complex interchange between human and non-human actors.[8] Barbara Adams argues that the consequence of Modernity has been to treat time and space as objective and external to human experience.[9] Such claims efface the possibilities of time's very contingency and the ways in which actors, institutions, structures and normative systems can actively produce it. The invisibility of Platonic time's contingency, or this process of its naturalisation, conceals and obfuscates the possibilities of multiple temporalities and the processes of governance which emerge from them. If the claims of this book are convincing, then the problematisation of these undertheorised and under-demystified mechanisms of governance are more pressing. From here, the claim of adjudicative temporalities shaping pasts and futures and therefore fact construction can germinate.

Within legal scholarship, the absence of time as a subject of sustained inquiry[10] currently pales in comparison to what others have described as the privileging of space and spatiality in socio-legal research.[11] A temporal-turn, as it were, seeks to upend this naturalisation of Platonic time and argue of its contingency, moving 'beyond notions of time as always linear, containing social action...developing approaches to time that explore law's ambivalent, yet constitutive, roles in broader social and political ontologies'.[12] It is a contention of this book to re-iterate that, because of the naturalisation of time generally, this has often shaped our (scant) discussions of law and time. Therefore, some of what we may tentatively call a 'law-substantivalist time' field, in fact, claims law as ontologically distinct and situated against the backdrop of time as a transcendent *a priori* form (foregrounding the container metaphor). Instead, what invites the attention of this book is 'laws participation in the materialization of time',[13] including the linear, container configurations. Taking this to be what we mean by 'legal temporalities' (as distinct from law-substantivalist time), what is clear from surveying the literature (though by no means an exhaustive review) are 'law's polytemporalities'.[14] In other words, I argue that there are a multitude of modes, forms and techniques in which laws and legal institutions produce time, creating a disparate landscape. In fact, I jump a little further by claiming that the commitments of what I have called a law-substantivalist time literature, which assigns them as distinct entities, are a conceit, predicated on social constructions and contingencies of time forms. In fact, this chapter argues that law-substantivalist time insists on a *triple movement* in its *production* of metaphysical time, its *naturalisation* and then used as a *standard* against which laws are measured.

Locating itself firmly within the camp of 'legal temporalities' this book can proceed to examine what adjudicative temporalities are, how they are productive of legal events and legal subjectivities and whether alternative adjudicative temporalities reveal possibilities of radical social transformation. If the appeal in *Ahluwalia* can be read as illustrative of a particular type of adjudicative temporality that produced a certain type of past and therefore a partially agential subject of law that was constituted by histories of violence (or indeed any other types of juridically formed pasts), then adjudicative temporalities have all sorts of possibilities: not only in demystifying the politics of conventional legal judgement by illustrating how judicial fact construction is not centred on rules but by juridically produced temporalities, but also articulating what a radically oriented legal judgement may look like.

In this chapter, I will then begin with outlining this apparent bifurcation, law and substantivalist time and legal temporalities. The former exteriorises time, generally as a standard against which law can 'measure'. The latter instead sees law and judicial techniques as producing time and temporal forms of governance. After having created the categorisation as a way to illustrate the general themes of how law and time are discussed, I then proceed to do away with this distinction. I start by arguing how 'law and substantivalist time' is itself contingent. The next part of the chapter focusses on a particular type of legal temporality, which has heretofore been referred to as adjudicative temporalities. This provides a summary of writing that has focussed on the interrelation between time and reality construction in adjudication that I develop in the book.

Multiple legal temporalities

It is telling that, until recently, there had been a general poverty in exploring legal temporalities in socio-legal scholarship. One explanation that could be proffered has to do with the hegemony of the seemingly naturalised linear, container metaphor of time – often referred to as substantivalist time.

Additionally, the preference for space over time in the literature partly derives from their separation. While Mariana Valverde's *Chronotopic* analysis of the workings of governance processes[15] sought to 'thicken' understandings of space with time, any systematic exposition of legal times was found wanting.

The following two sub-sections briefly synthesise writing on law and time in two, apparently separate, general categories. The first considers examples that treat law and time as apparently distinct entities, re-enforcing the substantivalist conceptions of temporality.[16] The second sub-section draws on implicit and explicit discussions of legal temporalities – in the manner which forms the focus of this book – in that law produces time. The reasons for this categorisation are to systematise and then to break down the ways in which law and time are often discussed. The reason for this is for us to consider ruminations of law and time that are common and intuitive before highlighting the contingency of so-called substantivalist time and law. In other words, time discussed in the first category is just as contingent as time discussed in the second.

Law and substantivalist time

Writings that fall under this general category are characterised by two features. The first, and perhaps most important, is that they, as Renisa Mawani states, exteriorise time as something distinct from the law itself[17] rather than centring laws' production of time and temporalities. The second is that the 'exterior time' often refers to a linear, container form of time, that is, a universal invariant, irreversible, uniform and independent of events (legal or otherwise) that take place 'in it'.

Writings on Law and Substantivalist Time are surprisingly numerous, though not always visible or explicitly articulated. Earlier, I mentioned how Lon Fuller wrote about the perpetual future oriented-ness of law,[18] the normativity of which provides reasons for practical actions of self-directing, intelligent agents in guiding their future conduct.[19] While considered a theory of adjudication (though not in the same way that forms the focus of this book – on judicial fact construction), Dworkin makes use of temporal descriptors in the presentation of his chain novel analogy[20] that underwrites his theory of fit. The best (present) decision, as he writes, is one that respects the (past) rule and presents it and the legal systems in its best (future) light.

Perhaps the clearest examples of law and substantivalist time one often comes across are the explicit expressions of time or time periods – often using calendrical time[21] as the main quantifiable unit of measure, though sometimes triggered by events – in statutes. Indeed, the Office of the Parliamentary Counsel provides guidance on how to incorporate time periods into law,[22] which may refer to Statutes of Limitations[23] that apply to certain offences, often against the general principle of *nullum tempus occurrit regi.*[24]

Relatedly, a perennial question that criminal law has to confront at both the domestic and international level is whether the law ought to punish crimes committed many years ago.[25] The Rome Statute, for example, imposes a *ratione tempores,* determining the earliest point from when an alleged crime is actionable by the International Criminal Court.[26] In a 2015 decision by the then Independent Police Complaints Commission to not pursue a further investigation into the events of the Orgreave Coking Plant, its report submitted that 'given the passage of time, some material is apparently no longer available, having been lost or destroyed',[27] adding that 'the significant passage of time may limit others' ability to recall exactly what happened with accuracy'.[28] A similar problem emerged in the case of *Keyu and others v Secretary of State for Foreign and Commonwealth Affairs*,[29] where the courts refused to allow an appeal to order a public inquiry of the Batang Kali massacre, which occurred in 1948 when the area was under British Colonial administration, because 'it had been brought too late'.[30] Relatedly, this also begs the question as to whether such distantly past acts ought to be adjudicated on by the rules of the present legal system or laws contemporaneous with it – a question largely addressed by intertemporal law,[31] which also touches upon debates around contentious retroactive laws.[32] There are also formal legal requirements with time bars such as the condition for the UK government to lay international treaties before Parliament for 21 days.[33]

Similarly, sunset provisions, which define the duration of a law,[34] provide that laws expire at a certain date or can compel governments and parliaments to review the merit of a current law, particularly if it is in relation to delegated legislation.[35] This can often invite much criticism, particularly in the case of time-lengthy emergency legislation such as the recently enacted *Coronavirus Act* 2020.[36] The doctrine of desuetude,[37] a custom whereby a law is judicially abrogated after a prolonged period of non-use, is particularly controversial in light of what constitutes non-use and the constitutional implications of such a principle.[38] There are also other inflections of time in principles governing the timely delivery and expedition of justice.[39]

Heretofore, time is taken as an independent, invariable standard, against which laws and legal principles measure. There have been efforts to systematise this understanding of the law-substantivalist time nexus. Liaquat Ali Khan, for example, identifies several principles: of temporal correlation, of temporal inertia, of temporal triggers and of temporal co-operation.[40] The first, of temporal correlation, examines how proximity between different events can strike up legally significant inferences about causal relations.[41] We see this played out in provocation and self-defence in the use of force, whereby proximity can often, though not always, infer responsibility or lack thereof.[42] The second, of temporal inertia, describes a legal system's propensity towards or against change,[43] responding to a perennial debate in law and society studies, arguing that 'the evolution of law does not occur at the same pace as the evolution of man'.[44] This theme, in which the asymmetries of 'a society accustomed to instant gratification and constant flux...confronted with a legal system that must operate deliberately and change by design',[45] is diffuse in other so-called law and substantivalist time literature – which we may describe as the law being 'out of synch'.[46] For example, Andrew Wistrich attributes this temporal asymmetry to the law's veneration of the past, a 'respect for tradition, status quo biases, path-dependence, escalation of commitment, a desire to avoid making tough decisions, a reluctance to invest in improving upon past solutions to similar problems, a preference for intertemporal consistency, an inclination to follow the example of others and a penchant for pre-commitments'.[47] Instead, drawing on Kant's notion of foresight as a condition of practical activity, he argues for a future life in law, deriding interpretive strategies that venerate the past, such as formalism or constitutional originalism, and instead adapting a future-directed pragmatism.[48] Elsewhere, this has been described as 'calibration and synchronisation of law by zeitgeist'.[49] This is the ability for a legal order to either change or stabilize in accordance to paradigm shifts, or the *Zeitgeist*, defined as the 'real or hypostasised societal consensus on values, moral judgments, the need for changes and innovation as well as the justification for preserving the past and the status quo'.[50] The nature of a legal order's response to this meta-legal reference[51] realises a temporality: either *calibration*, which is 'the point of departure for interpreting or deliberating on a given norm or legal concept in order to maintain logical consistency and to ascertain if the intention and purpose of the law had been appropriately defined at the outset',[52] or *synchronisation* which 'ensures that a society's legal framework comprising rules, regulations and reasoning is in tune with the developments in the social, economic and cultural environment of its application'.[53] Indeed, the judges are the gatekeepers of the status quo.[54] The third of Khan's principles are temporal triggers[55] which refer to both the commencement of statutory schemes, limitation laws and sunset provisions.

It appears therefore that Khan's systemisation of law and time places him squarely among the writers that treat the two as largely self-contained and ontologically separate. While accepting the Durkheimian premise that the social world is comprised of multiple temporalities, which he refers to as a 'scalenic consciousness of being',[56] Khan is clear in his substantivalist temporal commitments. On his own terms, he is not talking about a legal production of time, but the inferences that clock time can make in attributing legal rights and responsibilities.

This is especially interesting in foregrounding the unravelling of the exteriorisation of time. As Greenhouse and others have argued,[57] substantivalist time, articulated through a linear-container metaphor, is itself a production of particular juridical techniques. What we may refer to as temporalities-as-exteriorised or temporalities-as-a priori are legal forms that legal techniques can produce. In other words, the naturalisation of substantivalist time is enacted through a triple movement by law: first by its production (of linear, container time), then by its naturalisation (through socialisation, prolonged use, various ideological or discursive techniques and thus judicial legitimation) and finally by measure (using this 'time' as a standard against which laws are measured, evaluated, quantified or inferences made). Grabham summarises the position of Greenhouse pertaining to the process of production and naturalisation well:

> In Greenhouse's account, linear time expresses law's effects, so that a sense of what "comes next" could be understood, as much as a result of governing, as it follows what appear to be "naturally" sequential events in time. In other words, law and legal temporalities assist in the fabrication of "social" and "natural" time.[58]

Linear, container time is a production of juridical mechanisms that produce a chronology of often singularly related causal events. Take Khan's theory of temporal inertia which identifies latent problems with law and its lag behind society, the lag which can be called such as it is measured by clock time. David Engel instead describes a similar asynchronicity, not one that is between law and clock time but one that is between different constructions of juridically produced temporalities. Engel explains how competing temporalities produced by laws can explain commitments, preferences and predilections of societies and their supposed asynchronicity or synchronicity. Exemplified through the opening of a new Cosmo plant, what Engel refers to as an event of articulation, are conflicting models of time. One iterative, in which 'recurring images of sameness, which re-affirm and reinforce essential and enduring qualities of nature'.[59] The other, based on linear models that are always committed to progressivism. For the former, progressive modes of temporality may be perceived as cultural disintegration while iterative models are perceived by the latter as cultural stagnation.[60] Legal norms have a normative ambivalence towards both temporal formations but can be used to produce and articulate either/or of the temporal mechanisms. In other words, law and legal technique can be instrumentalised to enact iterative or non-iterative modes of time. Time is not merely epiphenomenal but central to structuring 'efforts to shape opinion and assert control'.[61]

It is worth quoting Gordon C. Winston's distinction between analytical and perspectival time as it helps to illustrate how analytical time, seemingly natural, is as contingent a framework than any other construction of time:

> Time orders events. A fundamental complication in social analysis is that the same events must always be ordered under two different, though compatible, schemes. Under one ordering, any event can be described with respect to another event as taking place before, after, or simultaneously. Under the other ordering, a person or society is introduced, whereupon the same events can also be ordered as future,

> now, or past...it is useful to make this difference stark by describing these alternative orderings of events as two different kinds of time. An analytical time involves only the before-simultaneously-after ordering. A perspective time shows events the way people experience them in future-present-past ordering...Analytical time...permits analytical mind games, thinking about events that take place in time, while ignoring the constraints placed on an actual participant in those events. Analytical time lets us wander over the time freely...But if we think in analytical time, we can live, act, and decide only in perspectival time.[62]

As Rebecca French writes, 'time...is both a relationship between people and a mechanism for ordering experience. While we tend to take the concept of time for granted in the law and presume that it is simply the equivalent to the chronological passage of time, this image robs us of seeing that we socially structure and construct the way we see time'.[63] In the end, law and substantivalist time are what I have briefly described (and shortly go onto) as legal temporalities. In other words, *linear, substantivalist time is juridically produced.* This section has tried to separate out the way in which this happens through a triple movement. The *production, naturalisation* and *measure* of substantivalist time enables seemingly sequential, linear and causal logics of events and the effects. If linear-container time is less a metaphysical reality and more a metaphor, then one is opened up to the possibilities of other juridically formed temporalities.

Legal temporalities

The focus on Legal temporalities is to pay 'attention to law's shaping of time in diverse forms and through multiple techniques...the variegated means by which law and time materialise'.[64] Indeed, as Rebecca French states in her meticulous exegesis of the different multiple forms and models of legal temporalities, 'law is deeply embedded with ideas about time that deserve our attention- our legal notions of time are more complex and varied than simple linear clock time'.[65] There are important examples through which laws and juridical techniques produce time as well as the effects it has on subject formation, event formation and governmentality. This book borrows from this crucial way of thinking about time and law, which not only demystifies – as has been alluded in the reading of the *Ahluwalia* litigation – but also illuminates the possibilities of law and social transformation through thinking about time.

Given I have claimed that law produces pasts and futures, a good place to start is to think about the ways in which laws construct futures that can either follow predictable trajectories of linear progression or produce temporalities that are untimely. The following examples demonstrate logics that purport to construct or presuppose knowable futures on the basis of antecedent (and often unrelated and/or remote) acts. These can produce racialised governance strategies that criminalize legal subjects before any *act* that would typically be considered criminal has been committed and has presaged an angling towards a pre-emptive schema in law. Marieke De Gooede describes this as having 'the consequence of creating an extra-legal field of intervention in which administrative bureaucracies, immigration officials, consultants and financial dataminers are authorised to make sovereign decisions concerning the normality and abnormality of particular persons, behaviours and transactions, and to detain, question, monitor and freeze those considered abnormal'.[66] This is distinct from proscriptions and prescriptions for future acts- as that, as Lon Fuller says, is the 'normal' temporality of legal normativity- but enacts a mode of governance where a far more distant and often ambiguous future is seemingly knowable. Such modalities of prophetic governance and the politics of possibility[67] are commonly inhered in theories of risk[68] that inform predictive policing. In the fields of criminal law theory more generally, some have argued of a fully-fledged emergence of a preventive turn[69] beyond the developed principles of inchoate and associational crimes.[70] For example, the controversial 'gangs matrix', a database containing information of 'gang nominals', uses algorithms to generate an automated violence ranking system that informs racialised policing strategies, manifesting in invasive and multiple stop and searches of young Black men.[71] In Global Counter-Terrorism and Security law, Gavin Sullivan argues whether there has been an emergence of a marked transnational legal ordering process through the temporal and spatial logics of sanctions regimes. He examines how sanctions 'function as a form of pre-emptive security temporally driven by the exchange and use of intelligence-as-evidence...to provide a concrete analysis of how exceptional global governance is embedded and sustained in and through law'.[72] Relatedly, conveyor belt theories explaining the causes of terrorism (which consequently structure counter-terrorism strategies) are similarly informed by obtuse anticipatory logics that attempt the 'certain-isation' of future potentiality by reference to disparate past acts. This is often articulated as extremism or, even more remote, vulnerability to extremism as the primary litmus test for potential terrorist activity. Section 26, *Counter Terrorism and Security Act* 2015 imposes obligations on public sector workers to seek out those that are vulnerable to extremism which would then lead towards terrorism.[73] The guidelines issued by the Secretary of State outlining how to exercise this power, enabled through Section 29 of the act, impose the obligation to 'prevent people from being drawn into terrorism'[74]- not to prevent them from terrorism, but an imagined antecedent stage, of preventing them from being drawn into terrorism.

Elizabeth Freeman has developed the term "chrononormative" to refer to 'the use of time to organize individual human bodies toward maximum productivity'.[75] Building on this, Emily Grabham's work, so central to the intersections of law and temporality, began looking at time-related legal provisions and constructs as specific examples of biopolitics, in particular the UK's *Gender Recognition Act's* requirement for transgender people to stay as their "acquired" gender "until death".[76] Her later work then began to engage with materials, specifically "things", and 'their lively time-creating actions'.[77] Grabham argues how our relationship with things such as case reports, medical reports, medical tests, drugs files as well as a way of doing law with these things, like adjudicating, litigating, documenting, also contribute to the materialization of time in legal networks.[78] Her unpacking of temporalization through objects, draws on a broad scholarship of object-related anthropology that explain the ways in which things exert effect- including the role of clocks, railways, calendars and the ways in which they have created and stabilised hardened conceptions of clock-time.[79] What Grabham's brilliant analysis enables is break free of the limits that the temporalising effects of legal temporalities were entirely productions of legal mechanisms, and in fact emerged from objects.

Another important example that is equally critical to the aspirations of this book is Kathryn McNeilly's radical reconceptualization of human rights[80] as a transformative project that upends governance structures predicated on knowable futures, locating the potential for radical social change in a future that is not predetermined in present legal forms. The radical commitments of CLJ, as will be later argued, disrupt a lineal teleology of predictability of the future and instead, like McNeilly, locate the hopes for a radical transformation in untimely futures.

However, unknowable futures, as she recognises, are not necessarily radical. The temporalities of capitalism, for example, building on the work of E. P. Thompson, locate the obsession with the unknowable future with risk and speculation in financialised forms of capitalism: 'an orientation towards the future and concomitant attempts to make the future more governable, to hedge against dangers with new concepts and a new language of risk, risk management and the politicization of uncertainty as a threat to entrepreneurship of all sorts, are indeed important hallmarks of modernity'.[81] Unknowability lends to speculation and speculation can produce massive surplus value and all the attendant externalities with profit-maximisation.

Legal mechanisms and juridical techniques have also produced particular and variegated pasts. The voluminous studies on Law and Memory examine the governance of history and state-centred interpretations of key historical events.[82] Here, rather than law as merely a passive object of history, the field often adopts an 'internal perspective...that would examine law for the way it uses and writes history as well as for the ways in which it also becomes a site of memory and commemoration...an active participant in the process through which history is written and memory is constructed'.[83] Memory laws therefore actively produce pasts which often have material effects, not just in terms of potentially criminalising certain speech, but also in the production of state-approved texts and national commemorations. One[84] of the paths that the turn to history in international law has taken considers the role that past events have in providing insights on contemporaneous relevance. However, the retrieval of the past to advance a normative practice is 'deliberately sieved and compressed':

> It is not uncommon to find discourses concerning humanitarian intervention, for example, a brief historical account of 'state practice' (Bangladesh, Uganda, Kampuchea, Iraq, Sierra Leone and Kosovo perhaps) which will identify 'key events' and the positions adopted by 'relevant actors' (States and international organisations for the most part) followed by a conclusion that purports to law down when, if at all, intervention on such a basis might be regarded as legitimate. This tends to involve distinguishing between those factors that form part of the normative proposition (such as, perhaps, the severity of the humanitarian crisis and the inability of the UN Security Council to take action) and those which whilst historically significant, do not (such as might related, for example. To the origination of the crisis, the relationship between intervener and intervened, the experience of those facing intervention, or the perceptions of other non-State actors)·[85]

The so-called historical turn in international law has also enabled a critical revisionism of 'modern' international law's emergence from the colonial encounter[86] and capitalist modernity.[87]

As Keebet Von Benda-Beckmann writes, 'in the process of constructing and shaping collective memory, specific points of time in history tend to be highlighted while other periods of history are edited out in order to legitimize governance regimes, racial categories, or to assert claims to political positions under local law'.[88] Recalling Sarah Keenan's writing on the temporal governance mechanisms of the Torrens land registry system, such juridical techniques produce a general erasure of certain types of past land claims, and instead is constantly recreated through new registered titles – a memory-free colonial future.[89] Here, temporality operates as a form of racial governance denying entitlements to land that are elided through the production of certain temporalities. This is what one could liken to Rebecca French's descriptions of forms of legal time, particularly 'industrial time', which enables law to identify an important point whereby the law can 'erase, create, contract, expand, or even eliminate time'.[90]

Insisting on the triple movement that reveals the contingency of substantivalist time – of its *production, naturalisation* and *measure* – explains how that and other legal temporalities are produced through laws and judicial techniques. Importantly, therefore, they are not mere epiphenomena that provide novel, perhaps even valid, but fundamentally peripheral observation and introspection into law, legal normativity and governance, but in fact it is through the times that it produces that law governs. Law has its own constructions of time (whether that be 'time frames', knowable futures, *durée* etc.), and these are central to its mechanisms of governance. In particular, legal temporalities structure how it understands the legal subject and event formation, which may not always be the same as that of a non-legal subject:

> Law organizes and imposes time. It instils work and uniformity, all under the guise of systematicity and efficiency. While the common law recognizes other non-legal temporalities, including lived time as duration, it is often in conflict with them. Moreover, law not only responds to external temporalities; it also absorbs and obscures them. It expands and compresses time by emphasising, erasing, and recasting historical events. As law's time is imposed retrospectively, it is insufficient in capturing the ceaseless change that is life...by focusing on the relations that law has with other nonlocal temporalities, discussions of law's time may run the risk of obscuring and even homogenising the dynamic times of law.[91]

If we are to take seriously the claim that adjudicative temporalities shape fact construction and determine the articulation of legal events and subjects, it is important to see the work that legally produced times does.

Adjudicative temporalities

In this book, I talk about legal temporalities in one very specific sense. *Adjudicative temporalities*, it is argued, produce different types of pasts and futures that structure the facts of a legal case and thus its rendering of the legal subject and legal event rather than this work being done by the legal rule(s). Different adjudicative temporalities explain the variations in both the hearing of first instance and the appeal in the *Ahluwalia* case. The different adjudicative temporalities adopted, produced different pasts and futures, different legal events, legal subjectivities and produced different legal outcomes. If pasts and futures are contingent formations, as has been illustrated above, what types of pasts and futures are constructed in different types of legal judgement (previously called Abstract Legal Judgement [ALJ] and Concrete Legal Judgement [CLJ])? As will also become apparent, adjudicative temporalities also alter the form of legal rules. Attempts at unpacking the temporalities of adjudication have been occasional, less so in relation to judicial fact construction.[92] However, the following contributions illustrate some of the few attempts to do this.

Mark Kelman's 1981 paper entitled *Interpretive Construction in the Substantive Criminal Law*,[93] claims that judicial fact construction is structured by temporality. Legal argument proceeds in two successive stages: interpretive construction and rational rhetoricism. The first stage deals with the 'way we construe a factual situation and to the way we frame the possible rules to handle the situation'.[94] The second stage involves 'the process of presenting the legal conclusions that result when interpretive constructs are applied to the "facts"'.[95] It is the interpretive construction stage – construal of facts and framing of the possible rule – that countenance our attention.

The first stage of fact construal, according to Kelman, is composed of four unconscious interpretive constructs[96] which include (i) broad and narrow time frames, (ii) disjoined and unified accounts, (iii) broad and narrow views of intent and (iv) broad and narrow views of the defendant.[97] The first of these interpretive constructs, *broad and narrow time frames*, refers to whether adjudication may 'incorporate facts about the defendant's personal history' or whether to 'incorporate facts about events preceding or post-dating the criminal incident. An interpreter however, can readily focus solely on the isolated criminal incident, as if all we can learn of value in assessing culpability that can be seen with that narrower time focus'.[98] Drawing from Kelman's first interpretive construct, Alan Norrie[99] demonstrates the use of time frames through the US case of *State v Preslar*.[100] A woman, after having being beaten by her husband, left the family home with her child for her father's house. Some distance from her home, she decided to have a rest with the intention to continue the following morning but died of exposure. The court argued that she had exposed herself without necessity and was therefore fully voluntary. Had the courts applied a broader time frame, it might have been compelled to connect the woman's 'voluntary exposure' to the ill-treatment of her husband and perceive it as a constituted act of necessary self-preservation.

Second of Kelman's interpretive constructs is the apportioning of *disjoined or unified accounts* which may force judges and juries to look beyond an isolated incident say if a defendant made a decision at an earlier moment to act criminally. For example, 'is a negligent decision to kill followed by an intentional killing a negligent or intentional act? Is the person who misses X and shoots Y someone who commits two crimes – attempted murder of X plus, say, reckless homicide of Y – or one crime – an intentional murder of the person?'[101] This unsettles the seemingly perfunctory determination of intents to acts in adjudicative deliberation.

Third, *broad or narrow views of intent* reflect upon whether, in the commission of a crime, a person thinks singularly about each and every aspect in the execution of the criminal act which Kelman argues is not a simple matter. For example, when the defendant intends to undertake certain deeds constituting a particular crime, it feels both misleading in significant ways and perfectly proper in others to assert that the defendant intended the particular crime. When one acts, they may not have the categories of criminal laws as the telos of their intent, whereas in other situations it is clear.[102]

Finally, *broad or narrow views of the defendant* seeks to ascertain whether 'each defendant is a unique individual, with a unique set of perceptions and capabilities' where 'every crime is committed in a unique setting'.[103] To recall, this is analogous to William Lucy's description of ALJ, as having a presumed identity embodying the paradigmatic 'rational and so the legally competent...classic contractor',[104] what is later referred to as the liberal legal subject. Turning to Norrie once again, he writes that the paradigmatic rational legal subject[105] loses its special character when broader time frames are adopted.[106]

The conclusion that Kelman makes is that criminal law doctrine tends to adopt narrow time frames and, to quote Lindsay Farmer's reading of him, 'has particular political implications, buttressing a particular view of free-will, since it leads us to ignore earlier decisions or actions that could have an impact on our understanding of how free or determined a particular act actually was'.[107] Farmer continues that this is 'shaped by political considerations and serves certain social and class interests'.[108] Broader time frames, it seems, construct judicial facts that can destabilise the agential legal subject, one that is free-willed and autonomous, whereas narrower time frames appear to reify it. There are clear applications of this analysis and how it illustrates the politics of judging in the case of *Ahluwalia.* The difference between the cases appears to be the adoption of different time frames, as Kelman refers to them as, different renderings of legal subjectivity and the event and, consequently, responsibility ascription. We moved from an agential actor in the trial hearing to one who is constituted by a broader horizon of domestic violence.

There are several takeaways from Kelman's paper, therefore, that inform some of the claims of this book. In the tradition of displacing rule-centrism that was typical of LR and then CLS, he argues that 'time frames' structure factual determinations in adjudication, outlining a coterminous relationship between temporality, subjectivity and criminal responsibility. A narrow time frame, to use Kelman's nomenclature, constructs a defendant in such a way that they are criminally responsible for an act, as we see in *Ahluwalia.* However, a broad(er) time frame moves beyond the *mens rea* to include a qualifying trigger (say, in the loss of self-control defences) or, if one could envisage, a different *type of past* that pre-exists the narrow time frame that may mitigate responsibility. Time frames therefore are jurisgenerative. An immediate question arises as to what enables the process of time framing, what enables the adoption of narrow or broad time frames and finally how broad can time frames be.

Kelman, perhaps inadvertently, also stumbles upon a more extensive and consequential question about the relationship between temporality and subjectivity. If the constructions of legal subjectivity are contingent upon constructions of time, is the latter prior or *ex post* the former? To chronologise the question – that is, to think of them in a causal sequence – is perhaps a misstep. They in fact share a more complex, coterminous relation in which subjectivities are created in and through distinct temporalities. We have observed this earlier in the way Elizabeth Freeman's *chrononormativity* as a form of biopolitics captures the uses of temporal mechanisms to direct and organise bodies towards maximum productivity.[109] Other feminist incursions into subjectivity explore notions of the 'anachrony of being',[110] which involves a complex 'interpretation of subjectivity in temporal terms'.[111] Similarly, 'material practices, signs, figures, superstitions, images, and fictions' that belie the 'spirit' of an era provide the 'languages of life' through which subjectivity is formed, according to Achille Mbembe.[112] He writes that 'there is a close relationship between subjectivity and temporality – that in some way one can envisage subjectivity itself as temporality'.[113] One can forgive the evasion of such a point given that Kelman argues these are unconscious interpretive constructs which likely obfuscate the ways in which time prefigures subject formation. Among the changes in subjectivity in *Ahluwalia* is one from a fully agential subject to partially agential and constituted.

Further, legal subjectivity is often presupposed through a seemingly timeless standard of reasonableness.[114] However, what Kelman appears to be suggesting is that the normative assessment of responsibility is contingent on the time frames adopted which is underwritten by particular constructions of legal subjectivity. For example, a narrow time frame may apportion blame to the defendant in a negligence case. A broader time frame, however, may apportion partial responsibility to the claimant too. Would an even broader framing of the legal event and legal subject change a judge and jury's normative assessment of responsibility? If so, the question then becomes the extent and degree of broadening and what lends to the process of time framing that enables judicial discretion between narrow and broad time frames. Centrally however, reasonableness, agency, rationality appear to be shaped by temporality.

Another issue that forms part of the first stage, according to Kelman, is how judges 'frame the possible rules to handle the situation'.[115] The *form* of a legal rule is concomitant with the way in which the facts of the case are determined. This connects to Duncan Kennedy's thesis on the formal realizability of legal norms or, more appropriately for this inquiry, given its central focus on time, what Alexandre Lefebvre has referred to as sensed or senseless rules in his discussion on temporality and adjudication.[116] *Sensed* legal rules presuppose the facts as mere representations of the rule. In other words, legal norms which are 'sensed' anticipate or correspond to certain fact patterns as if they were inhered in the rule, leaving little possibilities for constructing new factual situations, which Kennedy refers to as *rule* forms. *Senseless* legal rules, however, bestow the primacy of new factual situations rather than subsuming them. New circumstances or 'background data'[117] may transpire that require a re-evaluation of the legal rule, which Kennedy refers to as *standards*. The legal form therefore is co-constitutive of the types of pasts and futures that particular adjudicative temporalities produce.

Finally, there is something else going on here, beyond what Kelman calls the arational choice over the indeterminacy of which time frames to adopt.[118] Judicial fact construction appears to be structured by the *indeterminate* choice of time frames adopted, but, as he argues, the very process of adoption 'keeps us from having to deal with more explicit political questions arising from one conscious interpretive construct – the conflict between intentionalism and determinism'.[119] Lindsay Farmer says that Kelman undercuts the political force of his argument (symptomatic of the US Critical Legal Studies movement writ large), leading him 'to see framing as a choice to be made in the process of constructing an argument, rather than understanding it as being linked in more systematic ways to the institutional practices of the criminal law'.[120] This is key. One can push further therefore and say that the political question can be drawn out *beyond* indeterminacy and the irresolute rendering of a social world as either the product of free-will or circumscribed by determinist logics. In fact, this locus of indeterminacy is, as will be argued, what enables the reproduction (or rupture from) particular social structures. This claim is predicated on what pasts and what futures are constructed by adjudicative temporalities and whether these are included in judicial fact determinations. For *Ahulwalia*, the pasts and futures produced were crucial in determining her criminal responsibility. More generally, it provides a new reading of these cases through the unproblematised and generally invisible axis of temporality. This provides one point of departure for this book. This is not a choice *per se*. Instead, it is that social structures can shape judicial temporalities either through the inclusion or elision of those very social structures in the courts rending of fact.

Related to this point of departure also requires providing an explanation as to what judicial technique enables *time framing* (à la Kelman). This is where the book borrows generously from drawing on philosophical inquiries into time and temporality that can begin to explain legal productions of temporality that structure subject and event formation. *Time frames* seem to suggest a conceptualisation of temporality that is divisible rather than interconnected, which allows one to 'carve up' reality into distinct parts.[121] Several questions can be asked. Given that adjudication takes place *ex post factum*, what enables these pasts to be constructed in either narrow or broad, unified or disjointed ways? How might this structure legal subject formation? Further, if adjudication is indeed law as politics by another means, does time and time framing conceal loci of power? How might other adjudicative temporalities produce pasts that are interconnected and thus resistant to time framing (as *Ahluwalia* in the appeal seemed to suggest)?

What might the effect of this be upon adjudication's construction of subjectivity, the resultant legal event and normative ascriptions of responsibility?

Some of the key arguments that Kelman makes were also written about elsewhere in a series of papers published from a symposium on *Time, Law and Society*.[122] One of its contributions, by Keväť Nousiainen in a paper titled *Time of Law – Time of Experience*, echoes some of Kelman's claims. Her paper examines the ways in which temporality structures reality construction, arguing that time is ontologically and epistemologically involved in the most basic questions of law[123] rather than affirming the tendency to exteriorise time. However, Nousiainen pushes further by beginning to provide an explanation as to how philosophical interrogations of time could explain time framing. She suggests that adjudication involves an interesting temporal challenge of being *ex post*, though attempting to reconstruct the view of the legal subject *ex ante*.[124] Thus 'subjective time', Nousiainen says, is operative alongside a universally accepted conception of time, and both inform the law. She thus establishes a triad of 'reality construction, text, time'.[125]

The triad offers the clearest exposition of how temporality conditions judicial factual construction through the use of broad or narrow time frames. Broad time frames consider incidents as constitutive of a unified whole and the narrow as separable, singular and disconnected. Crucially law, according to Nousiainen, naturally produces a 'subject structure that keeps apart the subject in its active and passive formulations. This seems to implicate two time structures – a subjective, active and *ex-ante* time, as well as an objective, passive and ex-post time'.[126] Proceeding to attach a phenomenological conception of time to the action subject, Nousiainen briefly outlines Henri Bergson's *durée*, as experiential time, as well as his critique of Kant's concept of time, accusing him of 'spatialising temporality'. Bergson sees time as qualitative, connected in a unified, mobile whole rather than a homogenous continuum that can be divided into parts,[127] which is characteristic, from the view of Bergson, of Kantian time. She uses Bergsonian time to suggest that changes and subsequent measurement (narrow or broad time frames) are impossible as one cannot 'measure differences in experience'. In other words, to delineate or 'time frame' is inimical to lived experience (*durée*). It's not surprising therefore that Nousiainen uses the example of Battered Woman Syndrome[128] and the choice of time frames adjudication uses in determining culpability.

The departure point that Nousiainen provides is to explore how one might *explain* juridical techniques of time framing and what alternative conceptualisations of temporality tell us about other adjudicative temporalities and their construction of reality. We can observe a transplantation of Nousiainen's erudition of broad and narrow time frames in *Ahluwalia* and its rendering of reality. For example, in the case of *Ahluwalia*, it is clear that in the appeal, the adjudicative temporalities produced pasts that were not structured *by time framing* but more by duration, à la Bergson.

It is through Bergson that this chapter segues onto the work of Alexandre Lefebvre, who provides a detailed account of how temporality can explain the creative impulses of adjudication in responding to new and innovative fact situations. The theory is complex and at times adventurous, but while many of the pages are spent ruminating over the temporal mechanisms of legal judgement, of particular interest are how innovative fact situations are co-creative of legal rules, which Lefebvre refers to as either sensed or senseless and which build on Kelman's first stage of interpretive construction, mentioned above. Of particular interest to this book is the way in which temporalities are coterminous with the form of legal rules and the work that 'the Encounter' and 'the Problem' will do in CLJ as a type of transformative legal judgement.

Lefebvre foregrounds Bergsonian temporality with Deleuze to provide a more accurate account of adjudication, one that explains the problems of legal lacunae created by hard cases and the inherent creativity of adjudicative practice to respond to them. The main claim of his work is that time in law is responsible for its creativity; and since Bergson's theory of time is one of creation, this lends towards an account of adjudication that is responsive:

> My major ambition is to use Bergson toward a theory of adjudication, one that creates a concept of judgment sufficient to explain how adjudication works, how creative it is and how law is necessarily transformative. Jurisprudence is a new path along which to renew Bergsonian metaphysics.[129]

Lefebvre begins by laying aim at three major theories of adjudication rendered by Hart,[130] Dworkin[131] and Habermas,[132] as varying permutations of 'judgment as subsumption'. In other words, all three fundamentally conceptualise judgement as the subsumption of sensible phenomena (case facts) to pure concepts (legal rules) – case facts are mere instantiations of the legal rule.[133] In these variations of the subsumptive theories, therefore, legal rules and concepts are said to have an anticipatory logic that pre-empts all legal events. The problem with this account is that it does not adequately explain how adjudication is an inherently creative enterprise that often responds to societal developments that exceed it. As legal concepts are by their nature abstract, Lefebvre therefore attempts to relocate jurisprudence in concrete cases.[134]

To do so, Lefebvre introduces the Deleuzian 'Encounter', which renders the creative and transformative impulses of adjudication possible. The Encounter is a moment which forces us to think rather than to act according to pre-ordained habits (like the anticipatory logic of subsumptive theories of judgement). Lefebvre deploys it to describe the relationship between the legal rule and the case, in which the latter is not a mere instantiation of the former (as per subsumptive theories of judgement) but singular and unique. For Deleuze, thinking has been unable to escape the dogmatic 'philosophy of recognition', in which phenomena are abstracted and placed in pre-ordained categories or concepts as if thinking operates on the basis of recognition. In effect, the phenomena or thing is cognised merely as an instantiation of the concept. Instead, the Encounter can be thought of as the 'unrecognised', as that which challenges the legal concept/rule and operates external to it rather than as an already anticipated interiority. Therefore, the Encounter can be more accurately described, not as a 'particularisation' of the rule but as a singularity[135] – in effect, a unique case. If adjudication is subsumptive, cases can only be, following the cases recognition, considered as 'interior' to the rule, limiting the capacity for legal rules to change. The subsumption theory therefore cannot deal with the Encounter in which the 'concept of the transcendental delimits the frame for every possible experience and event before it occurs and defines if not what occurs, then at least what can- or cannot- occur'.[136] Adjudication as a creative endeavour must therefore afford the *primacy* of the Encounter that forces rules to change in big or small ways in response to cases which are always different and unique. Deleuze thus calls his philosophy a 'transcendental empiricism'[137] that promotes a concrete judgement.

Lefebvre also introduces the notion of the 'Problem'[138] as a device which attempts to create rights to improve a situation. Though it should not be compared to a predetermined *telos*, the Problem is a specific puzzle of a case that confronts the legal rule towards a resolution.[139] Concepts and rules that are created in adjudication are responses to real Problems that the judge states. Indeed, 'they are the transcendental condition of creative adjudication'.[140] How a Problem is stated therefore holds the key for adjudication's transformative and creative potential – what will be central to CLJ.

To illustrate the dialogic relation between the Encounter and the Problem, Lefebvre focusses on the case of *Delgamuukw v British Columbia*.[141] The plaintiffs were First Nation Peoples that claimed ownership of a substantial size of land. The claims were dismissed by the Canadian Supreme Court, but a re-trial was ordered on the basis of a technical infringement. The court therefore took the opportunity to define the nature of Aboriginal Title. The title was referred to as *sui generis* which Lefebvre read as symptomatic of the Encounter – and thus hostile to recognition. Specifically, it resisted recognition under the traditional concept of fee simple property interest because of the unique origins of the title, partly because it was communally held.[142] The Problem was articulated by Lamer J as 'the reconciliation of the pre-existence of aboriginal societies with the sovereignty of the Crown'.[143] This meant that the Aboriginal Title, practiced through occupation, was proof of possession and enacted a right to the land itself. Unlike traditional fee simple property, this could not be alienated by any other party (bar the Crown) nor could it be used in a manner irreconcilable with the nature the First Nations attach to it. The Encounter provided the basis for the judge to identify the Problem, where the former was ostensibly the judicial determination of facts that created the legal event while concurrently highlighting the limitations of the current concept of fee simple. While certain types of legal judgement would have perceived this as incompatible with the traditional legal concept, Lefebvre argues, alongside his more detailed erudition of Bergsonian temporalities of Pure Pasts and Perception, the demands of the Encounter, made possible through the articulation of the Problem, produce a unique fact situation that ultimately reconstructs a new legal rule and the legal event.[144]

ENCOUNTER → PROBLEM → NEW CONCEPT/RULE

Taking stock of Lefebvre's theory of adjudication, while recognising the generous summaries in the brief foray into his book, there are important considerations pertaining to legal technique and its production of temporalities. Lefebvre locates the transformative loci of adjudication in the concrete cases which are made possible through the Encounter. In addition, the legal form or 'the framing of the possible rule' (to use Kelman's phrasing) is also contingent on elevating concrete cases. By concrete cases, one refers to the judicial determination of facts. While Lefebvre derides the rule-centric nature of positivist theories of adjudication, he still fundamentally argues that a re-construction of the rule, through taking parts of previous precedents, are what structures the legal subject and legal event. For Lefebvre, legal temporalities produce new rules that correspond to new fact situations. This book contrastingly, de-centres the rule and argues that adjudicative temporalities produce the fact situations.

Conclusion

Problematising time and the ways in which time and temporalities are produced by and through law reveal not only the contingency of linear and container time ('substantivalist time') but also the ways in which different temporal constructions are produced in different fields and domains of law. Counter-terror law appears to construct anticipated futures from the ether of uncertainty, while colonial land administration in Australia produces perpetually created new presents that extinguish historic land claims and entitlements. Radical re-conceptualisations of human rights jurisprudence are only possible in untimely futures, while predicted futures enable racialised forms of governance through the gangs matrix. Time frames instantiate the difference between the autonomous, agential legal subject and that which is situated and constituted by circumstance. Finally, Bergson's *durée*, almost certainly never envisaged or anticipated by the French thinker, appears to provide some explanation for why Battered woman syndrome was 'missed out' in the jury trial of *Ahluwalia.* This chapter has attempted to dissolve the boundary of legal time scholarship between one which fixes time as independent of law and another which sees time produced by it. From there, we can focus specifically on legally produced times in adjudication.

Accepting this principal claim – that law produces time – belies a greater and more revealing conceit of law and adjudication. Legal temporalities and their invisibilisation or under-problematisation conceal a locus of judicial power – and this is more than the determinist or free-will narratives of law. More generally, as it will be argued, these determine whether the law, specifically ALJ and CLJ, reproduce or may rupture social structures.

If we are to substantiate the claim that adjudicative temporalities structure subject and event formation, it will require a greater theoretical exposition of the theories of time which the book claims inform the different types of legal judgement – ALJ and CLJ. Nousiainen began to provide some erudition of how one can dissect and greater understand legal temporalities by making reference to Bergsonian temporality and Bergson's critique of Kant temporality. The following chapter picks up from that point and outlines theories of time that will help us to make sense of the different types of adjudicative temporalities.

Notes

1 Emily Grabham and Siân Beynon-Jones (eds), *Law and Time* (Routledge 2018) 2.
2 Carol Greenhouse, *A Moment's Notice: Time Politics across Culture* (Cornell University Press 1996) 87.
3 Carol Greenhouse, *A Moment's Notice: Time Politics across Culture* (Cornell University Press 1996) 4.
4 Renisa Mawani, 'Law as Temporality: Colonial Politics and Indian Settlers' (2014) 4 University of California Irvine Law Review 74.
5 For an overview, also Ned Markosian, 'Time' *The Stanford Encyclopaedia of Philosophy* (2002) <http://plato.stanford.edu/entries/time/> accessed 16 June 2019.
6 David Harvey, *The Condition of Postmodernity: An Enquiry into the Origins of Cultural Change* (Wiley Blackwell 1991) 204.
7 William Reddy, 'The Eurasian Origins of Empty Time and Space: Modernity as Temporally Reconsidered' (2016) 55 History and Theory 326.
8 Bruno Latour, *We Have Never Been Modern* (Catherine Porter tr, Harvard University Press 1993) 73.
9 Barbara Adam, *Time and Social Theory* (Polity Press 1990).
10 Renisa Mawani, 'The Times of Law' (2015) 40,1 Law & Social Inquiry 255.
11 Mariana Valverde, *Chronotopes of Law: Jurisdiction, Scale and Governance* (Routledge 2015) 37–43.
12 Emily Grabham and Siân Beynon-Jones (eds), *Law and Time* (Routledge 2018) 18.
13 Emily Grabham and Siân Beynon-Jones (eds), *Law and Time* (Routledge 2018) 18.
14 Donna Haraway, *Staying with the Trouble: Making Kin in the Chthulucene* (Duke University Press 2016) 60.
15 Marina Valverde, *The Chronotopes of Law: Jurisdiction, Scale and Governance* (Routledge 2015) 75.

16 Speaking to colleagues anectodally, this type of discussion appears to have intuitive appeal when one things about law and time.
17 Renisa Mawani, 'Law as Temporality: Colonial Politics and Indian Settlers' (2014) 4 University of California Irvine Law Review 40.
18 Lon Fuller, *The Morality of Law* (Yale University Press 1969) 53; the exception to this of course would be retroactive laws.
19 Lindsay Farmer, 'Time and Space in Criminal Law' (2010) 13,2 New Criminal Law Review: An International and Interdisciplinary Journal 342.
20 Ronald Dworkin, *Law's Empire* (Hart Publishing 1980).
21 *s.9, Interpretation Act 1978.*
22 Drafting Guidance (Office of Parliamentary Counsel, 2018) <https://assets.publishing.service.gov.uk/government/uploads/system/uploads/attachment_data/file/727629/drafting_guidance_July_2018.2..pdf> accessed 19 June 2019.
23 One example includes the *Limitation Act 1980* c. 58 which provides a time bar on various civil offences.
24 Time does not run against the Crown.
25 Tom Douglas, 'Should We Punish Crimes from the Distant Past?' (*Practical Ethics Blog*, 8 May 2015) <http://blog.practicalethics.ox.ac.uk/2015/05/should-we-punish-crimes-from-the-distant-past/>
26 *The Rome Statute of the International Criminal Court 1998, Article 11 (1)-(2).*
27 Sarah Green, 'IPCC Decisions on Matters Relating to the Policing of Events at Orgreave Coking Plant in 1984' <https://www.ipcc.gov.uk/sites/default/files/Documents/investigation_commissioner_reports/Ogreave_Decision_12–06–2015.pdf> accessed 30 May 2015, 9.
28 Sarah Green, 'IPCC Decisions on Matters Relating to the Policing of Events at Orgreave Coking Plant in 1984' <https://www.ipcc.gov.uk/sites/default/files/Documents/investigation_commissioner_reports/Ogreave_Decision_12–06–2015.pdf> accessed 30 May 2015, 17.
29 [2015] UKSC 69.
30 [2015] UKSC 69 [28].
31 See also Anthony D'Amato, 'International Law, Intertemporal Problems' R. Bernhardt (ed.), *Encyclopaedia of Public International Law* (1992) 1234–1236; Taslim O Elias, 'The Doctrine of Intertemporal Law' (1980) 74,2 The American Journal of International Law 500; Rosalyn Higgins, 'Time and Law: International Perspectives on an Old Problem' (1997) 46,3 International and Comparative Law Quarterly 501.
32 Retroactive legislation is prohibited by Article 7 (1) of the European Convention on Human Rights, clause 3 of Article I, Section 9 of the United States Constitution and is a staple of Rule of Law theories. For exceptions to this in the UK, see also Viscount Simmonds in *DPP V. Shaw* [1962] AC 220, the War Damage Act 1965 and *Burmah Oil Company Ltd v Lord Advocate* [1965] AC 75.
33 *s.20(2) Constitutional Reform and Governance Act 2010.*
34 Antonios Kouroutakis, *The Constitutional Value of Sunset Clauses* (Routledge 2016).
35 ss 75(1) & 76, *Coronavirus Act* 2020; Section 21 of the *Terrorism Prevention and Investigation Measures Act* 2011.
36 Paul Scott, 'Fighting COVID 19 – Legal Powers and Risks: The United Kingdom' (Verfassungs Blog 2020) <https://verfassungsblog.de/fighting-covid-19-legal-powers-and-risks-the-united-kingdom/> accessed 21 March 2020.
37 'Desuetude' (2006) 119,7 Harvard Law Review 2209–2229.
38 Richard Albert, 'Constitutional Amendment by Constitutional Desuetude' (2014) 62,3 The American Journal of Comparative Law 641–686.

39 In a recent UK High Court decision, for example, it was ruled that 'fast track rules' for asylum seekers incorporated structural unfairness due to the short amount of time for the appeals process. See also *Detention Action v. First-tier Tribunal, Upper Tribunal, Lord Chancellor* [2015] EWHC 1689, 58.
40 Ali Khan, 'Temporality of Law' (2009) 40,1 McGeorge Law Review.
41 Ali Khan, 'Temporality of Law' (2009) 40,1 McGeorge Law Review 71.
42 Proximity is less of an issue in cases of anticipatory or pre-emptive self-defence in use of force issues. Also, recall earlier case of *R v. Baillie (John Dickie)* [1995] 2 Cr. App. R where a lapse of time did satisfy the limb of 'sudden and temporary loss of self-control'.
43 Ali Khan, 'Temporality of Law' (2009) 40,1 McGeorge Law Review 80.
44 Brian M Stewart, 'Chronolawgy: A Study of Law and Temporal Perception' (2012) 67,1 University of Miami Law Review 304.
45 Brian M Stewart, 'Chronolawgy: A Study of Law and Temporal Perception' (2012) 67,1 University of Miami Law Review 304.
46 Sarah Keenan, 'Making Land Liquid: On Time and Title Registration' in Emily Grabham and Siân Beynon-Jones (eds), *Law and Time* (Routledge 2018) 145–161.
47 Andrew J Wistrich, 'The Evolving Temporality of Law Making' (2012) 44,3 Connecticut Law Review 740–741.
48 Oliver Wendell Holmes, 'The Path of Law' (1897) 10 Harvard Law Review 457.
49 Armin Höland, 'Calibration and Synchronisation of Law by Zeitgeist' (2014) 46,1 The Journal of Legal Pluralism and Unofficial Law 100.
50 Armin Höland, 'Calibration and Synchronisation of Law by Zeitgeist' (2014) 46,1 The Journal of Legal Pluralism and Unofficial Law 100.
51 Armin Höland, 'Calibration and Synchronisation of Law by Zeitgeist' (2014) 46,1 The Journal of Legal Pluralism and Unofficial Law 106.
52 Armin Höland, 'Calibration and Synchronisation of Law by Zeitgeist' (2014) 46,1 The Journal of Legal Pluralism and Unofficial Law 105.
53 Armin Höland, 'Calibration and Synchronisation of Law by Zeitgeist' (2014) 46,1 The Journal of Legal Pluralism and Unofficial Law 100.
54 Lord Devlin, 'Judges and Lawmakers' (1976) 39,1 Modern Law Review 1.
55 Ali Khan, 'Temporality of Law' (2009) 40,1 McGeorge Law Review 106.
56 Ali Khan, 'Temporality of Law' (2009) 40,1 McGeorge Law Review 79.
57 Rebecca R French, 'Time in the Law' (2001) 72 University of Colorado Law Review 705.
58 Emily Grabham, *Brewing Legal Times: Things, Forms and the Enactment of Law* (University of Toronto Press 2016) 13.
59 David M Engel, 'Law, Time and Community' (1987) 21,4 Law and Society Review 610.
60 David M Engel, 'Law, Time and Community' (1987) 21,4 Law and Society Review 611.
61 David M Engel, 'Law, Time and Community' (1987) 21,4 Law and Society Review 635.
62 Gordon Winston, 'Three Problems with the Treatment of Time in Economics: Perspectives, Repetitiveness and Time' in Gordon Winston and Richard Teichgraeber (eds), *The Boundaries of Economics* (CUP 1988) 32–33.
63 Rebecca R French, 'Time in the Law' (2001) 72 University of Colorado Law Review 695; See also Barbara Adam, *Time and Social Theory* (Polity Press 1990).
64 Emily Grabham and Siân Beynon-Jones (eds), *Law and Time* (Routledge 2018) 22.
65 Rebecca R French, 'Time in the Law' (2001) 72 University of Colorado Law Review 671.

66 Marieke De Goede, 'The Politics pf Preemption and the War on Terror in Europe' (2008) 14,1 European Journal of International Relations 163.
67 Louise Amoore, *The Politics of Possibility* (Duke University Press 2013).
68 Keebet von Benda-Beckmann, 'Trust and the Temporalities of Law' (2014) 46,1 The Journal of Legal Pluralism and Unofficial Law 11–14.
69 Henrique Carvalho, *The Preventive Turn in Criminal Law* (OUP 2017).
70 Lindsay Farmer, 'Time and Space in Criminal Law' (2010) 13,2 New Criminal Law Review: An International and Interdisciplinary Journal 334.
71 Patrick Williams, 'Being Matrixed: The (Over)Policing of Gang Suspects in London' (2018) Stop Watch <http://www.stop-watch.org/uploads/documents/Being_Matrixed.pdf> accessed 21 June 2019; See also Patrick Williams and Rebecca Clarke, 'Dangerous Associations: Joint Enterprise, Gangs and Racism'. Centre for Crime and Justice Studies (London 2016) <https://www.crimeandjustice.org.uk/>
72 See also Gavin Sullivan, 'Transnational Legal Assemblages and Global Security Law: Topologies and Temporalities of the List' (2014) 5,1 Transnational Legal Theory 81.
73 s.26 Counter Terrorism and Security Act 2015.
74 HM Gov, 'Revised Prevent Duty Guidance for England and Wales' (2015) <https://assets.publishing.service.gov.uk/government/uploads/system/uploads/attachment_data/file/445977/3799_Revised_Prevent_Duty_Guidance__England_Wales_V2-Interactive.pdf>
75 Elizabeth Freeman, *Time Binds: Queer Temporalities, Queer Histories* (Duke University Press 2010) 3.
76 Emily Grabham, 'Governing Permanence: Trans Subjects, Time, and the Gender Recognition Act' (2010) 19,1 Social and Legal Studies 107–126.
77 Emily Grabham, *Brewing Legal Times: Things, Forms and the Enactment of Law* (University of Toronto Press 2016).
78 Emily Grabham, *Brewing Legal Times: Things, Forms and the Enactment of Law* (University of Toronto Press 2016).
79 Michael O'Malley, *Keeping Watch- A History of American Time* (Smithsonian Institution 1996) 817–838.
80 Kathryn McNeilly, 'Are Rights Out of Time? International Human Rights Law, Temporality, and Radical Social Change' (2018) Social and Legal Studies
81 Vanessa Ogle, 'Time, Temporality and the History of Capitalism' (2019) 243,1 Past & Present 321–322.
82 Uladzislau Belavusau and Aleksandra Gliszczyńska-Grabias, 'Introduction' in Uladzislau Belavusau and Aleksandra Gliszczyńska-Grabias (eds), *Law and Memory: Toward Legal Governance of History* (OUP 2017) 1.
83 Austin Sarat and Thomas Kearns, *History, Memory, and the Law* (University of Michigan Press 2002) 2.
84 Matthew Craven, Malgosia Fitzmaurice and Maria Vogiatzi (eds), *Time, History and International Law* (Martinus Nijhoff Publishers 2007) 1–26.
85 Matthew Craven, Malgosia Fitzmaurice and Maria Vogiatzi (eds), *Time, History and International Law* (Martinus Nijhoff Publishers 2007) 16–17.
86 Anthony Angie, *Imperialism, Sovereignty and International Law* (CUP 2005).
87 Ntina Tzouvala, 'Civilisation'-in Jean d'Aspremont and Sahib Singh, eds., *Concepts for International Law: Contributions to Disciplinary Thought* (Edward Elgar, 2018).
88 Keebet von Benda-Beckmann, 'Trust and the Temporalities of Law' (2014) 46,1 The Journal of Legal Pluralism and Unofficial Law 7.
89 Sarah Keenan, 'Smoke, Curtains and Mirrors: The Production of Race through Time and Title Registration' (2017) 28 Law and Critique 97–87.

90 Sarah Keenan, 'Smoke, Curtains and Mirrors: The Production of Race through Time and Title Registration' (2017) 28 Law and Critique 707.
91 Renisa Mawani, 'The Times of Law' (2015) 40,1 Law & Social Inquiry 255.
92 Emmet Flood, 'Factual Construction and Judgment in Constitutional Adjudication' (1991) 100,6 Yale Law Journal 1795.
93 Mark Kelman, 'Interpretive Construction in the Substantive Criminal Law' (1981) 33,4 Stanford Law Review 591.
94 See also Mark Kelman, 'Interpretive Construction in the Substantive Criminal Law' (1981) 33,4 Stanford Law Review 593.
95 See also Mark Kelman, 'Interpretive Construction in the Substantive Criminal Law' (1981) 33,4 Stanford Law Review 593.
96 Benjamin Cardozo also accounts for the 'subconscious element in the Judicial Process' as the forces of 'likes and dislikes, the predilections and the prejudices, the complex of instincts and emotions and habit and convictions, which make man, whether he be litigant or judge'. See also Benjamin Cardozo, *The Nature of the Judicial Process* (Yale University Press 1921) 167–180.
97 Mark Kelman, 'Interpretive Construction in the Substantive Criminal Law' (1981) 33,4 Stanford Law Review 593–596.
98 Mark Kelman, 'Interpretive Construction in the Substantive Criminal Law' (1981) 33,4 Stanford Law 594.
99 Alan Norrie, *Crime, Reason and History: A Critical Introduction to Criminal Law* (CUP 2011) 141.
100 (1885) 48 NC 417 18.
101 Mark Kelman, 'Interpretive Construction in the Substantive Criminal Law' (1981) 33,4 Stanford 595.
102 Mark Kelman, 'Interpretive Construction in the Substantive Criminal Law' (1981) 33,4 Stanford 595.
103 Mark Kelman, 'Interpretive Construction in the Substantive Criminal Law' (1981) 33,4 Stanford 596.
104 Ngaire Naffine, 'Who Are Law's Persons? From Cheshire Cats to Responsible Subjects' (2003) 66, 3, Modern Law Review 362.
105 Ngaire Naffine, *Law's Meaning of Life: Philosophy, Religion, Darwin and the Legal Person* (Hart Publishing 2009) 64–65.
106 Alan Norrie, *Crime, Reason and History: A Critical Introduction to Criminal Law* (CUP 2011) 137–141.
107 Lindsay Farmer L, 'Time and Space in Criminal Law' (2010) 13,2 New Criminal Law Review: An International and Interdisciplinary Journal 340.
108 Lindsay Farmer L, 'Time and Space in Criminal Law' (2010) 13,2 New Criminal Law Review: An International and Interdisciplinary Journal 340.
109 Elizabeth Freeman, *Time Binds: Queer Temporalities, Queer Histories* (Duke University Press 2010).
110 Caroline Arni, '"Moi Seule" 1833: Feminist Subjectivity, Temporality, and Historical Interpretation' (2012) 2,2 History of the Present 117; See also Elizabeth Grosz and Grosz E, *Time Travels: Feminism, Nature, Power* (Duke University Press 2005).
111 Caroline Arni, '"Moi Seule" 1833: Feminist Subjectivity, Temporality, and Historical Interpretation' (2012) 2,2 History of the Present 114.
112 Achille Mbembe, *On the Postcolony* (University California Press 2001) 15.
113 Achille Mbembe, *On the Postcolony* (University California Press 2001) 15.
114 The thesis also claims that the reasonable man can be situated. See Chapters 4 and 5.
115 See Mark Kelman, 'Interpretive Construction in the Substantive Criminal Law' (1981) 33,4 Stanford Law 593.

116 Alexandre Lefebvre, *The Image of Law: Deleuze, Bergson, Spinoza* (Stanford University Press 2008) 102; Duncan Kennedy, 'Form and Substance in Private Law Adjudication' (1976) 89 Harvard Law Review 1687–1688.
117 Mark Kelman, 'Interpretive Construction in the Substantive Criminal Law' (1981) 33,4 Stanford Law 594.
118 Tanzil Chowdhury, 'Time Frames and Legal Indeterminacy' (2017) 1 Canadian Journal of Law and Jurisprudence 57–76.
119 Mark Kelman, 'Interpretive Construction in the Substantive Criminal Law' (1981) 33,4 Stanford Law 594.
120 Lindsay Farmer, 'Time and Space in Criminal Law' (2010) 13,2 New Criminal Law Review: An International and Interdisciplinary Journal 341.
121 Or 'spatial time'. See Chapters 2 and 3.
122 Jes Bjarup and Mogens Blegvad (eds), *Time, Law and Society: Edited Proceedings of a Nordic Symposium at Sandbjerg Gods* (Franz Steiner Verlag 1994).
123 Kevät Nousiainen, 'Time of Law, Time of Experience' in Jes Bjarup and Mogens Blegvad (eds), *Time, Law and Society: Edited Proceedings of a Nordic Symposium at Sandbjerg Gods*'(Franz Steiner Verlag 1994) 23.
124 See also Christopher Hutton 'Meaning, Time and the Law: Ex Post and Ex Ante Perspectives' (2009) 22 International Journal of the Semiotics 279.
125 Kevät Nousiainen, 'Time of Law, Time of Experience' in Jes Bjarup and Mogens Blegvad (eds), *Time, Law and Society: Edited Proceedings of a Nordic Symposium at Sandbjerg Gods* (Franz Steiner Verlag 1994) 24.
126 Kevät Nousiainen, 'Time of Law, Time of Experience' in Jes Bjarup and Mogens Blegvad (eds), *Time, Law and Society: Edited Proceedings of a Nordic Symposium at Sandbjerg Gods* (Franz Steiner Verlag 1994) 29.
127 Kevät Nousiainen, 'Time of Law, Time of Experience' in Jes Bjarup and Mogens Blegvad (eds), *Time, Law and Society: Edited Proceedings of a Nordic Symposium at Sandbjerg Gods* (Franz Steiner Verlag 1994) 31.
128 This will be explored in Chapter 5.
129 Alexandre Lefebvre, *The Image of Law: Deleuze, Bergson, Spinoza* (Stanford University Press 2008) 51.
130 Alexandre Lefebvre, *The Image of Law: Deleuze, Bergson, Spinoza* (Stanford University Press 2008) 5–21.
131 Alexandre Lefebvre, *The Image of Law: Deleuze, Bergson, Spinoza* (Stanford University Press 2008) 22–36, 107–114.
132 Alexandre Lefebvre, *The Image of Law: Deleuze, Bergson, Spinoza* (Stanford University Press 2008) 37–52, 107–114.
133 Alexandre Lefebvre, *The Image of Law: Deleuze, Bergson, Spinoza* (Stanford University Press 2008) 6.
134 Alexandre Lefebvre, *The Image of Law: Deleuze, Bergson, Spinoza* (Stanford University Press 2008) 56.
135 Karin Van Marle, 'Law's Time, Particularity and Slowness' (2003) 19 South African Journal on Human Rights 241.
136 Alexandre Lefebvre, *The Image of Law: Deleuze, Bergson, Spinoza* (Stanford University Press 2008) 71. See also Chapter 1, section 1.4.
137 Alexandre Lefebvre, *The Image of Law: Deleuze, Bergson, Spinoza* (Stanford University Press 2008) 71.
138 Alexandre Lefebvre, *The Image of Law: Deleuze, Bergson, Spinoza* (Stanford University Press 2008) 85.
139 This he borrows from Spinoza. See also Alexandre Lefebvre, *The Image of Law: Deleuze, Bergson, Spinoza* (Stanford University Press 2008) 197–259.
140 Alexandre Lefebvre, *The Image of Law: Deleuze, Bergson, Spinoza* (Stanford University Press 2008) 213.

141 [1997] 3 S.C.R. 1010.
142 Alexandre Lefebvre, *The Image of Law: Deleuze, Bergson, Spinoza* (Stanford University Press 2008) 209.
143 Alexandre Lefebvre, *The Image of Law: Deleuze, Bergson, Spinoza* (Stanford University Press 2008) 210.
144 For a thorough analysis of the case law through Lefebvre's account of adjudication, see also Alexandre Lefebvre, *The Image of Law: Deleuze, Bergson, Spinoza* (Stanford University Press 2008) 210–215.

Chapter 2

Times past and future, and the forms of adjudicative temporalities

Introduction

The litigation history of *Ahluwalia* is especially generative for this book as a way of thinking about judicial fact construction through legal temporalities. The differences at trial and appeal in the exemplar judgement was read, in the introduction, as manifestations of contrasting adjudicative temporalities rather than the straight application of the rules to corresponding fact. In the hearing of first instance, the judgement constructed the legal event as one which began at the point the mental element of the killing came into being, and ended upon the completion of her act. The subjectivities of the defendant, contained within the 'time framed' legal event, was of an agential and volitional legal subject, appearing only when the defendant formulated the intent and disappearing soon after they had committed the act. This judicial rendering of the legal event and subject – 'the facts' – presupposed a construction of reality in which the pasts were divisible. The court returned the verdict that apportioned criminal responsibility to the defendant. However, in the determination of the subject and event of law in the appeal, there was a qualitative change. Reality was no longer presupposed as divisible, but the entirety of the past was interconnected with the present. Emergent in this interconnected past and present was a history of violence that produced a subject of law that was situated and constituted. The adaptation of a 'different timing', beginning not when Kiranjit formulated the intention but 'much earlier', altered the structure of the legal event – and so changed the outcome. It was not the legal rule that instructed the judge when to, as it were, 'start the clock' in their determination of the facts, but the *legal* times that the judges adopted; what we might refer to as a 'temporal stretching of the legal subject'.[1] The general claims underwriting this book are that adjudicative temporalities, rather than legal rules, structure subject and event formation in legal judgement. Further, it is argued that this can have a corollary effect on rights entitlements, responsibility ascription, remedies and punishment. This position therefore presumes a general decentring of the rule (and their correspondence or subsumption of facts 'out there'), instead postulating a conterminous relationship between adjudicative temporalities (which determine judicial facts) and the framing of the rule to respond to the fact situation, either as a sensed or senseless rule. Further, in the absence of any metaprinciple as to which adjudicative temporalities to adopt, one observes a generally concealed and underproblematised loci of political judgement through law. Legally produced temporalities were crucial in *Ahluwalia* and are key, as will be argued, in all cases. Keeping this example in the foreground, this chapter seeks to elucidate the different adjudicative temporalities that characterise CLJ and ALJ by drawing on different theoreticians of temporality.

This chapter explores an expansive field of contrasting intellectual traditions, and seeks to use these as a way to observe the different *forms* of adjudicative temporalities. This will all be in anticipation of the later discussion in the book as to how they structure and determine judicial fact construction (structuring the legal subject and event, past and futures) in adjudication. Usefully, Rebecca French describes the *attributes* and *forms* of time that are used in law: the former 'are employed by lawyers in legal analysis and presentations',[2] and the latter, she divides into five provisional categories: 'industrial clock time, transcendent time, natural time, social formation time, and physicists' time'.[3] The nomenclature of 'Forms of time' provides a useful categorisation that will help us to prise apart its different features. Similarly, therefore, this chapter uses conceptualisations of temporality to illustrate the different *forms of adjudicative temporality* later discussed in the antipodal types of Abstract and Concrete Legal Judgement.

This book largely draws from two thinkers – Henri Bergson and Hans-Georg Gadamer – as well as the various contemporary formulations of their thinking. In addition to borrowing generously from their original incarnations, it will become apparent how more adventurous readings serve the purposes of this book. Kathryn McNeilly's deployment of Elizabeth Grosz's work, for example, is neo-Bergsonian in bent. Additionally, the later discussion of spatial temporality draws upon Bergson's critique of Kantian temporality while Gadamer's hermeneutics, in developing a theory of the past, has a clear Bergsonian temperament. However, for the purposes of clarity, the chapter is arranged first by types of pasts in adjudication and then by types of futures; they are all fundamentally drawn from Bergsonian and Gadamerian insights.

Taking up Nousiainen's thesis, the chapter begins with an exposition of Henri Bergson's *durée*. Bergson's phenomenological time centres our stream of consciousness as a temporality which is fundamentally indivisible and interconnected. This is later used in the book to describe a type of past – *the enduring past* – found in examples of Concrete Legal Judgement. Contrastingly, continuing to borrow from Bergson, the chapter then develops Bergson's reading of Kantian temporality which he describes as a 'spatialisation of time' (without necessarily subscribing to a general attack on Kantian legal subjectivity). This is referred to later in the book as forming the *spatial past* which is characteristic of Abstract Legal Judgement. These forms of past temporality – *durée* and spatial – will be developed later in the book to explain the ways in which subject and event formation are structured.

This chapter will then briefly explore the post-Romantic shift in Hermeneutics as articulated by Hans-Georg Gadamer and his work on 'effective historical consciousness'. Gadamer's hermeneutics provides another form of adjudicative temporality, likened to Bergsonian *durée* that necessarily underwrites exercises of interpretation within the confines of an all-encompassing past. Transcending the situatedness of the reader of a text is not possible, according to Gadamer. In the ontological inflections of his work, tradition necessarily colours the interpretive exercise. This will later be used to describe the *sedimented past*, which are found in examples of Concrete Legal Judgement.

Finally, reverting back to the Bergsonian course, the chapter draws on Kathryn McNeilly's important synthesis and application of *untimely futures* as sites of radical social change. In her reconceptualisation of International Human Rights Law, she draws from feminist engagements with temporality, in particular the work of Elizabeth Grosz, to 'propose that a productive future…in facilitating radical social change can be envisaged by considering more closely the relationship between human rights and temporality and by thinking through a conception of rights which is untimely'.[4] These *untimely futures*, as is later discussed, also emerge in Concrete Legal Judgement. This will then be contrasted with the lineal teleology of knowable futures that centre knowability, predictability and certainty. These are known as *teleological futures* and are characteristic of decisions that tend towards Abstract Legal Judgement, discussed later in the book.

Bergson and *Durée*

Henri Bergson was once considered one of the most brilliant thinkers of his generation. Radiating polymathic credentials, he started life as a mathematician, before turning to philosophy, and later winning the Nobel Prize for Literature. Among his cavalcade of novel ideas was 'the life-force' or *élan vital*, inhered in his evolutionary biology and theory of creativity. Bergson attempted to reconfigure the Cartesian dualism as a difference of time rather than space. After his final book, *Two Sources of Morality and Religion*, his work faded into obscurity, some attributing this to a debate that others claimed he had lost to Albert Einstein, though others ascribing it to the ascendancy of Hegelian idealism as a competitor and eventually successor canon. However, Bergson's work has seen a resurgence of late with not only a renewed interest in the Deleuzian readings of his work[5] but also varied expeditions into feminist theory[6]; common law[7]; theories of adjudication[8]; and, more recently, postcolonial readings.[9]

Despite his mathematics background, Bergson was reticent of the scientific method encroaching into the fields of social sciences. He derided the ascendancy of Associationist Psychology, which sought to quantify behaviour and emotions, as well as Gustav Fechner's Phonometrics, which similarly tried to measure feelings and sensory effects. The brain and consciousness, according to Bergson, ought to invite separate intellectual treatment, observing the intrusion of science as relegating humans to the level of automatons, anathema to the central axiom of his life's work, which was creativity. As the fundamental impulse of his work championed the consciousness as the site of free-will, his rejection of the determinism of science was not surprising – scientific laws sought to render the future certain and predictable. Bergson rejected what he saw as arresting theories of teleological reasoning,[10] declaring such fatalistic conceptions of time as incompatible with free-will. Instead, the course of our own histories did not pull us from the future into it; rather it was the 'life source behind us', the compulsion or *élan vital.*[11] Time was energy, to use the phrase coined by Suzanne Guerlac,[12] and it liberated humans from the fatalistic determinism of science, replacing it with a future that is plural, open and unknowable.

The influence of Bergson's musically inured father was apparent in both his poetic style of writing and his philosophical analogies.[13] His popular theory of time, *Durée*, is saturated with artistic and musical references, aiming to clarify his complex ideas which are often resistant to simple explanation. *Durée* or time as duration is considered 'experiential time' and is thus 'real time', according to Bergson. It is not the Aristotelian measurement of change between two points, but seeks to invigorate the concept of time with movement and dynamism. Movement, according to Bergson, comes prior to that which moves. Indeed:

> Pure Duration is the form which the succession of our conscious states assumes when our ego lets itself live, when it refrains from separating its present state from its former states. For this purpose it need not be entirely absorbed in the passing sensation or idea; for then, on the contrary, it would no longer 'endure'. Nor need it forget its former states: it is enough that, in recalling these states, it does not set them alongside its actual state as one point alongside another, but forms both the past and the present states into an organic whole, as happens when we recall the notes of a tune, melting, so to speak, into one another.[14]

Durée as real, lived time then is characterised by the interpenetration of conscious states. It is not a series of separate states (such as the divisible units of 'clock-time' as per Aristotle[15]) but, as Bergson describes, 'so solidly organized, so profoundly animated with a common life, that I could not have said where any one of them finished or where another commenced'.[16] Though one might to think however, that time therefore is merely an interconnected linear form, Suzanne Guerlac likens it in a typically Bergsonian fashion to a melody[17] with an ever-accumulating past:

> Duration implies a mode of temporal synthesis that is different from the linear narrative development of past-present-future. It involves a temporal synthesis that knits temporal dimensions together, as in a melody. Melody, which implies a certain mode of organization, is a figure of duration. The identification of a melody implies an act of temporal synthesis. Melody performs this work to the extent that it binds past, present, and future together in a radically singular way...Melody is the figure of confused multiplicity, the figure of duration. We are dealing with a succession of qualities and nuances of feeling, but 'a succession without distinction.' Elements overlap and interpenetrate in a peculiar solidarity.[18]

In this way, time as *durée* is said to endure and the past is constitutive of a dynamic and moving present. This is exemplified by successive states of consciousness, which are confused or interconnected. To conceptualise of time in this way is to think of it as the intercalation of an accumulating past into an ephemeral and dynamic present. Past and present cannot be delineated *stricto sensu*; to understand it as the addition of successive states is to fall into the trap of immobilised spatiality. *Durée* thus may be likened to a whole, rather than composed of distinct parts, and is thus antithetical to Aristotelean-inspired units of 'clock-time' or a more general process of *chronologisation*. This is a term which one can understand as the *process of distinguishing, selecting, and placing adjacent to one another states into a sequence that are presumed to be causally related* and is one which will be referred to frequently throughout this book. The analogies between the facts in the trial hearing in *Ahluwalia* as being an example of chronologisation and the appeal as imbuing features of *durée* are clear.

Most significant to *durée* therefore, is the notion of interpenetration. Thus *durée* is resistant to division (unless it is reflected upon, in which it ceases to be durational time and therefore it resists analytic intervention). *Durée* differs from a past and present that sit adjacent to one another (like in chronologies); rather they dovetail one another into an indistinguishable whole. The relationship is one of symbiotic mutualism:

> Within myself a process of organisation or interpenetration of conscious states is going on, which constitutes true duration. It is because I endure in this way that I picture to myself what I call the past oscillations of the pendulum at the same time as I perceive the present oscillation.[19]

In addition to its indivisibility, *durée* is also associated with *motion*. One of Bergson's many analogies, this time of the shooting star, provides a useful illustration in which he writes that 'we have the sensation of the space traversed and the indivisible sensation of motion or mobility',[20] wherein *durée* refers to the latter of these descriptions:

> In short, there are two elements to be distinguished in movement, the space traversed and the action by means of which one has crossed this space, the successive positions and the synthesis of these positions. The first of these elements is a homogenous quantity. The second only has reality in our consciousness. It is...a quality or intensity.[21]

Some of the features of *durée* are of an accumulating past which shapes the consciousness of present perception. Rather than conceptualise consciousness as a *tabula rasa* or a subject with a transcendental ego, instead we are necessarily and constantly being made by ever-growing past states. One cannot consider *durée*, therefore, without considering the intrinsic link between what has been and what is becoming. Thus *durée* asserts that the entirety of an accumulating past is constitutive of an ever-changing present. Again, if we remind ourselves of the appeal in *Ahluwalia,* the connections between *durée* and the rendering of the legal event and subject are instructive of the relationship between adjudicative temporalities and judicial fact construction.

Bergson also describes *durée* as qualitative and resistant to quantification. The feature of quality is ascertained by the ever-changing and inimitable nature of the present; the past, as the accretion of former presents, consequently pigment the present. Thus no two 'presents' can be said to be the same and their difference is qualitative (based on the intercalated past) rather than quantitative (as in the difference between two points).[22] The combination of time's quality and its motion is what Guerlac calls *qualitative progress*. She imagines watching the oscillations of a pendulum, swaying from side to side, lulling oneself into a state of relaxation until eventually you sleep. *Durée* suggests that it cannot have been the last swing, singularly disconnected from the others that made you sleep; rather it is the combination of all the previous swings, 'the rhythmic organization of the whole'.[23] It was not the quantity of the notes, but the quality exhibited by them. Time thus cannot be reduced to magnitudes as this is a vapid representation of its rich heterogeneity. *Durée* is ultimately a time of quality.

The *form* of adjudicative temporality that imbues the features of *durée* can be characterised by motion, with an interpenetrative, accumulating and constitutive past and ephemeral present. It is analogous to experience and is resistant to any form of analysis which necessarily neutralises its interpenetrativeness. One can see resonances of this temporal form in the determination of facts in the *Ahluwalia* appeal. It is *durée* that later characterises the *durational past* in CLJ.

Spatial temporality

In Nousiainen's paper, in addition to briefly outlining Henri Bergson's *durée* as experiential time, she makes reference to his excoriating critique of Kant's concept of time, in which Bergson accuses him of 'spatialising temporality'. Where Bergson sees time as qualitative, connected together in a unified, mobile whole, Kant, according to Bergson, conceptualises time as a homogenous continuum that can be divided into parts.[24] Incidentally, in Kant's own terms, there is nothing to suggest that time is *spatialised.* Indeed, he explicitly separates the two[25] and theorises time as an *a priori* feature of the intellect that allows us to make sense of data to produce phenomena.[26] To understand time as spatial therefore is to read Kant through Bergson (though not to adopt this as Kantian time but spatial time) and to say that real time (*durée*) has been altered with features of space (and not that it becomes space).

Time as spatial, unlike Bergson's *durée*, is mediated through symbols and other representations. To explain how time introduces spatial features requires an understanding of what Bergson means by *intensity* and *extensity.* Consider the following: Elizah enjoys reading the poetry of Rabindranath Tagore, but seeing her friends makes her 'twice as happy'. Her happiness can be measured relative to the different tasks she undertakes during her day. It is this quantification ('twice') of affective 'internal states' ('happiness') that Bergson took issue with.[27] These intensities or 'psychic states', as Bergson refers to them as, cannot be measured in the same way as extensities.[28] To clarify the point, Bergson invites us to consider the following example.[29] If Elizah switches on one bulb, it will emit light which will create the sensation of brightness. If she proceeds to switch on another additional bulb or, better yet, imagine a dimmer switch where she can reduce the output of the light, the sensation of the brightness changes. Though light can be measured in watts or joules, the brightness is something different. It refers to one's feeling of the *quality* of the light, not the quantity. Elizah cannot measure the brightness of the light in the same manner as she can measure the light itself. This attempted alignment of intensity with extensity is understandably prevalent. For example, Elizah can appreciate that her muscles *feel* (intensity) under *more* strain with a *heavier* object (extensity) – hence the temptation to equate the increase in weight to the sensation she feels within herself; but Bergson took issue with equating the measurable external magnitude with the intensity. Such a process was what he termed *representative sensations.*[30]

This led Bergson to make the distinction between *difference in degree* and *difference in kind*[31]; the bulb changes in the former sense by units of measurement, the brightness in the latter based on sensations. Henceforth, brightness and light *are not* equivalent.[32] Bergson describes the changing states of these intensities as becoming richer in much the same way a melody does when other instruments join into an ensemble piece. Intensity, therefore, is a succession of different conscious states or feelings which naturally interpenetrate one another, what is known as 'qualitative progress'.[33] This particular phrase of Guerlac's captures two important aspects: first that the nature of the difference is qualitative and not measurable, and second that the succession of conscious states is a dynamic process. To recall the light bulb example once again, Bergson forces the distinction between the difference of brightness in its qualitative sense rather than confusing it with the quantity of the measurable light (in joules) in order to consider intensities of brightness (quality) which he terms 'qualitative multiplicity'.[34]

Having laid the groundwork explaining the differences between intensity and extensity, Bergson distinguishes between spatial time and *durée* in which extensities are representative of intensities. Simply put, *durée*, as a stream of interconnected conscious states, is intensity, and spatial time is extensity.

Temporality as spatial does not mean that it transmutes into space but rather that it imbues qualities of space. Unlike *durée*, spatiality is 'what enables us to distinguish a number of identical and simultaneous sensations from one another; it is thus a principle of differentiation other than that of qualitative differentiation, and consequently it is a reality with no quality'.[35] Objects obtain their exteriority from space. It is the 'medium which inserts intervals between them and sets off their outlines'.[36] Space is the empty, uniform scene for the representation of objects, a 'homogenous milieu detached from any content'.[37] Bergson, reading this, claims therefore that the thing that is spatialised (*durée*) is presumed to be the same.

To illustrate the point of uniformity, consider the process of counting sheep. In order to proceed beyond one, the individual must project homogeneity by ignoring the sheep's qualitative differences, assuming their uniformity. To do otherwise, would mean that they never proceed beyond one, as one sheep who is shorn is counted, then another 'one sheep' as it is slightly shaggier (and would have to be counted separately), and another 'one sheep' that is in fact a ewe, and so on and so forth. Counting (i.e. quantification) can therefore not proceed without the abstraction and the imposition of uniformity.[38] In the process of counting sheep 'we must retain the successive images and set them alongside each of the new units which we picture to ourselves: *now it is in space that juxtaposition takes place*'.[39] Objects in space are implicitly divisible, discrete and juxtaposed. Bergson also says that one is able to 'hold things in space' and conceive of them all at once. This is what is referred to as *simultaneity*.

To explain how the features of space (uniformity, divisibility, juxtaposition, simultaneity) are introduced into *durée*, Bergson identifies two types of consciousness: *immediate* and *reflective*. These explain not only how features of space corrupt *durée* but also, paradoxically, why spatial temporality is a seemingly necessary configuration of analytical judgement more generally.

Bergson says that *Immediate Consciousness* refers to the way something is perceived by us directly before one stops and thinks about it.[40] *Im*-mediate may translate as the *un*-mediated apprehension of an object. The *im*-mediate consciousness therefore senses data that stimulate the 'stream of consciousness' (*durée*). Once one reflects upon experience (*durée*), however, it undergoes mediation in representative (and thus spatial) forms and falls into the trap of immobility. The emphasis of the immediate consciousness therefore is on the immanence and purity of the sense data. The immediate consciousness occurs prior to the data's synthesis with concepts. In this way, immediate consciousness is raw data, free from any processing, computation and concept-subsumption.[41]

This type of consciousness can be contrasted with *Reflective Consciousness*. Bergson describes this as 'a medium in which our conscious states form a discrete series so as to admit of being counted'[42] in that 'it delights in clean cut distinctions, which are easily expressed in words, and in things with well-defined outlines, like those perceived in space'.[43] The very act of cognition (e.g. in the Kantian transcendental apparatus) that synthesises data with concepts to create phenomena (i.e. to subsume)[44] allows us to think and act. This means that pure data is merely represented and, within the Bergsonian metaphysics, not real. This data can be represented through 'language, logic, mathematics and other symbols or means of representation'.[45] Thus the very act of cognizing or reflection introduces spatiality (uniformity, divisibility, juxtaposition, simultaneity) into *durée* and also illustrates the problem of aligning extensity with intensity (or representations that describe interpenetrating conscious states).

How spatiality is introduced into *durée* to produce spatial temporality further requires an understanding of why words, symbols or other forms of reflection and representation are inherently static and spatial.[46] Reflexivity naturally requires contemplation about an object before one can represent it in some form. The representation mimics that which is akin to space as the object becomes homogenised. In other words, reflection strips the conscious states of their qualitative difference and places them against one another in discrete categories to create a quantitative multiplicity. To recall the example of *counting* sheep made earlier, this illustrates the inextricable link between reflexivity and spatiality. Numbers necessarily imply spatiality (divisibility, simultaneity, uniformity and juxtaposition) and thus discrete states rather than continuity or interpenetration; no two numbers can overlap (even though numbers can be divided *ad infinitum*, they will *always* be juxtaposed). Like extensive qualities, they are self-contained because of their uniformity. Thus uniformity suggests homogeneity and juxtaposition implies simultaneity. The counting of the sheep deprives them of their difference in kind. Indeed, 'we include them all in the same image, and it follows as a necessary consequence that we place them side by side in an ideal space'.[47] Counting is necessarily reflective and numbers are a representation of the conscious states which are a result of the cognitive process such that they are reflective rather than immediate. Bergson, however, reserves his most searing criticism towards language and he states it is that which alienates us most from direct experience.[48] The interpenetration or 'confused multiplicity' of our immediate consciousness is whittled into objects presented as words which reduce events to a distinct multiplicity, thus creating a chronology. It falls into the same trap of spatiality as number, in which time is presented as independent entities which are statically isolated. Any representation which necessarily involves some form of cognition will *always* introduce space into time. A. R. Lacey sums it up well, stating that 'since philosophizing is an intellectual activity, and therefore involves the "freezing" of what it is talking about, it would not be surprising if difficulties arose when we tried to talk about the inherently unfrozen'.[49]

Spatial temporality therefore can be understood as a representation of *durée*, in which durational time is reflected upon, mediated and represented to subsequently introduce properties of space into it. These include divisibility, simultaneity, juxtaposition and uniformity. Spatial time is operative in the reflective consciousness (reflected) that subsumes 'lived experience' (*durée*) under categories (mediated) in its cognitive process, thus introducing features of space into time (represented). Time considered in this respect is nothing more than the fourth dimension of space. Spatial time ignores the qualitative aspect that is characteristic of the inner conscious states (*durée*), instead replacing it with uniformity and simultaneity. Revisiting briefly *Ahluwalia* once again, the features of spatial temporality appear to describe the way in which the event and subject were produced in the trial hearing, one which cleaved the defendant from pasts that would have compromised her agency. To spatialise the past therefore is to produce certain types of fully agential subjectivities.

To surmise the *form* of adjudicative temporality that imbues the features of spatial temporality, one ought to recall from earlier what was referred to as *chronologisation*. One can understand this as the process of distinguishing, selecting and placing adjacent to one another states into a sequence that are presumed to be causally related. This is entirely consonant with the Bergsonian formulation of spatial temporality that is characterised by uniformity, divisibility, juxtaposition and simultaneity. Spatial temporality will later come to characterise the *spatial past* in ALJ.

Gadamer and effective history

Gadamerian hermeneutics can tell us much about the forms of other adjudicative temporalities. Working under the tutelage of Martin Heidegger and Edmund Husserl, Gadamer was inspired primarily by the former in seeing interpretation not as a method but as ontological. He was renowned for the post-Romantic shift in hermeneutics, observing the epistemic limitations in humans' inherent situatedness. Gadamer claimed that one always projected one's own prejudices or 'effective history' in their engagement of texts (though this was later extended to interpreting conduct). The task for the interpretive being was to challenge their 'horizons' with that of the text until there was a synthesis or 'fusion of horizons'.

Interestingly, much of his work has been deployed in various exegeses of statutory interpretation.[50] The conventional treatment of Gadamer therefore has tended to understand how his hermeneutics can unravel the interpretive gymnastics required in meaning of legal rules. Given this book rejects the exclusivity of correspondence theories or rule-centric adjudication, and instead contends that temporality primarily structures fact construction, Gadamer will be deployed in the service of how adjudicative temporalities that resemble the form of his hermeneutics determine judicial facts in event and subject formation.

Gadamer rejects objective, neutral or value-free[51] readings of legal texts, instead attempting to explain what the conditions are for intersubjective meaning or *Verständigung*. The focus purely on method evades what actually informs any hermeneutical practice. Gadamer's hermeneutics can therefore be understood in three ways – that interpretation is ontological, dialectical and critical.[52]

That interpretation is ontological derives from Gadamer's contention that epistemology is largely independent of any scientific or timeless method, and instead, adopting Martin Heidegger's historicity of our 'being-in-the-world as the fore-structure of Dasein', he argues that we are in fact interpretive beings:

> We are thrown into a world whose contexts moulds us and limits our imagination and, hence, our options. Our very being is a process of interpreting our past, which is projected onto us and to which we respond… not in what way being can be understood but in what way understanding is being…interpretation is the common ground of interaction between text and interpreter, by which each establishes its being…interpreter and text are indissolubly linked as a matter of being.[53]

To put it crudely, interpretation is not something one 'does', but rather something one 'is'. Hence, to think of variable methods of interpretation misses the point. Unlike the *tabula rasa* of the Cartesian spectator, what shapes one's understanding of a text is one's *horizon* which is described as 'the range of vision that includes everything that can be seen from a particular vantage point'.[54] This relates to what Gadamer calls the *history of effect*[55]; as our existence is inherently contextual, we project onto meaning the traditions of the world in which, to once again use Heideggerean parlance, we are 'thrown into'. One possesses an 'effective historical consciousness' by stint of awareness of this situatedness. To do otherwise demonstrates what Gadamer refers to as Enlightenment thinking's 'prejudice toward prejudice'.

That interpretation is dialectical (or dialogical) refers to the to-ing and fro-ing between the horizons of the interpreter and the text. Meaning does not automatically protrude from the text (like the hermeneutics of authorial intent present in strands of UK interpretive thinking that venerate parliamentary intent or US Constitutional originalism) but requires participation.[56] Probing and further penetration of the text challenges the interpreter's horizon.[57] To quote Brad Sherman's writing, 'the confrontation with the text and openness is willingness to expose, challenge and criticise prejudices highlighted by the text, this openness is achieved dialectically with a willingness to listen and also to admit error'.[58] Indeed, 'an important part of this testing occurs in encountering the past and in understanding the tradition from which we come'.[59] The dialectical process with the text will eventually result in a *Fusion of Horizons* in which the interpreters' prejudgements, generated by their effective history, are exposed and challenged, as is the text. Both provoke introspection into the effective history of the interpreter and the presumptions of the text. Through conversation, a synthesis of sorts is accomplished.

That interpretation is critical states that 'the interpreter questions the text, the presuppositions of which may be attenuated or undermined over time. In turn, the interpreter uses the experience to re-evaluate her own pre-understandings, to separate the enabling, truth-seeking ones from the disabling, false ones'.[60] Romantic Hermeneutics, Gadamer argues, was based on a misplaced claim of transcendental meaning which undermines the critical scope of hermeneutics where the author is only the first reader of the text.

Gadamer's utility in statutory interpretation varies among scholars. Some say that it exemplified hermeneutical understanding,[61] some were more reticent[62] and still others presented it as an honest account of statutory interpretation that avoided the limitations of other theories[63]; some suggested proponents of the Gadamerian understanding have yet to unlock its potential.[64] The main criticisms levelled at Gadamer therefore emanated from its apparent conservativism (which was most vocal in his debate with Habermas),[65] its apparent relativism[66] and its lack of critical bite.[67] Important though these are, these will not be developed at this point, though there will be some discussion as to how Gadamer's hermeneutics may enable radical social transformation by visibilising conditions or social structures in CLJs rendering of the legal event.

There are many resonances in Gadamer's work that can help to advance other forms of adjudicative temporalities through a novel re-reading of his hermeneutics and his various ontological claims. Legal event formation, it can be argued, is structured by a temporality in which the present is constantly being constituted by an overarching past horizon. Indeed, 'time is the productive possibility of custom and tradition aiding understanding by illuminating what presents itself'.[68] An adventurous extrapolation of Gadamer will therefore result in the following. First, he describes his hermeneutics as observing the *conditions* for understanding. The importance of this will become clear in the later chapters, but we can make a few preliminary points. Spatial temporality has thus far been discussed as foregrounding causal relations through its presaging of chronologisation. Gadamerian temporality, as it were, will therefore seek to render the visibility of conditions rather than causes in the rendering of judicial facts. Gadamer's effective history as the constitutive horizon of the natural persons in adjudication suggests a temporality resistant to chronologisation. Like Bergson, Gadamer harboured a similar reticence towards the encroachment of the natural sciences on human understanding, and playful readings of Gadamer may be able to construe him in some sense as 'neo-Bergsonian' or with whom many parallels between his and Bergson's work can be drawn. Further, it does not require a Herculean leap to see the similarities between Gadamerian temporality and the way in which subject and event formation occurred in the *Ahluwalia* appeal. The history of violence she underwent suffuses our understanding of her killing her husband, and as with Gadamer, the two cannot be separated.

A chrono-centric (rather than rule-centric, correspondence) theory of judicial fact construction informed by Gadamerian temporalities would likely structure legal subjects and legal events, which would be largely resistant to 'time framing', as Kelman writes. It would be one in which the *effective history* would constitute a typically narrow time-framed legal event and subject in ALJ. Such a form of adjudicative temporality would likely require legal judgement to introspect into the traditions ('effective history') that constitute the legal subject and buttress the legal event with 'the conditions of the possibility of understanding'.[69] It is Gadamerian hermeneutics, particularly his work on effective history, that later characterises the *sedimented past* as another type of past in CLJ.

Grosz on untimely futures

This chapter will now turn its focus away from types of past and explore the possibilities of different types of futures productive in adjudication. However, the Bergsonian influence still resonates with these different expositions of futures. Elizabeth Grosz's writings, for example, on untimely futures, are thoroughly neo-Bergsonian, locating agency and emancipatory feminist politics in Bergson's theory of creativity. Here, two types of futures are described, one which is untimely and the other teleological.

We can read Groszian futures, as it were, through the work of Kathryn McNeilly. In attempting to rescue International Human Rights Law from the stagnations of its sundry shortcomings, McNeilly attempts to re-orient it towards *untimely futures* in the service of radical social change. Acknowledging that law is not *in* (substantivalist) time but that it can produce and sustain multiple temporalities, she locates the shortcomings of international human rights law in its production of particular futures, which are predicated on a 'linear temporality towards a knowable future' that 'has characterised understandings of the "what" and "why" of this area'.[70] In other words, she convincingly argues that the diminution of their transformative impact that many have invested in human rights has been because of the predictive futures inhered in the production of its temporalities. As such, this has undercut their transformative effects. Instead, therefore, McNeilly argues for an *untimely human rights* which abandons an Aristotelean linear and progressive relation between past, present and future and invests in a future which is not anticipated or prepared for in the present. Absent the *telos*, untimeliness is unknowable and it is that unknowability that presages the potential for radical social change.

McNeilly borrows from the work of Elizabeth Grosz and 'the implications and effects of conceiving a temporality in which the future remains virtual and beyond the control of the present'.[71] Grosz therefore firmly rejects teleological time of a graduated temporality, wherein the future is largely defined by the strictures of the present, 'a concept of a temporality not under the domination or privilege of the present, that is, a temporality directed to a future that is unattainable and unknowable in the present'.[72]

Not surprisingly, Grosz borrows from Bergson's notion of *durée* and élan vital,[73] in which he writes that the course of our own pasts does not pull us from the future into it but rather is the 'life source behind us'.[74] Bergson locates free-will in the site of *durée* or the 'pre-eminence of an undetermined future'.[75] Relevant to the field of human rights jurisprudence and drawing from Grosz, therefore, McNeilly argues 'that it is not strictly possible to learn from the past for the future in a substantive sense'.[76] The future cannot be contained in the present's pursuit of reading from the past an extrapolated and teleological and predictable future. It is, as Grosz urges us, to 'push the present to generate an unknown'. Grosz locates the possibilities of change within the horizons of an unknowable future:

> While resisting the temptation to predict, to forecast, to extrapolate trends of the present into the future, they are all, in different ways, directed to how we can generate and welcome a future that we may not recognize, a future that may deform, inflect, or redirect our current hopes and aspirations. They welcome a concept of the future which we do not control but which may shape and form us according to its forces.[77]

We've already come across similar renderings of futures in the rejection of *sensed* rules, which similarly extol the virtues of predictability, knowability and certainty, ultimately limiting the possibilities for radical social change.[78] Grosz liberates the past from a future that is its 'natural' extrapolation to one which is instead disjointed, and therefore potentially transformative.

Correspondingly, therefore, 'teleological futures' bestow importance on knowable futures. The soundings of teleological thinking are commonly associated with Aristotle (with forebears in Hegel and Marx, among others) and his purposive inclinations. They also informed Modernity's trajectories of progressivism and Weberian linear rational development.[79] Similarly, as Greenhouse writes, law typically advances linear conceptions of time. This is most evident, for example, in common law systems which are typically understood to follow a linear teleology. This can be disrupted at moments to respond to exogenous shocks but is always thought to be following a linear trend towards a final cause.[80] Similarly, French, despite identifying alternative forms of time produced by law, notes the dominance of linearity. Contrasted with untimely futures, this renders a future that is predictable or knowable. As will later become clear, *untimely futures* are what distinguishes CLJ from ALJ, the latter of which is characterised by teleological futures.

Again, we can see the production of these different types of futures in the *Ahluwalia* litigation. In the appeal hearing, emerges the creation, at that time, of a *new or what we may call an untimely* grounds for diminished responsibility – battered women syndrome. Now what is particularly important about this, and will be developed at some length later, is that this untimely future is only possible with the incorporation of certain facts which are emergent in different types of pasts (i.e. *not* those in the spatial past). In other words, the new defence isn't possible in the trial hearing because the durational past – the history of violence – was elided. However, once that is recognised in the appeal, a new future is possible. Thus there exists a relationship between the different types of pasts and futures, as will be demonstrated in the later discussions on CLJ.

Conclusion

The aim of this chapter has been to use theories of time and temporality to explain the *forms of adjudicative temporalities* and how they distinguish ALJ and CLJ in structuring subject and event formation. One form is *durée*, characterised by an interpenetrative, accumulating and constitutive past and ephemeral present. Another temporal form, spatial temporality, is characterised by features that can distinguish, select and place adjacent to one another, states into a sequence that are presumed to be causally related. This is entirely consonant with the Bergsonian formulation of spatial temporality that is characterised by uniformity, divisibility, juxtaposition and simultaneity. The third form, informed by Gadamerian hermeneutics, would likely structure legal subjects and legal events which would be largely resistant to 'time framing'. It would produce a construction of the legal subject that would be immersed in its *effective history* that would form part of the legal event. Such a form of adjudicative temporality would likely require legal judgement to introspect into the traditions ('effective history') that constitute the legal subject and what conditions pre-figure the legal event, 'the *conditions* of the possibility of understanding'.[81] The fourth form produces futures of unpredictability, unknowability and uncertainty, which contrast with the fifth form that is underwritten by a lineal teleology, rendering the future certain and knowable. The first three forms of adjudicative temporality will enable us to see the *types of pasts* produced in legal judgement and the legal subjects and events they produce, while the last two refer to the *types of future* that are produced. Through this exploration of the features of these different formations of time, it will hopefully help us to detail the differences between ALJ and CLJ, specifically in their constructions of the legal event and legal subject (though their productions of pasts and futures) and how this effects the outcome of judicial decision-making.

Notes

1 James Boyle, 'Is Subjectivity Possible? The Postmodern Subject in Legal Theory' (1991) 62 University of Colorado Review 522.
2 Rebecca R French, 'Time in the Law' (2001) 72 University of Colorado Law Review 672.
3 Rebecca R French, 'Time in the Law' (2001) 72 University of Colorado Law Review 703.
4 Kathryn McNeilly, 'Are Rights Out of Time? International Human Rights Law, Temporality, and Radical Social Change' (2018) 28, 6 Social and Legal Studies 817–838.
5 Gilles Deleuze, *Bergsonism* (Hugh Tomlinson and Barbara Habberjam trs, Zone Books 1991).
6 Elizabeth Grosz, *Time Travels: Feminism, Nature and Power* (Duke University Press 2005).
7 Renisa Mawani, 'The Times of Law' (2015) 40,1 Law & Social Inquiry 253–263.
8 Alexandre Lefebvre, *The Image of Law: Deleuze, Bergson, Spinoza* (Stanford University Press 2008); See also Suzanne Guerlac, *Thinking in Time: An Introduction to Henri Bergson* (Cornell University Press 2006) 173–211.
9 Souleymane Bachir Diagne, *Postcolonial Bergson* (Fordam University Press 2019).
10 This relates to the point that Alexandre Lefebvre makes earlier which stated that Bergson would have had a *prima facie* enmity towards the 'goal-oriented' adjudication of American Legal Pragmatism. See also Alexandre Lefebvre, *The Image of Law: Deleuze, Bergson, Spinoza* (Stanford University Press 2008) 114.
11 Henri Bergson, *Creative Evolution* (Arthur Miller tr, Macmillan and Co Ltd 1922) 89.
12 See also Suzanne Guerlac, *Thinking in Time: An Introduction to Henri Bergson* (Cornell University Press 2006).
13 This has been a bone of contention for some. See also Bertrand Russell, 'The Philosophy of Henri Bergson' (1912) 22,3 The Monist 321.
14 Henri Bergson, *Time and Free Will: An Essay on the Immediate Data of Consciousness* (J H Muirhead ed, F L Pogson trs, Forgotten Books 2012) 100.

15 Aristotle, 'Time' in Richard M Gale (ed), *The Philosophy of Time: A Collection of Essays* (Harvester Press 1978) 9–23.
16 Henri Bergson, *An Introduction to Metaphysics* (T E Hulme trs, Hackett Publishing Company 1999) 25.
17 See also Gerald Postema, 'Time in Law's Domain' (2018) 31,1 Ratio Juris 160–182; Gerald Postema, 'Melody and Law's Mindfulness of Time' (2004) 17,2 Ratio Juris 203. See also David Luban, 'Time-Mindedness and Jurisprudence' (2015) 101 Virginia Law Review 903–917.
18 Suzanne Guerlac, *Thinking in Time: An Introduction to Henri Bergson* (Cornell University Press 2006) 66–67.
19 Henri Bergson, *Time and Free Will: An Essay on the Immediate Data of Consciousness* (J H Muirhead ed, F L Pogson trs, Forgotten Books 2012) 108.
20 Henri Bergson, *Time and Free Will: An Essay on the Immediate Data of Consciousness* (J H Muirhead ed, F L Pogson trs, Forgotten Books 2012) 111.
21 Henri Bergson, *Time and Free Will: An Essay on the Immediate Data of Consciousness* (J H Muirhead ed, F L Pogson trs, Forgotten Books 2012) 111–112.
22 This idea is developed further in *Matter and Memory* but for an overview, see also Suzanne Guerlac, *Thinking in Time: An Introduction to Henri Bergson* (Cornell University Press 2006) 106–172.
23 Henri Bergson, *Time and Free Will: An Essay on the Immediate Data of Consciousness* (J H Muirhead ed, F L Pogson trs, Forgotten Books 2012) 106.
24 Kevät Nousiainen, 'Time of Law, Time of Experience' in Jes Bjarup and Mogens Blegvad (eds), *Time, Law and Society: Edited Proceedings of a Nordic Symposium at Sandbjerg Gods* (Franz Steiner Verlag 1994) 31.
25 This is in contrast to Valverde's 'chronotopic analysis'. See also Marina Valverde, *The Chronotopes of Law: Jurisdiction, Scale and Governance* (Routledge 2015) 33–37.
26 Immanuel Kant, *Critique of Pure Reason* (Paul Guyer and Allen W. Wood eds. & trs, CUP 1998) 163.
27 Henri Bergson, *Time and Free Will: An Essay on the Immediate Data of Consciousness* (J H Muirhead ed, F L Pogson trs, Forgotten Books 2012) 1.
28 Bergson differs significantly from empirical or idealist epistemologies. See also Bergson Henri Bergson, *Time and Free Will: An Essay on the Immediate Data of Consciousness* (J H Muirhead ed, F L Pogson trs, Forgotten Books 2012); *An Introduction to Metaphysics* (T E Hulme trs, Hackett Publishing Company 1999).
29 Henri Bergson, *Time and Free Will: An Essay on the Immediate Data of Consciousness* (J H Muirhead ed, F L Pogson trs, Forgotten Books 2012) 4–5.
30 Henri Bergson, *Time and Free Will: An Essay on the Immediate Data of Consciousness* (J H Muirhead ed, F L Pogson trs, Forgotten Books 2012) 90.
31 Suzanne Guerlac, *Thinking in Time: An Introduction to Henri Bergson* (Cornell University Press 2006) 45.
32 This is made clearer with the idea of *pure sensations* which are seemingly independent of any external stimuli or extensive magnitude and avoids the trap of equating it with extensity. See also Bergson Henri Bergson, *Time and Free Will: An Essay on the Immediate Data of Consciousness* (J H Muirhead ed, F L Pogson trs, Forgotten Books 2012) 10–11.
33 Suzanne Guerlac, *Thinking in Time: An Introduction to Henri Bergson* (Cornell University Press 2006) 49.
34 Henri Bergson, *Time and Free Will: An Essay on the Immediate Data of Consciousness* (J H Muirhead ed, F L Pogson trs, Forgotten Books 2012) 40–41.
35 Henri Bergson, *Time and Free Will: An Essay on the Immediate Data of Consciousness* (J H Muirhead ed, F L Pogson trs, Forgotten Books 2012) 95.
36 Henri Bergson, *Time and Free Will: An Essay on the Immediate Data of Consciousness* (J H Muirhead ed, F L Pogson trs, Forgotten Books 2012) 98.

37 Suzanne Guerlac, *Thinking in Time: An Introduction to Henri Bergson* (Cornell University Press 2006) 64.
38 This important point relates to abstraction that Deleuze takes issue with his critique of the dogmatic philosophy of recognition. For the sheep to be counted, they have to be categorised in a manner that extinguishes them of their qualitative difference (abstraction) so that what remains is their sameness. Therefore, they can only be counted if they correspond to an abstract concept or that which is recognised.
39 Henri Bergson, *Time and Free Will: An Essay on the Immediate Data of Consciousness* (J H Muirhead ed, F L Pogson trs, Forgotten Books 2012) 77 (emphasis added).
40 Suzanne Guerlac, *Thinking in Time: An Introduction to Henri Bergson* (Cornell University Press 2006) 62.
41 This is not to suggest that *durée* and the immediate consciousness is an 'objective reality'. See note above.
42 Henri Bergson, *Time and Free Will: An Essay on the Immediate Data of Consciousness* (J H Muirhead ed, F L Pogson trs, Forgotten Books 2012) 91.
43 Henri Bergson, *Time and Free Will: An Essay on the Immediate Data of Consciousness* (J H Muirhead ed, F L Pogson trs, Forgotten Books 2012) 9.
44 Much like Lefebvre's critiques of Hart, Dworkin and Habermas's theories of adjudication.
45 Suzanne Guerlac, *Thinking in Time: An Introduction to Henri Bergson* (Cornell University Press 2006) 62.
46 See also Mark S Muldoon, 'Henri Bergson and Postmodernism' (1990) 34,2 Philosophy Today 179.
47 Henri Bergson, *Time and Free Will: An Essay on the Immediate Data of Consciousness* (J H Muirhead ed, F L Pogson trs, Forgotten Books 2012) 77.
48 Suzanne Guerlac, *Thinking in Time: An Introduction to Henri Bergson* (Cornell University Press 2006) 69.
49 A R Lacey, *Bergson* (Routledge 1989) 28.
50 Brad Sherman, 'Hermeneutics in Law' (1988) 51 Modern Law Review 386–402; See also William N Eskridge Jr. 'Gadamer/ Statutory Interpretation' (1990) 3832 Yale Law School Faculty Scholarship Series 614.
51 Indeed, like Thomas Kuhn's 'consensus, crisis, paradigm shift', Gadamer similarly rejects the objectivity of the natural sciences. See also Georgia Warnke, *Hermeneutics, Tradition and Reason* (Polity Press 1987) 3.
52 William N Eskridge Jr. 'Gadamer/ Statutory Interpretation' (1990) 3832 Yale Law School Faculty Scholarship Series 614.
53 William N Eskridge Jr. 'Gadamer/ Statutory Interpretation' (1990) 3832 Yale Law School Faculty Scholarship Series 617–618.
54 Hans-Georg Gadamer, *Truth and Method* (Joel Weinheimer and Donald G Marshall trs, 2nd edn, Continuum Publishing Group 2004) 301.
55 Hans-Georg Gadamer, *Truth and Method* (Joel Weinheimer and Donald G Marshall trs, 2nd edn, Continuum Publishing Group 2004) 299–300.
56 Georgia Warnke, *Hermeneutics, Tradition and Reason* (Polity Press 1987) 65.
57 Brad Sherman, 'Hermeneutics in Law' (1988) 51 Modern Law Review 390.
58 Brad Sherman, 'Hermeneutics in Law' (1988) 51 Modern Law Review 393.
59 Hans-Georg Gadamer, *Truth and Method* (Joel Weinheimer and Donald G Marshall trs, 2nd edn, Continuum Publishing Group 2004) 306.
60 William N Eskridge Jr. 'Gadamer/ Statutory Interpretation' (1990) 3832 Yale Law School Faculty Scholarship Series 614.
61 Francis Joseph Mootz, 'Hermeneutics and Law' in Niall Keane and Chris Law (eds), *The Blackwell Companion to Hermeneutics* (Wiley & Sons 2016) 595.
62 Brad Sherman, 'Hermeneutics in Law' (1988) 51 Modern Law Review 395.

63 See also William N Eskridge Jr. 'Gadamer/ Statutory Interpretation' (1990) 3832 Yale Law School Faculty Scholarship Series 609–681; George Wright, 'On a General Theory of Interpretation: The Betti-Gadamer Dispute in Legal Hermeneutics' (1987) 32,1 American Journal of Jurisprudence 191.
64 Francis Joseph Mootz, 'Hermeneutics and Law' in Niall Keane and Chris Law (eds), *The Blackwell Companion to Hermeneutics* (Wiley & Sons 2016) 1.
65 For a summary of the debate, see also William N Eskridge Jr. 'Gadamer/ Statutory Interpretation' (1990) 3832 Yale Law School Faculty Scholarship Series 630–632; Georgia Warnke, *Hermeneutics, Tradition and Reason* (Polity Press 1987) 92.
66 Georgia Warnke, *Hermeneutics, Tradition and Reason* (Polity Press 1987) 91.
67 See also Francis J Mootz, 'Gadamer's Rhetorical Conception of Hermeneutics as the Key to Developing a Critical Hermeneutics (2008) SSRN Electronic Journal 1–21.
68 Paul Regan, 'Hans-Georg Gadamer's Philosophical Hermeneutics: Concepts of Reading, Understanding and Interpretation' (2012) 4,2 Meta: Research in Hermeneutics, Phenomenology, and Practical Philosophy 300.
69 Georgia Warnke, *Hermeneutics, Tradition and Reason* (Polity Press 1987) 3.
70 Kathryn McNeilly, 'Are Rights Out of Time? International Human Rights Law, Temporality and Radical Social Change' (2018) Social and Legal Studies 4.
71 Elizabeth Grosz, *Time Travels: Feminism, Nature, Power* (Duke University Press 2005) 1.
72 Elizabeth Grosz, *Time Travels: Feminism, Nature, Power* (Duke University Press 2005) 1.
73 Henri Bergson, *Creative Evolution* (Arthur Miller tr, Macmillan and Co Ltd 1922) 89.
74 Henri Bergson, *Creative Evolution* (Arthur Miller tr, Macmillan and Co Ltd 1922) 89.
75 Elizabeth Grosz, 'Feminist Futures' (2002) 21,1 Tulsa Studies in Women's Literature 15.
76 Kathryn McNeilly, 'Are Rights Out of Time? International Human Rights Law, Temporality and Radical Social Change' (2018) Social and Legal Studies 823.
77 Elizabeth Grosz, *Time Travels: Feminism, Nature, Power* (Duke University Press 2005) 2.
78 On this very point of radical social change, McNeilly turns to the work of Drucillia Cornell and Judith Butler, to whom the book shall return to later when looking at the past and future temporalities of CLJ.
79 Max Weber, *The Protestant Ethic and the Spirit of Capitalism* (1930; London 1992).
80 Carol Greenhouse, A *Moment's Notice: Time Politics across Culture* (Cornell University Press 1996).
81 Georgia Warnke, *Hermeneutics, Tradition and Reason* (Polity Press 1987) 3.

Chapter 3

The temporalities of abstract legal judgment

Introduction

Legal Realism and Critical Legal Studies offer an important departure point for this book as they posit the peripheral role of legal rules in both legal decision-making and their determination of facts in legal judgement. This book tentatively argues that adjudicative temporalities occupy the role vacated by rule de-centring, in that *it* conditions judicial fact construction, specifically its production of the legal subject and legal event through its constructions of pasts and futures. These have corollary effects in how liability and responsibilities are determined (given the focus on criminal law). This book began by identifying two types of legal judgement – Abstract Legal Judgement (ALJ) and Concrete Legal Judgement (CLJ) – situated at antipodal ends of a spectrum rather than divided into binary typology of adjudication such that legal decisions could be distinguished by tending towards either side (rather than being examples of either/or). In addition to the features of ALJ that William Lucy outlines, which I will shortly restate, this chapter also details the adjudicative temporalities that inform ALJ – specifically the futures and pasts that it produces – as well as the events and subjects that it constructs and, in keeping with the two stages of interpretive construction that Kelman identifies, the way in which the legal rule is framed to handle the fact situation. The central argument of this chapter therefore provides an elucidation of Kelman's time framing that is characteristic of ALJ as well as arguing that the production of the archetypal legal subject – what is now referred to as liberal legal subject – in adjudication as well as the legal event is fundamentally a question about its temporal construction.

This chapter will start by providing a summary of some of the features of ALJ before detailing the types of pasts and futures, drawing on the previous chapter, that are latent in decisions that tend towards ALJ. Following this broader discussion, this chapter embarks on an exegesis of subject formation in ALJ and the ways in which its temporalities produce such legal subjects, which are 'contained' within the legal event and are 'born and reborn at each moment'. The next section then looks at cases where the time frames adopted by ALJ are broadened, say in cases such as loss of self-control or contributory negligence (in civil cases). While it may reasonably be presumed that a broader time frame or broader spatial past may compromise agency, this is not necessarily the case as I will later explain. Finally, the chapter finishes off with drawing on the merits and demerits of this conventional approach to judicial decision-making.

Features of ALJ

To recall Lucy's summation of ALJ, he defines it as having three components: it 'judges us (i) not in all our particularity but as identical abstract beings; (ii) by reference to general and objective standards equally applicable to all such beings; (iii) the application of these standards being mitigated only by a limited range of exculpatory claims'.[1] The three features of this type of judgement, this chapter argues, are conditioned by the adjudicative temporalities they produce for the reason that temporality structures event and subjective formation.

ALJ is defined by a *spatial temporality* (borrowing from Bergson's critique of Kantian temporality explained in the previous chapter) that, given adjudication takes place *ex post factum*, produces *spatial pasts*. The features of spatial pasts underwrite what Kelman refers to as time framing in which spatiality enables the use of narrow or broad(er) time framing in judicial fact construction. This chapter also foretells how spatial temporalities enable the elision of *other types of pasts*, referred to later as *variegated pasts*, which are produced by non-spatial adjudicative temporalities.

Further, the production of the liberal legal subject in adjudication is fundamentally a question about its temporal construction. Subject formation in ALJ is contingent on the production of spatial pasts and produces a legal subject which is desituated and deracinated. Indeed, it is what Lucy terms as *presumptive identity*,[2] in that ALJ structures the liberal legal subject as having 'the same in terms of those capacities, cognitive and physical, which enable humans to comply with achievable and intelligible legal standards'.[3] Notably, the term 'presumptive' is an interesting one, with clear temporal connotations that inhere an anticipatory logic of sameness and knowability of the legal subject in advance of adjudication. The argument here is that this anticipatory logic of sameness is maintained in the constructions of past, through legally produced spatial time, in adjudication.

Ultimately, the production of the liberal legal subject in ALJ is such that it elides pre-existing physical and mental health ailments as well as the social, cultural and economic situatedness of the persons – which are revealed in other non-spatial temporalities. More specifically, as it will be later explained, the liberal legal subject is typically *contained* in a spatially time-framed legal event in which the legal subject it constituted by a series of repetitive new beginnings, born and reborn at each moment. This overarching temporality of the liberal legal subject makes more sense in cases where the legal event adopts a broad time frame, as will be illustrated later.

Finally, the way in which the legal rule(s) is framed in ALJ, is that they are *sensed*. This means that the rule(s) presupposes the judicial facts as mere representations of the rule. Relatedly, therefore, this means that ALJ is characterised by futures that are knowable (rather than 'untimely'), bearing a lineal teleology, reinforcing the certainty of the legal rule and legal system overall and reducing ALJ to a type of legal formalism. Lefebvre in fact refers to this as *inattentive judgement*, in which a judge treats the facts of the case as a familiar situation, a mere instantiation of the general legal rule so that the facts operate as a representative sign of a general rule.[4]

Spatial pasts and knowable futures of the legal event

Given that adjudication takes place *ex post factum*, ALJ's spatial temporalities produce spatial pasts that primarily lend to categorising reality into discrete events that can be distinguished, placed adjacent to one another and selected to generate a chronology. If we recall the features of spatial temporality – uniformity, divisibility, juxtaposition and simultaneity – this provides the theoretical underpinnings of Kelman's (as with Nousiainen's) *time framing* as the unconscious construct in criminal law adjudication, which allows it to construct the world and natural persons in narrow or broad time frames. This affords the judge and juries in trial cases the ability to *chronologise* the legal event. This is the process of distinguishing, selecting and placing adjacent to one another states into a sequence that are presumed to be causally related. To use the Bergsonian nomenclature, ALJ produces a past-ness externally in space that translates the construction of an indivisible and interconnected consciousness of the world into discrete units capable of being counted and measured. Importantly, by thinking of ALJ's temporality as spatial, enabling the chronologising of the past, also allows the courts to consider certain types of pasts immaterial and thus 'framed out'.

Spatial temporality allows for reality to be measured, numbered, sequenced and manipulated, and to demarcate the commencement-termination of the boundaries of facts which are considered relevant for a court case. Judges will use temporal triggers[5] that appear to suggest time (*qua durée*), when in actual fact this is nothing more than ordering in spatially inflected time. Such temporal triggers can either be dates or conduct which denote the initiation of legal relations, such as acceptance of a contract (and the other pre-requisites) or *mens rea* and so forth. The temporalities of ALJ therefore imbue a difference of degree, not of kind, a difference between broad or narrow time frames.

If one accepts the apparent necessity of spatial temporality, that is, if we take Bergson's critique seriously that reflection necessarily spatialises time – crucially important, given that adjudication always takes place *ex post factum* – then in effect all cases necessarily chronologise the determination of the facts of a case. Spatial temporalities are inevitable. While most fact paragraphs in legal reportage will provide an example of such chronlogisation, the popular case of *McLoughlin v. O'Brian* and Lord Wilberforce's statement can help illustrate the point:

> My Lords, this appeal arises from a very serious and tragic road accident which occurred on October 19, 1973, near Withersfield, Suffolk. The appellant's husband, Thomas McLoughlin, and three of her children, George, aged 17, Kathleen, aged 7, and Gillian, nearly 3, were in a Ford motor car: George was driving. A fourth child, Michael, then aged 11, was a passenger in a following motor car driven by Mr. Pilgrim: this car did not become involved in the accident. The Ford car was in collision with a lorry driven by the first respondent and owned by the second respondent. That lorry had been in collision with another lorry driven by the third respondent and owned by the fourth respondent. It is admitted that the accident to the Ford car was caused by the respondents' negligence.[6]

Speculating as to how Bergson would describe this passage, it could be that it is a representation of the lived experience of the litigants, articulated (and thus operant in the reflective consciousness) through the judicial production of spatial temporalities. The very act of expression severs *durée* into separate parts (time frames) such that the judge is able to provide points of application.

Spatial pasts therefore enable temporal triggers that initiate or terminate a legal event, within which laws, powers, rights and obligations are activated.[7] Spatiality, as uniformity, divisibility, juxtaposition and simultaneity, allows pasts to be separated from broader time frames – but also, as it will be argued later, *other types of pasts*. Thus, more concretely, time framing enabled through the dividing and juxtaposing logics of spatial temporality is what facilitates the elision of other types of past (and therefore facts) in adjudication. This is what Patrick Nerhot more broadly describes when he says that 'a fact is the result of an operation whereby a particular element is taken out, isolated from a context of its own to be placed in another context that gives it a particular meaning'.[8] Oliver Wendell Holmes wrote about adjudication that:

> The process is one, from a lawyer's statement of a case, eliminating as it does all the dramatic elements with which his client's story has clothed it, and retaining only the facts of legal import, up to the final analyses and abstract universals of theoretic jurisprudence.[9]

The spatial temporalities of ALJ enable events to be rendered as a chronology that gives it a particular meaning, presumed to be causally related and largely independent of other types of pasts. The qualities of space are needed to time frame factual construction and subsequently to ascertain rights and responsibilities. The production of spatial temporality permits the creation of indices that allow for the formation of the legal event. It apportions control in determining what is and what is not relevant in the determination of facts enabling 'a provisional hooking together of elements into something that looks cohesive'.[10] Time as spatial therefore is a form of sorting into a seemingly coherent representational narrative. Once again, to chronologise what Kelman refers to as time framing is the process of distinguishing, selecting and placing adjacent to one another states into a sequence that are presumed to be causally related.

Finally, ALJ produces knowable futures, following a lineal teleology that ensures legal certainty. In other words, as will become apparent, spatial pasts ensure the sameness or the presumptive identity of the legal subject. This increases the likelihood that the incumbent case is treated like 'similar cases' or cases that similarly deploy spatial pasts, eliding contingency, situatedness and difference in the formation of the subject and event of law. Certainty, predictability and knowable futures are therefore produced through the presumptive identity of the legal subject that is ensured in eliding difference which would otherwise only be emergent in non-spatial pasts.

Legal subjectivity formation in ALJ

The presumptive identity of legal subjects produced in ALJ – that are 'the same in terms of those capacities, cognitive and physical, which enable humans to comply with achievable and intelligible legal standards'[11] – can more fundamentally be explained with reference to spatial temporalities, specifically spatial pasts, produced by ALJ. This section attempts to explain how the paradigmatic *liberal legal subject*[12] – abstracted, deracinated and rational – is structured by ALJ's spatial pasts. In turn, this also helps to explain how particular *types of pasts*, in which contingency, situatedness and difference are emergent, are considered immaterial in ALJ's determination of fact.

Generally, the term legal subject is used interchangeably and can often refer to different bodies, things or persons within legal proceedings. These include legal persons,[13] legal participants,[14] legal entity,[15] juridical man[16] or juristic person.[17] To add to the confusion, the legal subject can refer not just to litigants but to judges,[18] and this does not entertain a more perennial debate about non-human legal persons[19] as the subject of rights as well as hierarchies of humanities in rights discourse.[20]

While a legal subject maybe someone who attempts to understand the law, legal doctrine and the legal system,[21] the legal subject is understood here as:

> how law or legal culture constructs how we think about people—how law and legal culture ascribe particular identities and features to people, defining some characteristics as salient and others as irrelevant.

> The "legal subject," in this sense, is a subject as seen (and dealt with) through the eyes of the law or legal culture.[22]

That the legal subject is a social construction is by no means revelatory.[23] Ngaire Naffine provides a useful taxonomy of legal subjectivity in common law jurisdictions, identifying three types with varying commitments to whether they maintain a correspondence with a presumed objective personhood or whether legal subject formation recognises its constructivist epistemologies. Indeed, 'should it even be law's task to try to capture and preserve and protect what it takes to be our essential natures, to mirror life? Or should the life of the legal person remain an independent legal reality, not part of the non-legal world of fact'.[24]

The first type of legal persons Naffine refers to anecdotally as 'the Cheshire Cat', defined later in her writings as the 'Legalist position'[25]:

> ...nothing more than the formal capacity...it does not depend on metaphysical claims about what it is to be a person. Subscribers to this definition of person tend to insist on the abstract and purely legal nature of the concept and in so doing they appear to set law apart from moral theory and also from the social, political and historical sciences.[26]

Simply, to be a legal person is to be the subject of legal rights and duties. Thus, to confer legal rights or to impose legal duties is to confer legal personality.[27] Bryant Smith similarly argues that personhood is 'an abstraction of which legal relations are predicated, or as a name for the condition of being party to legal relations'.[28] This conception of the legal person operates at its highest level of abstraction and presupposes a normative closure of law that does not care for metaphysical speculations of personality or subjecthood.[29] Because of its abstraction, this functions as the most inclusive conception of the person whilst being the most empirically bankrupt and morally empty.[30]

Second is 'any reasonable creature in being', which 'in this context means a human someone, becomes a legal person...at birth, which is also legally defined, and stops being a legal person at whole brain death, legally defined... it is necessarily linked with biological and also metaphysical definitions of humanity'.[31] Naffine later describes this in her work as the religionist[32] and the naturalist[33] approaches to legal personality. Here the law contemplates conceptions of human-ness, absorbing insights from medicine,[34] but also theological and philosophical inquiries. Its most enduring presence is obviously within human rights discourse, in which legal personality precedes positive rights, though discussions around the genealogy of human rights have often contested who constitutes the human of human rights, as well as whether or not to extend the taxonomy of persons of law to animals.[35]

Third, perhaps the most pervasive,[36] is the paradigmatic rationalist[37] or 'responsible subject' that is 'an active, autonomous actor: someone who is positively able to bear legal duties and to assert legal rights in their own capacity. This person is imagined as an attentive, articulate litigant or defendant, who can appreciate the complexity of law's demands and respond directly and personally, for his own reasons'.[38] She/he is essentialised with attributions of will and foresight, the 'normal person'.[39] They represent 'to many the ideal (if not the actual) legal actor'.[40] Specifically in criminal law exists a highly rational agent[41] that seeks to sustain a coherent theory of responsibility: 'the central organising idea, which is accepted by leading criminal law theorists, is that criminal law communicates its freedom-limiting norms directly to us, as rational agents'.[42] It is *this* construction of legal subjectivity, produced by spatial temporalities in ALJ, that is synonymous with the paradigmatic subject of law and the basis upon which the chapter proceeds.

One may refer to this paradigmatic legal subject as the archetypal *liberal legal subject*, who 'is a highly accountable, independent, and socially de-contextualised agent'[43] and can be likened to the presumptive identity characterised in ALJ. There is analytical convenience in this rendering of legal subjectivity, a unitary, autonomous, impermeable, deracinated, rational and agential subject '"back there" in control of analysis and reason'.[44] Indeed, it is perhaps one of the most saleable aspects of Modernity, linked to our own individual physicality while also preserving the idea of the world as the extension of the thinking ego. Indeed, the engine history proceeds largely through the ideas of man.[45] This produces an interesting situation, in which the individual makes history, but they can also transcend it, along with their situatedness and contingency – the latter two of which Lucy says is otherwise elided in the presumed identity of legal subjects. The liberal legal subject is not only centred but seemingly 'objective' in that it has the ability to shear its own idiosyncrasies.

It is worth briefly noting the attempts of varying intellectual traditions to upend what Critical Legal Studies refers to as a theoretical fiction.[46] In an effort to problematise the presumed essences of a unified, autonomous and rational self, it has most emphatically been denounced within postmodernist circles as a discursive construct.[47] Writing that 'it is not the consciousness of men that determines their existence but their social existence that determines their consciousness',[48] Marxian notions of legal subjectivity also recognise the contingency of subject-hood. Specifically in relation to how the capitalist mode of production renders subjectivity of equal and abstract personality in the realisation of exchange-value, Marxists have critiqued how juridical subjectivity[49] elides the concrete conditions of commodity exchange and therefore obfuscate the relations of exploitation and domination.[50] Despite the ubiquity of these attacks, the liberal legal subject largely prevails.

The deracinated liberal legal subject in law is also rational and often referred to as the 'reasonable man'. Though a legal fiction, he[51] provides the presumed hypothetical standard for legal conduct. Consider the tort of negligence where 'we must judge the defendant by the standards of a reasonable person who is undertaking the task or activity in the course of which negligence is said to arise. The "reasonable person" test is generally an objective one, which is not adjusted to fit the particular qualities of the defendant'.[52] Lord Macmillan in *Muir v. Glasgow Corporation* identifies the reasonable man as follows:

> Some persons are by nature unduly timorous and imagine every path beset with lions. Others, of more robust temperament, fail to foresee or nonchalantly disregard even the most obvious dangers. The reasonable man is presumed to be free both from over-apprehension and from over-confidence, but there is a sense in which the standard of care of the reasonable man involves in its application a subjective element. It is still left to the judge to decide what, in the circumstances of the particular case, the reasonable man would have had in contemplation, and what, accordingly, the party sought to be made liable ought to have foreseen.[53]

The problems, however, with the *presumed identity* of the liberal legal subject can surmised as follows:

> When we insist on formal equality, we can do so only by drawing a very narrow picture of what it is to be a legal subject, the universal and formally defined actor of civil society. I am equal to one of the Rockefellers because we are both political subjects, we are both formally equal, and the 'form' is very narrow. Disparities of wealth, power, and status are defined out of existence precisely because they are placed outside the realm of political subjectivity. Does he have the vote? Is he a citizen? Does he have the right to speak freely? Then of what relevance is it that he has no political power, that he is effectively disenfranchised and that he does not have the resources to make himself heard? As a political subject he is equal to anyone.[54]

The argument here is that the production of the liberal legal subject in ALJ is fundamentally a result of its temporal construction.

In other words, spatial temporalities, enabling time framing, produce the paradigmatic, deracinated, liberal legal subject by 'transcending' particular types of pasts that would otherwise render the situatedness and constituted nature of the legal subject visible. This is possible given the features of spatial temporality (divisible, uniform, juxtaposed and simultaneous) that enables the framing out and elision of these other types of pasts.

In the context of ALJ, the presumptive identity of the liberal legal subject is constructed by spatial temporality, enabling the production of pasts that are divisible, uniform and selectable – that is, the selection of narrow or broad time frames – contrasted with a theory of adjudicative temporality that is necessarily interconnected and resistant to division. Thus, contingency and situatedness of the liberal legal subject can be ignored through the non-selection of different types of pasts such as pre-existing conditions (i.e. mental, physiological conditions or social structures) – more on this later. ALJ assumes the presumptive identity of the liberal legal subject through the production of a past that elides other types of pasts that reveal its contingency and situatedness. Spatial temporality therefore provides the theoretical underpinnings of narrow and broad time frames that Kelman suggests is the difference between intentionalist and determinist discourses in criminal law adjudication.

To be clear, it is not that adjudicative temporalities make the subject of law rational or deracinated, but rather that it constructs it in such a mode, in its determination of the legal event, to presume that it is rational. However, there is more to merely the juridical production of a spatial past that constructs a legal subject that transcends its difference (through time framing). The legal subject in ALJ only *appears* within a (typically, though not always) narrow time-framed legal event. In effect, the liberal legal subject is contained within the time frame of the legal event that the legal judgement has adopted. In the fullest embrace of ALJ, therefore, everything, such as more remote antecedent moments (e.g. loss of self-control, unless of course a broad time frame is adopted) and pre-existing conditions (e.g. mental, physiological conditions or social structures), are elided or framed out in the construction of the legal event and legal subject. In determining responsibility, the trial judge (or the jury under the judge's direction) will consider the action only within the confines of said spatially-temporally constructed legal event (ignoring more antecedent moments or pre-existing conditions).

Though there may be some reference in the law reports to more remote events, the liberal legal subject only emerges within the confines of a spatial past constructed legal event: what Kelman understands by the narrow time frame that presumes the 'free-will' discourse of criminal law. It follows that 'cutting off' from broad time frames or other types of past (what is now referred to as the *variegated past*, to which I shall return to in the following chapter) leaves only that past which is considered material and allows the natural person to retain the 'reasonable man' edifice. Indeed, 'in order that we may lay hold upon and describe the living process within ourselves, we are obliged to direct attention upon selected and therefore fragmentary parts of an undivided whole'.[55] Outside of these indexes, the liberal legal subject is not able to engage their legal rights. Indeed, 'right regimes are therefore often conceived and implemented through temporal mechanisms that rely, at least, on a "before" and an "after"'.[56] Outside of these indexes, they cease to be paradigmatic liberal legal subject. With no other types of past produced by the temporalities of ALJ (ignoring pre-existing conditions or the variegated past), it is as if the *liberal legal subject is born, killed and reborn at each moment*; this is particularly pertinent when we look at the adoption of broad time frames. Borrowing from Sarah Keenan's writings on the temporalities of the Torrens Land registry, we might describe the liberal legal subject that ALJ produces as having 'an overarching time of repetitive new beginnings, a series of staccato-like slices of time'[57] that are detached from variegated pasts (i.e. more antecedent moments or pre-existing conditions).

Importantly, therefore, this also means that even if a broad time frame is adopted (i.e. to incorporate an antecedent moment such as Loss of Self-Control) to create the legal event, as will be detailed shortly, it still maintains the paradigmatic deracinated, agential and rational liberal legal subject. This pertains to the final feature of ALJ that Lucy ascribes that there are only a limited number of exculpatory claims that may reasonably mitigate responsibility. Normative ascriptions of responsibility can and do change with broader time frames, but it is still considered so with the frame of the liberal legal subject that is created through a series of repetitive new beginnings. Such defences are considered normative because of the reasonable person's logic underwriting them. As William Lucy writes, 'when accepting exculpatory claims, the law rarely delves into the particularities of the defendant's context or character as reinforced by something else: such exculpatory claims are usually only valid if reasonable. Reasonableness requirements are the principal means by which the law treats those before it as abstract beings rather than the beings they actually are'.[58]

Thus one can begin to conceptualise and redefine the legal subject along the lines of legal temporalities. *In ALJ, the liberal legal subject is the containment of the litigant(s) within the boundaries of a spatial past-legal event, a subject that is born, killed and reborn at each moment.*

Spatial temporality (which is divisible, uniform, able to be juxtaposed and simultaneous), as that which enables time frames and by extension the selection (and elision) of pasts, allows the courts to include and exclude, incorporate and extinguish, other types of pasts (ignoring more antecedent moments, unless a broad time frame is adopted) or pre-existing conditions (the variegated past) to produce a liberal legal subject that transcends contingency and situatedness (which destabilise or problematise its presupposed agency) through that very selection. Elsewhere, this has been referred to as chronologisation, which is the process of distinguishing, selecting and placing adjacent to one another states into a sequence that are presumed to be causally related.

Spatial temporality tries to construct certainty everywhere[59] through the production of a legal subject who is a highly accountable, independent and socially de-contextualised agent. ALJ does this by enabling the possibility of adjudication to disconnect from contingency and situatedness emergent in the variegated pasts which are produced by other adjudicative temporalities (argued in the following chapter). The effect of spatial temporality is to delineate a retrospective reality that enables ALJ to dissect and divide a natural person's life into events and to contain them within the confines of a spatio-temporally constructed legal event.

To further describe the spatial past, the following sections will be dedicated to three of its salient features. These include the process of broadening the legal event, the nature of the broadening and the nature of its past-ness.

Broadening the legal event in ALJ

While having explained the legal event and (the more typically adopted[60]) narrow time frames through the production of spatial pasts, there still requires an explanation of broad(er) time frames that are operative in the legally produced spatial pasts. Broadening is the process of switching from the adoption of a narrow time frame of the spatial past in judicial fact construction to the adoption of a broader time frame. This also means broadening still engages spatial pasts as opposed to variegated pasts. This attempts to make sense of the third feature of ALJ, which Lucy spells out as the mitigation of responsibility through a limited range of exculpatory claims. This tends to occur with some defences in criminal (i.e. loss of self-control) as well as civil law (i.e. consent, contributory negligence). Contrast this, for example, with strict liability cases. They tend to contain the legal subject within a very narrow time-framed legal event. Narrowness presumes rationality (and thus responsibility) as it 'cuts off' contingency, situatedness and thus potentially exculpatory facts emergent in different types of pasts that may otherwise compromise the agency of the legal subject. Consider section 5 of the *Sexual Offences Act 2003*, which considers sexual intercourse with a child under 13 a strict liability crime of rape, irrespective of the age of the defendant. All that is required for the offence is proof of the intentional penetration of the child under 13. This is based on the principle that intentional sexual activity such as that proscribed in section 5 with children below that age should not be permitted in any circumstances. In the case of *R v.G*,[61] the appellant, 15 at the time of the offence, had intercourse with the complainant, who told him that she was 15 when she was actually 12. He was convicted and appealed on the grounds, first, that an offence of criminal strict liability pursuant to section 5 infringed his Article 6(1) and (2) right to a 'fair and public hearing' and presumption of innocence rights, respectively, and, second, that the conviction was incompatible with his Article 8 rights such that 'as he was only 15 at the time of the offence, the Crown acted unduly harshly by prosecuting him under section 5 rather than under section 13, which deals with sexual offences committed by persons under 18 and carries a maximum penalty for imprisonment for 5 years'.[62]

What facts are deemed judicially relevant? As far as constructing the legal event and subject goes, the appellant is contained within the spatial past-constructed legal event, 'starting' from when he intentionally penetrated the complainant. Everything else is extinguished (or framed out) and thus no other types of pasts are weaved into this retrospective narrative. Though the courts at both appellate stages accepted the applicant's version of the events, namely that he believed her to be 15 when she had expressed words to that effect, the 'eyes through which the law saw the legal subject' was in a 'sensed' and thus strict application of that rule (what Lucy refers to as the 'uniformity component') that only considered relevant the facts that are presupposed in the rule. This may seem entirely reasonable, given moral and practical considerations in protecting child welfare, but could one envisage a situation in which there ought to be some discretion? What may emerge if other types of variegated pasts (or pre-existing conditions) were incorporated into the construction of the legal event? Indeed, Lord Hope hinted indirectly at the absence of other types of pasts which would seek to contextualise the transgression by identifying the difficulty confronting prosecuting authorities in 'discriminating between cases where the proscribed activity was truly mutual on the one hand and those where the complaint was subjected to an element of exploitation or undue pressure on the other'.[63]

In effect, the case is seen merely as a particularisation of section 5 such that the rule was sensed. For strict liability cases, therefore, other types of variegated pasts (pre-existing conditions), structured by non-spatial adjudicative temporalities (as it is later argued)[64] that would problematise the free-will paradigm of the archetypal liberal legal subject, are an anathema. The absence of moral blameworthiness is irrelevant as are the unique circumstances. Even though there may be course to mitigate responsibility of the appellant, only emergent in other types of past, strict liability for 'reasons of principle' ignores these.

R v. G may be contrasted with the 'asbestos litigation'[65] for their noticeably different use of time frames in the formation of the legal event. In the latter, the natural persons as claimants (rather than just defendants) *appear earlier.* These cases sought to bring actions against the parties' old employers for negligently exposing them to asbestos. Over a period of time, they had worked for several companies and contractors which had exposed them to the fibres. The issue, however, was that the latent period for the onset of pleural mesothelioma contracted from the asbestos fibres took many years and it wasn't clear which of their previous employers were responsible. Lord Bingham said that the 'balance of probabilities test' for establishing causation was inappropriate for this particular case and instead ruled that causation could be established if the defendant(s) had materially increased the risk of harm.

At first, it may appear that such a comparison is not warranted, given that the contrast between these cases lie in the use of obviously different legal rules. However, as has been stated from the onset, this book claims that judicial fact construction is contingent on the adjudicative temporalities that structure it, rather than a correspondence theory of rule-centric adjudication. A further response to this would be to ask why one legal rule is sensed in such a way to adopt a narrow time frame and largely ignore other types of variegated pasts (which Lord Hope in *R v. G* appeared to be hinting at such), yet another legal rule is able to construct the legal event in the asbestos litigation on the basis of medical knowledge using a broader time frame. This may provide some insight into what types of variegated pasts are deemed acceptable in the process of broadening. Are only physiological causes worthy of broad time frames? What about other enduring conditions that we may liken to Johann Gaultung's structures of violence? Or persistent forms of economic exploitation in materialist readings of history? Indeed, does this ruling on causation entrench a particular vision of social and economic organisation?[66] Do strict liability crimes tend to target a particular disenfranchised class of society?

Though broader time frames, used to accommodate the latent period for the onset of mesothelioma, contrast to the narrow time frames adopted in *R v. G*, what is particularly interesting about these cases is that despite both claimants and the defendants *appearing earlier*, this did not necessarily entail an analysis mitigating the liabilities of the defendant employers. Indeed, they were still constructed as responsible agents who had 'materially increased the risk of harm' to the claimants, the reason being that the litigants were still seen in a narrow time frame, of repetitive new beginnings, a series of staccato-like slices of time.

Another example of a broadening of the legal event includes the partial defence of contributory negligence that mitigates the defendant's tortious liability due to the claimant's action as a contributory factor. This particular act differs in degree from a normal negligence claim by a magnitude of uniform units from the point in time of the defendant's negligent (in) action (hence features of spatial time). In the case of *Froom v. Butcher*,[67] the defendant sought a reduction in damages after he had crashed into the claimant's car, injuring the driver and his wife and daughter, because they were not wearing seat belts. The judges allowed the appeal and reduced the damages accordingly. In terms of the construction of the legal event, Mr Froom's actions (or, rather, inaction of not wearing his seat belt) *preceded* Mr Butcher's crashing into him. The event and thus the liabilities of the legal subject(s) similarly changed. Broadening of the legal event along the axis of spatial temporality mitigates responsibility in the case of contributory negligence for the defendant.

A fair question would be to ask whether this construction of the legal event in ALJ's determination of judicial facts is the work of a political choice of time frames, structured by spatial temporality, or primarily the normative assessment of relative responsibility? A weak reply would be to admit that the judges were primarily motivated by making a normative assessment and that Kelman's 'time frames' are *unconscious* interpretive constructs or mere retrospective justification. A stronger reply, however, would be to ask in the case of *Froom* why the judge thought it pertinent to stop at the point of contributory negligence despite undertaking a process of broadening. Perhaps there is something that Mr Froom had interpellated from his past which meant he would not wear his seat belt (interestingly, this was not a legal requirement at the time). This may seem tenuous in this particular case, but the impetus behind the question is to inquire as to the value of 'cutting off' or framing out at this moment, particularly following a process of *broadening* the legal event and why a past that is separable rather than interconnected (as far as is possible) is normatively useful. How would a normative judgement change with a considerably broader time frame, as it clearly changed with the claimant's antecedent action?

Importantly, the *process of broadening* occurs with *instances or points in spatial time*. Instances refer to a particular fact(s) that the courts consider relevant, which form points in spatial time – entirely resonant with the *divisibility* of spatial time. For example, the contributing negligent act in *Froom* – the inaction of wearing seat belts – broadens the legal event back to this earlier *point*. It is called an instant because it refers to a *point in time* which *starts and ceases*, a fleeting moment. The significance of this will now be explained.

It is worth making a final point as to the nature of spatial pasts which will help to illustrate more clearly its difference from the variegated pasts that are produced in CLJ. Spatial pasts (and the events and legal subjects they produce) are past by virtue of adjudication being *ex post factum*. This means that when the event was happen*ing*, these pasts were by definition present. The reason for making this point will be developed in more detail later[68] but briefly. The spatial past can be contrasted with the *variegated past*, what we understand as conditions, which can be either physiological or mental (such as insanity, battered woman syndrome) or structural. Unlike the spatial past, the *variegated past*[69] cannot be considered *past* in the same way as the constituents of the legal event operant in the spatial past. This is because when the event was happening, these conditions *were* and continue to *be*. In other words, they preceded the legal event when it was present and continue to be a condition of the world. In that sense, they are not fleeting like the spatial past, but *enduring* (like *durée*); and though they are a *type* of past, unlike the spatial past, this is *not* by virtue of adjudication's positioning *ex post factum*. This key difference between the spatial past and the variegated past, which is emergent in CLJ, relates to differences between *causes* and *conditions* as typologies of pasts.

The containment of the legal subject in the spatial past legal event produces futures that are knowable as each subject of law, in a legal decision that tends towards ALJ, is presumed to be the same. This will mean that the legal subject acts in the same way and will produce the same outcome, ensuring the legal form as sensed and the certainty of the system of law.

Merits

ALJ's spatial temporalities enable the recollection and contemplation of facts that are not present but can be reflected upon. Thus spatial time allows the decision maker in ALJ to circumvent this problem, proceeding to speak and adjudicate on matters that are no longer present (which Bergson would describe as becoming). The result of spatialising time is therefore to re-create a representative past 'in extensity' from which one can select and establish an order of what happened:

> We could not introduce order among terms without first distinguishing them and then comparing the places which they occupy; hence we must perceive them as multiple, simultaneous and distinct; in a word, we set them side by side, and if we introduce an order in what is successive, the reason is that succession is converted into simultaneity and is projected into space.[70]

This is what has earlier been referred to as chronologising, which is the process of distinguishing, selecting and placing adjacent to one another states into a sequence that are presumed to be causally related.

Spatial time also prevents some apparent absurdities. The main one is that if adjudication's temporality is one that resembles the features of *durée* (an accumulating past interconnected with a dynamic present that is fundamentally resistant to division), all legal events would surely start *ab aeterno*. This is where spatial temporality derives its practical import, protecting one from the nauseating dynamism and indivisibility of reality. Indeed, 'our intelligence in fact, is so constituted that it attends by preference to rigidity- to fixed points taken out from the flowing current of reality. Manuel Castells points out that 'in the modern world in particular, time is conceived of in spatial terms: it is continuous and measurable, divided into spaces that can be filled, it can be vacant or unoccupied, and it is taken to imply limits or deadlines'.[71] Particularly on this claim that, Kelman, Norrie and Farmer argue, broad time frames can have exculpatory value, which surely means that there has to be a necessary time framing out of certain pasts. Indeed, imagine the quagmire of difficulties if judges and juries had to navigate the multiple causes, conditions and effects of events from the beginning of time. Representations therefore serve significant analytical ends for the adjudicatory exercise 'because of their iterability; this means that they stabilize, or fix our experience when they attach names to it'.[72] Whilst the language of the judge or law maker immobilises lived time, there is merit to the legal system of representations, particularly language, 'as the self thus refracted, and thereby broken to pieces, is much better adapted to the requirements of social life in general and language in particular, consciousness prefers it, and generally loses sight of the fundamental self'.[73] From the testimonies of witnesses, the examinations of the defendant and most crucially, the judgements that establish new laws or the legislators in Parliament, law is a discipline that demands fixity which language, premised on an apparent stability of meaning, is able to offer. Crucially, it helps to determine which facts are facts.

Another of the merits is that if cases are seen as particularisations of rules, and thus as *factually analogous*, spatiality can also provide precedent for demarcation points for future analogous cases which promote overall stability, legal certainty, determinacy and ultimately legitimacy. Indeed, this is a way to read temporality into the indeterminacies that are claimed by Legal Realism.[74] These are the promises that stem from the inertia of formalist adjudication that is predicated upon spatial temporality.

A legal decision that tends towards ALJ therefore lends towards a process of abstraction. Spatial temporalities enable the courts to identify junctures of when legal relationships, or rights, or duties or infringements have been established within the boundaries of the legal event. The normative benefits of ALJ therefore are in its ability to abstract and chronologise the complexities of life into the legal event; to prevent the absurd *ab aeterno* legal event; to produce the paradigmatic abstract, deracinated, willed subject of law which it can attach rights and responsibility to; and to ensure stability of the legal system by creating factually analogous cases.

Demerits

While spatial time is practically necessary, it can also be viewed as one which alienates the judge and jury from real time as *durée*, a tradition which is based on a form that *represents time* and naturally introduces aspects of space into it, targeting its imperative focus on analysis rather than concreteness. For example, some may say[75] that the law is simply not interested in capturing concreteness. Chronologisation therefore has its attendant problems. The decision to adopt either broad or narrow time frames, to produce distinctions and divisions in the construction of the legal event, is an eminently indeterminate process, which Kelman refers to as the arational choice,[76] an indeterminacy that reveals the power of the courts to delineate reality in a such manner that is entirely political. For example, does the 'reasonable man' standard consider the varying levels of experience of drivers in negligence cases,[77] the pre-existing conditions in which legal subjects inhabit[78] or social structures that generally silence women, all of which would only be emergent in other adjudicative temporalities? Indeed, 'these results are practically efficacious, but not true…they falsify the actual character of the world in the interests of action…reality is known…not discursively'.[79] Greenhouse further adds that linear time (as analogous to chronology) 'intrinsically demands a single principle of selection… but real life is not so neatly arranged'.[80] Nancy Margaret Paul and W. Scott Palmer's side note in their translation of Bergson's *Matter and Memory* put it well, saying, 'objects and facts have been carved out of reality…That which is commonly called a fact is not reality as it appears to immediate intuition'.[81]

It also appears that in the absence of a metaprinciple that determines whether to adopt narrow or broad time frames (or, as will later be discussed, variegated pasts), indeterminacy emerges which can be rearticulated through the unproblematised temporalities of adjudication.[82] A. R. Lacey's assessment of spatial time identifies the arbitrariness of 'picking out points', which underwrite Kelman's time frames as an arational decision-making process:

> Take a coloured expanse varying smoothly in hue from one end to the other, or an experience similarly varying over time. It may be arbitrary how many colours we distinguish but we can still distinguish and count them, and even if they are non-denumerable like the points on a line we still presumably have a multiplicity; we certainly call them points (plural). The variegated experience can only be called a multiplicity in so far as we do consent to single out stages of it and count them, but Bergson could be justified in pointing to the arbitrariness of how we do this.[83]

Are these temporal triggers, the beginning and end of a legal event, determinate (legally ascribed), arbitrary (random) or political (buttressing a particular worldview)? As will be claimed, this indeterminacy or 'arational choice' is influenced by social structures which can determine this choice, either through its incorporation in the legal event or their elision, which spatial temporalities enable.

This element of indeterminacy can be bound in an amended version of the perennial debate over legal indeterminacy. If spatiality produces time frames that are reproduced in cases that are seen not as unique singularities but as particularities of the legal rule, then ALJ ought to be able to make a claim as to the determinateness of law. For example, if two cases are factually analogous, ALJ will delineate the legal event and produce the liberal legal subject in the same consistent manner in both cases. This is, after all, what we understand as the uniformity component and presumed identity of ALJ, but reconceptualised through time frames.

Determinacy is important for many reasons, but primarily because it ensures legal certainty (i.e. knowable futures). It presupposes that laws constrain a judge's decision in adjudication and that there is always one right answer to every case. Any apparent fissure in the coherent tapestry of law, often characterised by the so-called 'hard cases', can be mended with reference to various sources, interpretive methods or forms of reasoning. Brian Leiter identifies four components of what he calls the Class of Legal Reasons.[84] First is legitimate sources; second is legitimate interpretative operations performed on sources to derive rules from[85]; third is the legitimate rational operations that are used to synthesise facts and law to produce judgements[86]; and last is the legitimate interpretive operations on the facts of record in order to generate facts of legal significance – in other words, how one frames legal events for analysis. The last of the Class of Legal Reasons is of particular interest in that it refers to the interpretive operations that generate facts of judicial significance – what is argued here as being contingent on adjudicative temporalities.

The relation of temporality to adjudication and how temporality generates facts of legal significance in its construction of the judicial fact determination is central here. A legal rule or concept will outline facts which it gives legal meaning to, but the level of abstraction required to make laws as general as possible will mean, at the very least, some cases will exist which contain certain situations that have not been legislated upon. Here, the determinacy debate rears its head, attempting to formulate a *legal* response to this case that is not referred to explicitly in the text. This kind of indeterminacy, however, is different from the 'natural indeterminacy' of language (e.g. whether golf carts or roller skates are vehicles) but looks at whether judges are bound in their determination of the facts which are deemed relevant *or, to put this another way, whether broad or narrow time frames are adopted.* This is a question of temporality rather than how the rule exclusively generates the determination of facts. Spatial temporality allows for selection which is a central element of ALJ. To demonstrate this particular type of indeterminacy within the framework of temporality and reality construction, it is worth reintroducing Kelman's interpretive constructs once again.

Recall that Kelman posits that legal argument in criminal law proceeds in two stages: first is by way of 'interpretive construction', which is how courts determine fact construction and how they frame the legal rule to handle it (either as a rule or standard, senseless or sensed); and second is 'rational rhetoricism', which gives the first part of the legal argument a 'quasi-reasoned/rational' patina of legitimacy.[87] Interpretive constructs can either be unconscious or conscious. Unconscious interpretive constructs include the use of broad or narrow time frames:

> We prosecute particular acts-untoward incidents-that these people commit. But even these incidents have a history: Things occur before or after incidents that seem relevant to our judgment of what the perpetrator

> did. Sometimes we incorporate facts about the defendant's personal history. Other times, we incorporate facts about events preceding or post-dating the criminal indent. But an interpreter can readily focus solely on the isolated criminal incident, as if we can learn of value in assessing culpability can be seen with that narrower time focus.[88]

It also includes 'broad or narrow views of intent'[89] of the 'defendant'[90] or 'disjoined or unified accounts'[91] that describe the separating of events as a coherent coalesced whole. Thus 'by varying our interpretive focus, by particularizing at times and categorizing at others, substantive criminal law reaches all manner of results'.[92]

What is interesting about these unconscious interpretive constructs is that they can either invoke an intentionalist or determinist analysis[93] contingent on the basis of the judge's arational choice. For example, establishing the responsibility for criminal damage is an exercise of adjudication's arational choice rather that an exercise dictated by the legal rule; The judge may either select a narrow time frame- such that the legal person only appears within the boundaries of the spatial past-constructed legal event (starting from the *mens rea*)- or the judge may either broaden the time frame of the legal event such to include a more antecedent point or instant in spatial time from which to begin the legal event. The judge may even engage another types of past all together, both of which may mitigate responsibility. Note that in this hypothetical situation, it is not a defence or a normative ruling that broadens the construction of the legal event, but the time frames used.

Recall the argument of indeterminacy that Leiter describes as legitimate interpretive operations on the facts of record in order to generate facts of legal significance: for adjudication to be determinate in this respect, it ought to have a uniform method of how it generates such legally relevant facts, its construction of the legal event in identifying which cases it adopts narrow time frames for and in which cases it adopts broad time frames. Kelman has demonstrated that there is an extra-legal discretion in deploying narrow and broad time frames that can be predicated upon the same legal rules and can consequently produce disjoined or unified accounts of the legal event and how the legal rule is framed to handle it. The examples cited earlier of *R v. Ahluwalia* and *R v. Baillie*[94] illustrate the indeterminate use of time frames, despite the same provocation defence being used in both cases. Therefore, the same legal rule can be actualised to construct two antonymous legal events, ideas of intent or the defendant, both narrowly and broadly, which ultimately have very real consequences in ascriptions of responsibility. This particular type of indeterminacy is inexorably linked to adjudication and temporality, where responsibility is linked to the arbitrary use of time frames.

That the courts are able to shift from broad to narrow time frames of the event, intent and defendant in criminal law adjudication, and that it is able to oscillate between the deeply differential complexions of the legal event and legal subject as either 'unified or disjoined accounts', is attributable, this book claims, to ALJ's spatial temporality. Indeterminacy derives from the phenomenon of relatively unconstrained selection, to choose whether the legal event is inclusive or exclusive, narrow or broad in its time frames. By articulating a theory of adjudicative temporality that separates and individuates rather than expressing a time of adjudication that tends towards capturing central elements of its interconnectedness (such as in *durée*), ALJ lends towards arbitrariness. It allows courts to reign over what is and what is not considered significant for legal analysis, 'to create, alter, distort, or even destroy time itself'.[95]

However, there is a further additional element that we need to add to the indeterminacy thesis that departs from Kelman's claim that this is an arational choice. Lindsay Farmer, on restating Kelman's *arational* account of criminal law adjudication, describes it as 'non-rational processes of selecting from all potentially available facts, which excluded certain possible arguments which favours a particular ideological view of the criminal law'.[96] Thus in addition to arbitrariness and indeterminacy, spatial temporality and the time framing that it lends credence to is a *political* act. What it illustrates is the pliability of legal rules and adjudicative temporalities to construct legal events and legal subjects in broad/narrow-unified/disjoined ways and to illustrate the interests in interpretation[97] and how this has an overall impact on ascribing responsibility. However, this pliability is not decided in a vacuum as radical indeterminacy suggests. Such indeterminacy is influenced by social structures which will govern whether a narrow, broad or other type of past in used in the rendering of the legal event and fact. The contrast between *Baille* and *Ahluwalia* on the provocation grounds arguably illustrates the gendered construction of adjudicative temporality, where it was reasonable for the defendant, gendered as a man, to have a 'lapse of time' between the provocation and the *actus reus* but not reasonable to enact the same slow burn approach for the female victim of domestic violence.

Therefore, it is not just that spatial temporality provides for the possible extinction of antecedent moments that the legal event could be extended towards (creating longer causal chains as it were) or that it produces a vapid representation that also ignores the legal subjects constituted (as well as constituting) proclivity which are ostensibly inhered in forms of past that exist beyond spatiality, but that it produces knowable futures that socially reproduce social structures that are generally ignored in ALJs production of the legal event. This is a point to which we shall return to later when discussing CLJ. However, the limits of ALJ, despite the analytical conveniences inhered in spatial time, are well summed up by Karin Van Marle.

> The time that is followed by the law and legal institutions is a time that generalises and universalises and fails to embrace particularity and difference. Therefore, the law will always attempt to create false new

communities, urge us to forget, or at least construct memory in a way that forces us to negate all risk. Such an institutional approach, because of its limits, will strive for speed and closure.[98]

Conclusion

ALJ sacrifices concreteness for the sake of analytical convenience. While the shortcomings of ALJ may appear damning – the elision of other types of pasts, a process which is arguably political, the hollowed-out representation of the legal subject and the overall effects this has on liability – the practical import of its adjudicative temporality cannot be easily dismissed. Facts, conditions and other events have to be bracketed out in adjudication's production of the legal event and subject formation. Further, we have attempted to locate this argument of time frame selection within the larger literature on legal indeterminacy with, however, one important qualification. Unlike Kelman, this does not suggest that the selection of time frames is either unconscious or entirely free from the judges' perspective. What we argue is that this decision is influenced by social structures. The elision (and therefore ignorance of these social structures) would produce generally narrow time-framed legal events, whereas their incorporation would produce qualitatively different types of pasts and, consequently, legal events. It is to these different types of pasts that we now turn.

Notes

1 William Lucy, 'Abstraction and Equality' (2006) 62,1 Current Legal Problems 23.
2 William Lucy, *Law's Judgement* (Bloomsbury 2017) 4.
3 William Lucy, *Law's Judgement* (Bloomsbury 2017) 4.
4 Alexandre Lefebvre, *The Image of Law: Deleuze, Bergson, Spinoza* (Stanford University Press 2008) 167.
5 Ali Khan, 'Temporality of Law' (2009) 40,1 McGeorge Law Review 87.
6 [1983] 1 A.C. 410 [1].
7 Ali Khan, 'Temporality of Law' (2009) 40,1 McGeorge Law Review 87.
8 Patrick Nerhot, 'The Fact of Law' in Gunther Teubner (ed), *Autopoietic Law: A New Approach to Law and Society* (Walter de Gruyter & Co 1987) 326.
9 Oliver Wendell Holmes, 'The Path of Law' (1987) 10 Harvard Law Review 991.
10 Emily Grabham, *Brewing Legal Times: Things, Forms and the Enactment of Law* (University of Toronto Press 2016) 35.
11 William Lucy, *Law's Judgement* (Bloomsbury 2017) 4.
12 Taina Cooke, 'Seeing Past the Liberal Legal Subject: Cultural Defence, Agency and Women' (2017) 42,2 Suomen Anthropologi 23–40; See also Anna Grear, "Sexing the Matrix': Embodiment, Disembodiment and the Law –Towards the Re-Gendering of Legal Rationality' in J Jones, A Grear, R A Fenton and K Stevenson (eds), *Gender, Sexualities and Law* (Routledge 2011) 39–52.
13 Bryant Smith, 'Legal Personality' (1928) 37,3 The Yale Law Journal 283.
14 Ronald Dworkin, *Law's Empire* (Hart Publishing 1980) 14.
15 Alexander Nekam, *The Personality Conception of the Legal Entity* (Harvard University Press 1938).

16 Alexander Norrie, *Crime, Reason and History: A Critical Introduction to Criminal Law* (CUP 2011) 21.
17 Ngaire Naffine, *Law's Meaning of Life: Philosophy, Religion, Darwin and the Legal Person* (Hart Publishing 2009) 33.
18 Pierre Schlag, 'The Problem of the Subject' (1991) 69 Texas Law Review 1627.
19 See also s.14 *Te Awa Tupua (Whanganui River Claims Settlement) Act* 2017, which gives the Whanganui River legal personality – 'Te Awa Tupua is a legal person and has all the rights, powers, duties, and liabilities of a legal person'.
20 Carl Schmitt, *Constitutional Theory* (J Setizer trs, Duke University Press 2008 (originally published in 1928)) 264–267.
21 J M Balkin, 'Understanding Legal Understanding: The Legal Subject and the Problem of Legal Coherence' (1993) 103 Yale Law Journal 107.
22 J M Balkin, 'Understanding Legal Understanding: The Legal Subject and the Problem of Legal Coherence' (1993) 103 Yale Law Journal 106.
23 Robert Summers, 'Formal Legal Truth and Substantive Truth in Judicial Fact-Finding: Their Justified Divergence in Some Particular Cases' (1999) 18,5 Law and Philosophy 497.
24 Ngaire Naffine, *Law's Meaning of Life: Philosophy, Religion, Darwin and the Legal Person* (Hart Publishing 2009) 30.
25 Ngaire Naffine, *Law's Meaning of Life: Philosophy, Religion, Darwin and the Legal Person* (Hart Publishing 2009) 31–58.
26 Ngaire Naffine, *Law's Meaning of Life: Philosophy, Religion, Darwin and the Legal Person* (Hart Publishing 2009) 350–351.
27 Bryant Smith, 'Legal Personality' (1928) 37,3 The Yale Law Journal 283.
28 Bryant Smith, 'Legal Personality' (1928) 37,3 The Yale Law Journal 284.
29 Naffine indulges in the problems with this conception of legal personality in its theoretical (in)consistency. See also Ngaire Naffine, *Law's Meaning of Life: Philosophy, Religion, Darwin and the Legal Person* (Hart Publishing 2009) 45–58.
30 Ngaire Naffine, *Law's Meaning of Life: Philosophy, Religion, Darwin and the Legal Person* (Hart Publishing 2009) 351.
31 Ngaire Naffine, *Law's Meaning of Life: Philosophy, Religion, Darwin and the Legal Person* (Hart Publishing 2009) 357.
32 Ngaire Naffine, *Law's Meaning of Life: Philosophy, Religion, Darwin and the Legal Person* (Hart Publishing 2009) 23, 99–118.
33 Ngaire Naffine, *Law's Meaning of Life: Philosophy, Religion, Darwin and the Legal Person* (Hart Publishing 2009) 119–162.
34 See also John Harrington, 'Time as a Dimension of Medical Law' (2012) 20,4 Medical Law Review 491–515.
35 Ngaire Naffine, *Law's Meaning of Life: Philosophy, Religion, Darwin and the Legal Person* (Hart Publishing 2009) 24, 119–142.
36 The Rational legal subject is 'the paradigmatic rights holder'. See also Matthew Kramer, 'Do Animals and Dead People Have Legal Rights?' (2001) 15,1 Canadian Journal of Law and Jurisprudence 36
37 Ngaire Naffine, *Law's Meaning of Life: Philosophy, Religion, Darwin and the Legal Person* (Hart Publishing 2009) 24, 59–98.
38 Ngaire Naffine, *Law's Meaning of Life: Philosophy, Religion, Darwin and the Legal Person* (Hart Publishing 2009) 60.
39 John Chipman, Gray, *The Nature and Sources of the Law* (Columbia University Press 1909) 27.
40 Ngaire Naffine, *Law's Meaning of Life: Philosophy, Religion, Darwin and the Legal Person* (Hart Publishing 2009) 364.
41 Ngaire Naffine, *Law's Meaning of Life: Philosophy, Religion, Darwin and the Legal Person* (Hart Publishing 2009) 69–72.

42 Ngaire Naffine, *Law's Meaning of Life: Philosophy, Religion, Darwin and the Legal Person* (Hart Publishing 2009) 71.

43 Taina Cooke, 'Seeing Past the Liberal Legal Subject: Cultural Defence, Agency and Women' (2017) 42,2 Suomen Anthropologi 23–40; See also Anna Grear "Sexing the Matrix': Embodiment, Disembodiment and the Law –Towards the Re-Gendering of Legal Rationality' in J Jones, A Grear, R A Fenton and K Stevenson (eds), *Gender, Sexualities and Law* (Routledge 2011) 39–52.

44 Gary Minda, *Postmodern Legal Movements: Law and Jurisprudence at Century's Ends* (NYU Press 1995) 241.

45 Margaret Meek Lange, "Progress' Stanford Encyclopedia of Philosophy' <https://plato.stanford.edu/entries/progress/#OveConIss> accessed 10 May 2019.

46 See also J M Balkin, 'Understanding Legal Understanding: The Legal Subject and the Problem of Legal Coherence' (1993) 103 Yale Law Journal 105; James Boyle, 'Is Subjectivity Possible? The Postmodern Subject in Legal Theory' (1991) 62 University of Colorado Law Review 489; Pierre Schlag, 'Fish v. Zapp the Case of the Relatively Autonomous Self' (1987) 76 Georgetown Law Journal 37; Pierre Schlag, 'Normative and Nowhere to Go' (1990) 43 Stanford Law Review 167; Pierre Schlag, 'Normativity and the Politics of Form' (1991) 139 University of Pennsylvania Law Review 801; Pierre Schlag, 'The Problem of the Subject' (1991) 69 Texas Law Review 1627; Steven L Winter, 'Indeterminacy and Incommensurability in Constitutional Law' (1990) 78 California Law Review 1441; Jennifer Wicke, 'Postmodern Identities and the Politics of the (Legal) Subject' (1922) 19,2 Feminism and Postmodernism 10.

47 For a short introduction on the problems of the rational actor, see also Ngaire Naffine, *Law's Meaning of Life: Philosophy, Religion, Darwin and the Legal Person* (Hart Publishing 2009) 76–80.

48 Karl Marx, *A Contribution to the Critique of Political Economy* (Progress Publishers 1977).

49 Evgeny Pashukanis, *Marxism and Law: A General Theory* (Transaction Publishers 2001).

50 Richard Kinsey, 'Marxism and the Law: Preliminary Analyses' (1978) 5,2 British Journal of Law and Society 213.

51 See also Mayo Moran, *Rethinking the Reasonable Person* (OUP 2003).

52 Jenny Steele, *Tort Law: Text, Cases and Materials* (OUP 2010) 113–114.

53 [1943] A.C 448 [10].

54 James Boyle, 'Is Subjectivity Possible? The Postmodern Subject in Legal Theory' (1991) 62 University of Colorado Law Review 512.

55 Algot Ruhe and Nancy Margaret Paul, *Henri Bergson: An Account of His Life and Philosophy* (Macmillan and Co Ltd 1914) 56.

56 Emily Grabham, 'Governing Permanence: Trans Subjects, Time, and the Gender Recognition Act' (2010) 19,1 Social and Legal Studies 107–108.

57 Sarah Keenan, 'Smoke, Curtains and Mirrors: The Production of Race through Time and Title Registration' (2017) 28 Law and Critique 97–87.

58 William Lucy, *Law's Judgement* (Bloomsbury 2017) 7.

59 Steven L Winter, 'Indeterminacy and Incommensurability in Constitutional Law' (1990) 78 California Law Review 1449.

60 There is general hostility towards chains of causation which are not proximate. Lindsay Farmer quotes Scott Veitch, saying that 'legal conceptions of responsibility are organized according to conceptions of proximity and foresight, which refer to particular roles and duties, and according to a narrow conception of foreseeable consequences'. See also Lindsay Farmer, 'Time and Space in Criminal Law' (2010) 13,2 New Criminal Law Review: An International and Interdisciplinary Journal 343.

61 [2008] UKHL 37.
62 [2008] UKHL 37 [8].
63 [2008] UKHL 37 [14].
64 See Chapter 4.
65 *Fairchild v. Glenhaven* [2002] 3 WLR 89.
66 Mark Kelman, *A Guide to Critical Legal Studies* (Harvard University Press 1987) 91.
67 [1976] 1 QB 286.
68 See Chapter 4.
69 See Chapter 4.
70 Henri Bergson, *Time and Free Will: An Essay on the Immediate Data of Consciousness* (J H Muirhead ed, F L Pogson trs, Forgotten Books 2012) 102.
71 Manuel Castells, *The Information Age: Economy, Society and Culture: The Power of Identity* (Wiley & Sons 2011) 441.
72 Suzanne Guerlac, *Thinking in Time: An Introduction to Henri Bergson* (Cornell University Press 2006) 69.
73 Henri Bergson, *Time and Free Will: An Essay on the Immediate Data of Consciousness* (J H Muirhead ed, F L Pogson trs, Forgotten Books 2012) 128.
74 Tanzil Chowdhury, 'Time Frames and Legal Indeterminacy' (2017) 30, 1 Canadian Journal of Law and Jurisprudence 57–76.
75 Ngaire Naffine, *Law's Meaning of Life: Philosophy, Religion, Darwin and the Legal Person* (Hart Publishing 2009) 2–3. A 'jurisprudence of concreteness' or 'general jurisprudence' is examined in detail by Douzinas and Gearey. See also Costas Douzinas and Adam Gearey, *Critical Jurisprudence: A Political Philosophy of Justice* (Hart 2005) 40.
76 Mark Kelman, 'Interpretive Construction in the Substantive Criminal Law' (1981) 33,4 Stanford Law Review 594.
77 *Nettleship v. Weston* [1971] 2 QB 691.
78 Alan Norrie, *Crime, Reason and History: A Critical Introduction to Criminal Law* (CUP 2011) 137–141.
79 Henri Bergson, *An Introduction to Metaphysics* (T E Hulme trs, Hackett Publishing Company 1999) 15.
80 Carol Greenhouse, 'Just in Time: Temporality and the Cultural Legitimation of Law' (1989) 98,8 Yale Law Journal 1636.
81 Henri Bergson, *Matter and Memory* (Nancy Margaret Paul and W Scott Palmer trs, Digireads.com Publishing 2010) 99.
82 Tanzil Chowdhury, 'Time Frames and Legal Indeterminacy'(2017) 30, 1 Canadian Journal of Law and Jurisprudence 57–76
83 A R Lacey, *Bergson* (Routledge 1989) 26.
84 Brian Leiter, 'Legal Indeterminacy' (1995) 1 Legal Theory 481.
85 Interpretive methods such as the literal interpretation, 'mischief rule', 'golden rule', precedent.
86 Such as deductive/analogic reasoning.
87 Mark Kelman, 'Interpretive Construction in the Substantive Criminal Law' (1981) 33,4 Stanford Law Review 591.
88 The arational choice between narrow and broad time frames helps to avoid, according to the author, the conflict between the free-will paradigm and determinism. However, rather than seeing this as the difference between free-will and determinist analysis, I will take Kelman's time framing as being the difference between the liberal legal subject and a contingent, situated and constituted legal subject. Also, the interpretive choice between narrow and broad time frames affects not only doctrinally tricky legal cases, but also easy cases as narrow

time-framing fends off, at the methodological level, the possibility of doing situational analysis. See also Mark Kelman, 'Interpretive Construction in the Substantive Criminal Law' (1981) 33,4 Stanford Law Review 594.

89 Mark Kelman, 'Interpretive Construction in the Substantive Criminal Law' (1981) 33,4 Stanford Law Review 595.

90 Mark Kelman, 'Interpretive Construction in the Substantive Criminal Law' (1981) 33,4 Stanford Law Review 596.

91 Mark Kelman, 'Interpretive Construction in the Substantive Criminal Law' (1981) 33,4 Stanford Law Review 595; see also Kevät Nousiainen, 'Time of Law, Time of Experience' in Jes Bjarup and Mogens Blegvad (eds), *Time, Law and Society: Edited Proceedings of a Nordic Symposium at Sandbjerg Gods* (Franz Steiner Verlag 1994) 23; Christopher Hutton 'Meaning, Time and the Law: Ex Post and Ex Ante Perspectives' (2009) 22 International Journal of the Semiotics 279–292.

92 Mark Kelman, 'Interpretive Construction in the Substantive Criminal Law' (1981) 33,4 Stanford Law Review 596.

93 The varying time frames will not be understood as the difference between determinism and the free-will paradigm, but the difference between the natural persons as constituted and the free-will paradigm.

94 See also *Introduction.*

95 Rebecca R French, 'Time in the Law' (2001) 72 University of Colorado Law 693.

96 Lindsay Farmer, 'Time and Space in Criminal Law' (2010) 13,2 New Criminal Law Review: An International and Interdisciplinary Journal 340.

97 See also Paul Brest, 'Interpretation and Interest' (1982) 34,4 Stanford Law Review 765.

98 Karin Van Marle, 'Law's Time, Particularity and Slowness' (2003) 19 South African Journal on Human Rights 255.

Chapter 4

The temporalities of concrete legal judgment

Introduction

Karin Van Marle's writing on law's time states that the violent and reductive nature of law stems from its tendency to make the particular general and the concrete abstract.[1] This chapter therefore attempts to articulate what the temporalities of a Concrete Legal Judgement (CLJ) – non-conventional and under-utilised – would look like. CLJ is one that is oriented towards concreteness – or contingency, situatedness and complexity – rather than the analytical expediency that underwrites ALJ and its elision of certain types of pasts (through time framing) and its production of the liberal legal subject (contained within the legal event). CLJ lies at the antipodal end of the adjudicative spectrum from ALJ. It is in CLJ, productive of variegated pasts (with potentially exculpatory effects given our focus on criminal law) and untimely futures, that legal judgement may inhere the potential for radical social change. Attempting to advance an account of CLJ as a radically contrarian type of legal judgement, draws on Bergson's time of *durée*, Gadamer's effective history and Elizabeth Grosz's untimely futures. Whereas ALJ produces spatial pasts and knowable futures, CLJ invokes Bergsonian ideas of interpenetration and Gadamer's 'effective history', which are resistant to division, and produce, as will be explained, situated legal subjects that are embedded in variegated pasts. Further, CLJ also produces untimely futures, which result in new, unanticipated outcomes and provide a mechanism through which adjudication can potentially advance radical social change. As part of the judicial craft of CLJ, the Encounter, the Problem and their effects on legal form, all as interdependent facets of this judicial process, are also central to how CLJ is operationalised.

The chapter begins by outlining the features of CLJ, drawing on the second chapter's reading of Bergsonian and Gadamerian temporalities, and the ways in which they are connected to judicial fact construction. The following section is then dedicated to describing the types of pasts produced in CLJ, contrasted with ALJ, which this chapter refers to as the *variegated past*. After which, discussion is dedicated to certain operational features of CLJ: *the Problem*, *the Encounter* and *Legal Form*. In particular, the form of legal rules requires attention, given that the central presupposition of this book has been to displace the rule as the basis for judicial fact determination. What transpires from this discussion is the coterminous relationship between adjudicative temporalities and the form of the legal rule. Finally, the chapter ends by exploring further the production of untimely futures in CLJ and the possibilities (and limits) for radical social change.

Contrary to ALJ, the adjudicative temporalities of CLJ, taking from the writings of Bergson, Gadamer and Grosz, produce variegated, as opposed to just spatial, pasts and untimely, as opposed to teleological, futures. Rather than the spatial features of ALJ's temporality that render a legal subject that is born and reborn at each moment, CLJ produces a legal subject that is necessarily embedded and constituted by other types of pasts. Specifically, CLJ produces *variegated pasts* that are qualitatively different from spatial pasts. Whereas spatial pasts are characterised by features of space – uniformity, divisibility, juxtaposition and simultaneity – in which time frames are the fragmentations of experiential time (*durée*) and derive their past-ness, as it were, by virtue of their relation to adjudication being *ex post factum*, variegated pasts refer to a typology of past that are resistant to time framing and, importantly, enduring such that they were *also* past in relation to the proximity of the legal event when it was *happening*. Variegated pasts refer to conditions that either may be physiological or mental (such as insanity, battered woman syndrome) or socio-structural (gendered, racialised, classed). Whereas ALJ's spatial time attempts to chronologise the past – the process of distinguishing, selecting and placing adjacent to one another states into a sequence that are presumed to be causally related – CLJ augments the legal event with conditions which reveal the complexity, contingency and situatedness of the legal subject as well as revealing potential exculpatory claims in legal judgement. CLJ therefore is more than merely adopting broader time frames, operant within the spatial temporalities produced by ALJ, but the engagement of variegated pasts which, as will be explained, are qualitatively different.

Finally, the way in which the legal rule(s) is framed in CLJ is that they are *senseless*. Unlike in ALJ, where the rule(s) presupposes the judicial facts as mere representations of the rule, the production of variegated pasts provide new content for legal norms and undermine ostensibly rule-like forms to produce standard-like forms or senseless rules. Borrowing from Deleuzian thought, this chapter will also introduce the Problem and the Encounter as features of CLJ which summon the use and incorporation of the variegated past in judicial fact determination and alters the form of the legal rule from one which is sensed to senseless. Relatedly, therefore, this means that CLJ is characterised by futures that are untimely (rather than knowable), sacrificing certainty of the legal rule and legal system overall, to instead open up the possibilities of CLJ as a site of radical social change. This is, as Grosz states, resisting the attempt to predict the future and a linear continuation of the present, but 'to welcome a concept of the future which we do not control but which may shape and form us according to its forces'.[2]

Gadamerian and Bergsonian temporalities and judicial fact construction

Gadamer's hermeneutics have primarily been deployed in the field of statutory interpretation,[3] and have tended to focus upon the contingences of that exercise and the inevitable projection of judges and their *effective history* into the reading of legal texts. This chapter, however, shifts from the finitude of the judge and her understanding of the legal rules,[4] and instead extends this to how Gadamerian temporalities would prefigure judicial fact determination as well as structure event and subject formation. It seems pertinent, given this shift, to make some preliminary comments on how this might shape the construction of the legal subject and legal event – through the production of pasts and futures – and thus effect legal judgement overall. This will pre-empt the later, more detailed discussion on the *variegated pasts* that are produced by the adjudicative temporalities of CLJ.

Unlike the liberal legal subject of ALJ, a legal subject structured by Gadamerian temporalities would be shaped by an immanent *effective history*, which it is necessarily immersed in and constituted by. Its past would project into its present and shape its own understanding and experience. For Gadamer, this is not mere technique but an ontological inflection. The past and present, therefore, are necessarily indivisible, and introspection into the traditions that shape the legal subject's experience is central to any judicial determination of fact. This also means that because the entirety of the past is constitutive of the legal subject, CLJ is resistant to time framing. ALJ's incredulity towards this effective history (as was the case in *Ahluwalia* in the hearing of first instance) would be to ignore the *a priori* situatedness of the legal subject. Take ALJ's construction of the liberal legal subject *qua* the reasonable man; it would generally be illiterate of the subject's effective history which constitutes it. The legal subject of CLJ is not fully agential but situated:

> Situatedness is, rather, a way of describing the epistemological ecology in which we are simultaneously constituting and constituted. We are constituting because meaning arises in the imaginative interaction of the human being with the environment. We are constituted because the situated quality of human existences means that both the physical and social environment with which we interact is already formed by the actions of those who have preceded us.[5]

The world is not the extension of the thinking ego, as Cartesian framing would have it, but rather to take the Marxian position – our social being structures our consciousness.[6] We are always situated in circumstances not purely of our own making. A legal event structured by Gadamerian temporalities would be more than the adoption of broad(er) time frames. Rather, as Gadamer is concerned not with method but with the *conditions* of the possibility of understanding,[7] as with the above, CLJ, productive of Gadamerian temporalities, would introduce effective history as the horizon for understanding and for the context which would enrich the legal event. Whereas ALJ is principally concerned with *causal relations*, as a result of chronologising, CLJ would also include *conditions* or what may be understood as social structures in which the legal persons are situated. Conditions therefore can be understood as the incorporation of variegated pasts – conditions that may be physiological or mental (such as insanity, battered woman syndrome, etc.), or socio-structural (and enforce violence which is gendered, racialised and/or classed).[8]

The process of CLJ is complex, one which recognises the *anti-method* of Gadamer's interpretive approach. It may bear some resemblance to Lefebvre's *attentive* judgement or Karin Van Marle's strategy of delay, in which what she refers to as the 'particularity of the event' or its difference and contingency, emergent in the variegated pasts, reveal themselves. In its more conventional application to statutory interpretation, it operates through a *dialogic process*[9] where there is 'to-ing and fro-ing' between the situated interpreter and the legal text. Rather than the interpreter attempting a futile quest to recover authorial intent, for example, she 'instead challenges and questions its assumptions to get at its truth-value. Similarly, the interpreter places her own pre-judgments at risk, by opening them to questions and challenges from the text'.[10] Thus there is a dynamic back and forth between the present text and the effective history of the interpreter. Assuming that the interpreter is aware of her temporal situatedness, and thus embodies what Gadamer calls an 'effective historical consciousness', the dialogic process continues until there is a *fusion of horizons*.[11] In CLJ, however, effective history refers to conditions or social structures as a component of the legal event and therefore that which constitutes the legal subject. In the conventional deployment in interpreting legal texts, an awareness and challenge by the text of the effective history of the interpreter demands one to be critical of how ones pre-understandings shape the horizon of their present.[12] In CLJ, however, judgement that produces Gadamerian temporalities can challenge the truth claims of the legal text with the effective history *not* of the judge but of the legal subject in order to create and enrich its rendering of the legal event in this dialogic movement.[13]

Durée – as motioned time – is important for the reasons that it intercalates an accumulating past with a dynamic present. Like Gadamer, Bergson, through Lefebvre, has been used primarily to recognise the contingencies of the judge's technique, where both theories approach adjudication as variations of hermeneutical endeavours wherein the sites of interpretive contestation are the legal rules. Indeed, when Lefebvre refers to *durée*, he refers to duration in law as legal rules' continuous difference from itself.[14] As with the shift in focus of Gadamer, one may understand Bergson's *durée*, not in the context of the legal rules but that in the production of the legal subject and how this enriches the construction of the legal event.

In his reading of Bergson's durational time, Deleuze identifies *durée* as an ontological concept or *internal difference*.[15] *Durée* is not exterior or superior to the thing, but crucially, 'difference is the thing itself'.[16] Indeed:

> It is the very being of the subject. A being is neither an indifferent and stable subject, nor is it modified through multiple states; instead, a being is nothing other than its continuous modification in time...Beings are, and express nothing other than, difference (duration). This is the meaning of Bergson's most famous concept, duration: time as internal difference, as becoming.[17]

This suggests a conceptualisation of the legal subject that lacks fixity, stabilisation and is qualitatively different at each 'moment' (contrary to a liberal legal subject that is born and reborn at each moment). To put it crudely, one is not the same today as one was yesterday because of an accumulating and constituting past. Internal difference suggests a fluid, constituted and changing self,[18] in which an ever-changing present being is ephemeral. To fix the self, or contain them within the spatial past-legal event as ALJ does, is to ignore this accumulating (and thus constituting entirety of the whole) past and ephemeral present.[19]

Durée, as both contemporaneous with a dynamic present and pre-existing it in its entirety, is *qualitatively* different from the spatial past and thus it varies in kind rather than in degree (it pre-*exists* it rather than *precedes* it). As an ontological concept and thus extending it to our understanding of the legal subject, several themes emerge. First, when understanding and constructing the legal persons in CLJ's determination of fact, they cannot simply *appear* in the spatial past legal event as they are fundamentally characterised by an immanent and whole past. Second, where *durée* is used by Lefebvre as a site of creativity and freedom, the role of *durée* will be reconfigured as the constitutive horizon of the individual (like Gadamer). Suzanne Guerlac says:

> In inner experience there is an analogy to the necessary ordering of things in space. He [Bergson] calls this 'character' and it conditions, without determining, our present state. Our previous psychological states live on in this condensed manner because we carry them with us all the time. The past is always with us. It informs everything we do.[20]

This has very clear resonances with what has so far been referred to as 'conditions', particularly those which are physiological or mental. One may think of battered woman syndrome, for example, as that which endures, a whole past that is always present and is therefore something that ought not to be 'time framed' out – albeit that is not the case if the basis of adjudication is analytical convenience as is with ALJ. Further, as adjudication is a retrospective endeavour, *durée* provides a useful way to describe how disconnected events ('disjoined accounts', to use Kelman's lexicon) become connected and cohesive ones ('unified accounts') and how one must incorporate *enduring pasts*, like battered woman syndrome, as the constitutive horizons of the legal subject into the legal event. *Durée* can shed light upon the conditions for action and not exclusively focus upon causes, as is typically the case in legal judgement that tends towards ALJ. Herein lies the claim that temporality can produce typologies of past. Causes operate in spatial time while conditions, or what is shortly referred to as variegated pasts, are produced by *durée* and effective history; thus they are qualitatively different. Like Gadamer's effective history, the natural person is always situated. The relation, therefore, is one of constitution, as Guerlac's describes it, rather than a fatalistic determinism, thus moving beyond the 'free will-determinist paradigm' suggested by Kelman and others.[21]

Durée works in the service of legal judgement, intercalating the past and present to enrich the process of CLJ 'with their contour, their colour and their place in time'.[22] The role of CLJ would be to explore the content of the *durée* of the legal subject and how this is incorporated into the rendering of fact determination in CLJ. This would not be limited to variations of the spatial past (asbestos litigation contra strict liability, qualifying trigger in Loss of Self-Control Defence etc.) but include the enduring qualities of the legal subject (specifically physiological and mental conditions). Thus, it will adopt a critical and potentially transformative attitude by introspection into the enduring pasts of the legal subject.

The principal shift in these novel applications of Bergson and Gadamer has been to attribute them not to the judge *qua* interpreter, but to CLJ's production of the legal subject and resultant configuration of the legal event. This follows from the natural extension of ontological understandings of Gadamerian interpretation and Bergsonian *durée* as internal difference. CLJ becomes an undertaking not just of establishing (non-)casual relations but of looking at the *conditions* in which human agency is situated and how this may change designations of responsibility, if at all. Also, it aims to illustrate 'what is missed out' in ALJ's principle selection and why. Thus CLJ adopts critical and introspective attitudes into these different types of past that correspond to conditions as well as causes. To return back to Marx once again, the legal event and subject is made 'under circumstances already, given and transmitted from the past'.[23]

The next section is dedicated to detailing the *types of past* that the adjudicative temporalities of CLJ produce in its rendering of the legal subject and legal event before embarking on a discussion on the role of the Problem and the Encounter as necessary elements of CLJ and their effect on legal form, without which, the variegated pasts cannot be engaged and potentially incorporated into the CLJ's determination of fact.

The variegated past of CLJ

In the earlier discussion, one reason why the case of *R v. G* seemed problematic was in its construction of the past. The narrow time-framed legal event, containing the legal subject that is born and reborn at each moment, meant that there was no possibility for revealing their contingency or situatedness in the case to present itself as unique (e.g. the possibility of the defendant's mistaken belief or their situatedness in a social structure) and their potential exculpation. Instead, it was just another mechanised instantiation of the general legal rule of strict criminal liability. It produced analogous liberal legal subjects, made possible through a spatial temporality that is conducive to 'framing out' difference, contingency and situatedness. Law's judgement, to borrow a phrase from William Lucy, viewed the 15-year-old appellant as fixed, contained and defined prior to and independent of such constitutive physiological or mental conditions or social structures. Now it is especially importantly to state this: this is not to say that an enriched judicial determination of facts – enriched through the engagement of variegated pasts – ought to necessarily result in exonerating or mitigating responsibility, only that within this approach, it may reveal facts with potentially exculpatory effect which are worth considering as well as illustrating how and why certain pasts are excluding from judicial-factual analysis. This is a point to which the book shall return to later.

The aim of this section seeks to explain what other types of past are produced by Gadamer and Bergson's theories of time underwriting CLJ. In ALJ, fact construction is characterised by the production of spatial pasts. CLJ (or decisions that tend towards it) instead is epitomised by an altogether different type of past that is collectively described as *variegated*. The variegated past consists of *the spatial* but also *the enduring* and *the sedimented pasts*, with the latter two sharing features of *durée* and effective history, respectively. A case which has been decided in a manner that tends towards CLJ therefore can be identified by reference to the facts it considers relevant in its rendering of the legal event. Different types of past are conditioned by these adjudicative temporalities, as will soon become apparent.

The Spatial Past: to recall, the spatial past can vary by degree (i.e. calculable units of clock/calendrical time or narrow or broad time frames), which is initiated and ceased by instants (*mens rea-actus reus*). Such a category of past is characterised merely by virtue of adjudication's positioning *ex post factum*. In other words, when said legal event was happening, these pasts were by definition also happening (i.e. present). The spatial past is presumed to be causal and may undergo broadening along its spatial axis (such as the qualifying trigger in loss of self-control defence or contributory negligence claims). The legal subject is produced by virtue of its containment within the spatial past-legal event, born and reborn at each moment, outside of which it does not exist for the purposes of law's ascription of responsibility.

The Enduring Past: enduring qualities of the legal subject resemble the immanent entirety of a past that is necessarily constitutive. Unlike the spatial past, which is composed of instants (illustrated in particular with broadening time frames of the legal event) and whose past-ness is explained by virtue of adjudication's positioning *ex post factum*, the enduring past is altogether different. The enduring past precedes (or more accurately *pre-exists*) the legal event when it was happen*ing* (unlike the spatial past) and, resembling the accumulatory nature of Bergson's *durée*, it is not a fleeting moment, a point in time that starts then ceases (such as contributory negligence) but endures. Take *Ahluwalia* once again to illustrate this point. It would be unusual to say that the fact of the defendant's Battered Woman Syndrome is a past that is characterised by a *point in time*, but rather that it actually pre-existed the legal event (formulating the intent and carrying out the action of pouring petrol onto her sleeping husband) while it was happening. Instead, it seems entirely reasonable to describe it as enduring and having pre-existed the legal event in question – an internal difference to use the Deleuzian reading of Bergson. This is how pre-existing conditions, mental or physiological, materialise as pasts in CLJ's determination of facts, independent of any legal rule (or this was certainly the case when it was established). Indeed, this particular past of a defendant (e.g. BWS) is qualitatively different from a qualifying trigger, for the reasons that the former is enduring and the latter is fleeting. In other words, the former embraces the characteristics of *durée*, while the other embraces the features of spatial time.

The Sedimented Past: this third type of past, borrowed from the rereading of Gadamer, establishes a constitutive horizon or effective history as the situational context of the legal subject. In his anti-method approach, Gadamer describes his hermeneutical ontology as providing the *conditions* for understanding. The conditions for understanding can be suitably applied to enrich the legal event, which, given our focus on criminal law, may result in changes of responsibility attribution. Whereas the spatial past is presumed to be weaved together by causal logics, the sedimented past introduces *conditions* (or social structures) to enrich the understanding of the legal event in CLJ. The term sedimentation is understood as 'the deposit of the subjects past interactions with its physical and social situation'.[24] Rosemary Coombe, in describing what Gadamer means by context, says that 'it would seem to include historical and social factors'.[25]

To expand upon how the variegated past introduces conditions into the legal event in CLJ, it is worth looking at Alan Norrie's account of the distinction between causes (what is argued as emergent in the spatial past) and conditions or what he refers to as 'deeper causes' and his effort to problematise the causal and voluntary underpinnings of criminal law. To help illustrate this point, he refers to the Scarman Report, published in 1981 following the Brixton Riots, and quotes Lord Scarman, saying that 'deeper causes undoubtedly existed, and must be probed: but the immediate cause of Saturday's events was a spontaneous combustion set off by the spark of one particular incident'.[26] Norrie then goes on to analyse the report:

> Which factor 'makes the difference', the 'deeper causes' or the 'immediate cause'? If those 'deeper causes' (relating to poor social environment, racial discrimination, police harassment) are part of the 'normal conditions of life in the late twentieth-century, are they for that reason excluded from our account of what caused the riot? It would perhaps be convenient for the law, with its emphasis on the individual, if they were. Elsewhere in his report, Lord Scarman did draw a distinction between the 'causes' and the 'conditions' of the riots (1981, 16). This was shortly before he argued that the conditions of young black people cannot exclude their guilt for grave criminal offences which, as causal agents, they have committed.[27]

It is interesting to note that Norrie's description of 'deeper causes' is also satirically referred to as the 'normal conditions of life'. It is also noteworthy how he differentiates this from 'immediate causes'. One could convincingly interpret that deeper causes are equivalent to the sedimented past and that 'immediate causes' share the characteristics of the spatial past. In this example, the immediate causes refer presumably to the intention to damage property that was caused during the riot. Like the spatial past, these immediate causes (the adoption of narrow time frames) are past by virtue of adjudication's positioning *ex post* and are characterised by fleeting moments. The 'deeper causes' *qua* conditions, however, which includes the 'poor social environment, racial discrimination and police harassment' like the variegated past, are qualitatively different. These conditions do not derive their pastness from inquire's positioning, because unlike the immediate causes, they pre-exist the rioting when it was happen*ing and continue to exist.* This is the defendants' horizon, their effective history. Indeed, this particular fact of young Black men (poor social environment etc., i.e. their sedimented past) is again qualitatively different from, say, a qualifying trigger because the former is enduring, and the other is fleeting, and the former embraces the characteristics of 'effective history', while the other embraces the features of spatial time. Variegated pasts all imbue the features of temporality drawn from Gadamer and Bergson.

Arguably, the sedimented past would be the most controversial and radical inclusion into CLJ's rendering of the facts of the case, specifically its construction of both the legal subject and the event. It is generally argued, for example, that socio-economic circumstances, social structures of racial class or gendered violence do not form the basis of causation in law and are thus not grounds for mitigation of legal responsibility. Robert Sullivan makes an important point about Norrie's 'relational account' that attempts to envisage a defence of social duress, which would necessarily weave the sedimented past into CLJ's production of the legal event and subject:

> Many will agree with Norrie that large inequalities of resources and power are a bad thing...the link between social deprivation and the incidence of criminal offending is undeniable...Norrie argues that if the criminal justice system is to advance the case of justice for defendants, the grip of the Kantian model must be eased. Norrie does not dismiss as chimeras the Kantian values of autonomy and freedom...his argument is that an exclusive stress on personal agency excludes far too much of the whole picture. He emphasises time and again that conduct is a compound of the social and the personal. Accordingly, the pressures and exigencies of social circumstances and forces should feature in determining criminal liability...this perspective would allow claims that at least certain criminal acts are justified forms of defiance and/or appropriate exercises in distributive justice...Norrie insists he is not bent on a dismissal of legal ordering and legal values. In keeping with that, he nowhere claims directly that social disadvantage justifies criminal acts... his position seems to be that social factors should constitute grounds of *excuse* and that these excuses currently go unheard because of the Kantian model. Thus we are not dealing with a macro rejection of the right of the institutions of an unjust society to condemn and punish. We are within the realm of the micro examination of the circumstances of individuals, the realm of excuses.[28]

Whilst this is not an attack on Kantian legal subjectivity but abstracted, deracinated, rational legal subjectivity – the liberal legal subject – this description by Sullivan of Norrie's relational account embraces the features of CLJ. One may liken the 'whole picture' to which Sullivan refers to the variegated past and the 'compound of the social and personal' as referring specifically to the sedimented past. When Sullivan writes 'he nowhere claims directly that social disadvantage justifies criminal acts', this corresponds with the idea that a variegated past is not to absolve, but to reveal, contextualise and understand conduct and unearth the *potentially* exculpatory effects of that. Finally, the point of the 'micro examination of circumstances' is resolutely a reference to the Encounter as a prelude to the strategy of delay or attentive judgement, an appreciation of a case in its unique and concrete singularity rather than a manifestation of the general rule, which we shall come on to shortly.

The sedimented past is therefore meant to refer to conditions that are typically ignored in ALJ. Contrastingly, sociological and social theory has expended far more effort in making visible these often indiscernible social structures. We may liken the sedimented past to Johann Gaultung's lauded thesis of structural violence, which is 'present when human beings are being influenced so that their actual somatic and mental realizations are below their potential realizations'.[29] In other words, social structures, rather than individuals, make certain social groups less well off than they could be (i.e. life expectancy, access to education, jobs, material security etc.). In terms of the temporal production of social structures in the legal event, they are neither an 'instant' nor a 'point', but something which forms the horizon of the subject and would pre-exist the (legal) event while it was happening. Indeed, it has all the hallmarks we associate with the productive temporalities of Gadamer and Bergson. Developing the work of Gaultung in her work on Structural Injustice[30] and 'Five Theses of Oppression', Iris Marion Young similarly identifies oppression as a structural concept that *condition* groups:

> oppression designates the disadvantage and injustice some people suffer not because a tyrannical power coerces them, but because of the everyday practices of a well-intentioned liberal society....systematic constraints on groups'... Its causes are embedded in unquestioned norms, habits, and symbols, in the assumptions underlying institutional rules and the collective consequences of following those rules. It names, as Marilyn Frye puts it, "an enclosing structure of forces and barriers which tends to the immobilization and reduction of a group or category of people.[31]

Similarly, Susan Marks refers to these as 'background conditions, enabling frameworks and overarching systems'.[32] Does engaging the sedimented past in CLJs judicial determination of fact therefore require analysis of such social structures that recognise socio-economic duress, the potential epigenetic effects of slavery and the legacies and continuities of imperial domination? Are courts to also acknowledge the social reproduction of classed patriarchy too for they are produced by the temporalities of CLJ? This poses potentially serious problems of increased and potentially paralysing complexity for a liberal legal system. As Gramsci notes, 'the starting-point of critical elaboration is the consciousness of what one really is, and is "knowing thyself" as a product of the historical processes to date, which has deposited in you an infinity of traces, without leaving an inventory'.[33] Critical elaboration is central to CLJ, through its incorporation of social structures which go beyond the spatial temporality of the legal event in ALJ and reveal a complexity that ALJ, arguably conveniently, elides. It is the job of critical legal scholarship to reveal both the elisions presupposed in liberal legal judgement and the ways in which alternative legal processes, like CLJ, can both visibilse these social structures and incorporate them into its forms of judgement.

The enduring and sedimented pasts inculcate difference and destabilise the imposition of sameness, imparting the idea of each case being unique, departing from the presumptive identity of the liberal legal subject constructed by the spatial pasts of ALJ. Indeed, this is the perennial structure-agency[34] debate re-framed in their production through adjudicative temporalities.

Again, CLJ is not about including all facts that, given our focus has been on criminal law, may operate as mitigating factors[35] through a richer determination of what happened. Instead, it helps to illustrate the productive work of adjudicative temporalities and to observe what is missed in the absence of the variegated past, and to what political ends, as well as how an enriched determination of fact, through the variegated past, may mitigate responsibility. This is exactly what Lucy, quoted at the start of this chapter, refers to when arguing that more exculpatory claims are revealed in the 'fine-grained assessment of her particular capacities on this particular occasion, in these precise circumstances'.[36]

This process of normalising conditions, as Norrie refers to it as, is what allows a decision to tend towards ALJ through the production of spatial pasts. Indeed, one may recognise them as 'normal everyday events or circumstances that were a precondition but not the reason why the consequence happened at the time and in the manner it did'.[37] Therefore, the inclusion of the sedimented past in CLJ's event and subject formation poses tough questions that not only challenge 'traditional' ideas about the boundaries of what is and what is not law/legally intelligible but also question *beyond law* about the very fabric of society, the process of normalising conditions through the production of spatial temporality and their subsequent elision (and thus their institutional and social reproduction through adjudication). Therefore, ALJ's spatial temporalities, in its subject and event formation, are primarily concerned with immediate causes, whereas CLJ is also concerned with the incorporation of conditions and social structures emergent in the variegated past (enduring and sedimented). Causes and conditions have been described as products of different adjudicative temporalities and the qualitatively different types of past they produce.

What is especially useful about introducing conditions that are emergent in engaging the variegated past is that it responds to the problem of legal events beginning *ab aeterno*. The legal event in CLJ derives its richness and complexity not from an excessive broadening of the spatial past (i.e. adopting broad time frames; this would still contain the natural persons *qua* legal subject which is born, killed and reborn at each moment) but rather by supplementing it with the qualitatively different pasts – enduring and sedimented – in legal subject and event formation.

The determination of facts in CLJ, produced from the multiple pasts that correspond to different forms of temporality, is ignored in a decision that otherwise tends towards ALJ. Trapping the natural persons in the spatial past-legal event of ALJ requires extinguishing the enduring and sedimented pasts. CLJ, producing temporalities that resemble *durée* and effective history, embraces these three types of pasts, in which difference is emergent, the singularity of the case is affirmed and the possibility of new outcomes present. However, the exigencies of these variegated pasts cannot be engaged without recognition by the courts. By recognition, we mean incorporation into the judicial determination of facts. For this to happen, it is now pertinent to turn to the Encounter and the Problem.

The problem, the encounter and legal form

In his theory of criminal law adjudication, not only does Kelman argue about how facts are determined relevant for legal analysis, but he also makes reference to 'the way we frame the possible rules to handle the situation'.[38] The book thus far has rejected a rule-centric correspondence theory of judicial fact determination, instead arguing that it is based primarily on adjudicative temporalities. Significantly, however, variegated pasts, in the form of enduring and sedimented pasts, can provide new content for legal norms and undermine ostensibly rule-like forms to produce standards[39] or senseless rules. This also means, therefore, that the form of the legal rule can dictate what futures are produced in CLJ and, much more significantly, whether this provides a possibility for radical social change. To describe the relationship between legal forms, untimely futures and radical social changes will also require explaining the Deleuzian *Encounter* and the *Problem*. The complex interconnection of all these features along with the variegated pasts is symptomatic of CLJ. Importantly, however, they cannot be thought of as separate and causally linked but instead should be thought of as part of an interweaving, coterminous process. First, to explain the Encounter and the Problem.

Deleuze derides philosophies of recognition as 'an approach that seeks only to *recognize*...because it *a priori* assigns a representational form to the outside; it presumes that the encountered thing is only another identifiable instance of an existing concept'.[40] Such an approach, for our purposes, is the suppression of the contingency and complexity of a fact situation emergent in variegated pasts that may not correspond with or may be subsumed by the legal rule. A philosophy, or better yet, ALJ as an adjudication of recognition (what we have elsewhere referred to as subsumptive or correspondence theories) is concept or rule-centric. In effect, the fact situation exists only for the purposes of the legal rule; the fact situation being thought about by the courts and its appropriateness are only so *within* the broader category or concept. Anything thought about outside the general concept is either not recognised, or its unique differences are extinguished, such as the variegated past in ALJ. If philosophy is about the resistance and disposal of *doxa* (common beliefs), then a philosophy of recognition, according to Deleuze, is woefully inadequate. Thinking along these parameters is less about creativity and more about recognition. Deleuze's more general attack on modern philosophy is that it is marred by a ubiquitous, dull logic of recognition in which unique differences – fact situations which are not recognised from within a broader category or rule and which would otherwise be emergent in the variegated past – are omitted. On this account, 'the elementary concepts of representation are the categories defined as the conditions of possible experience. These, however, are too general, too large for the real'.[41]

The Deleuzian *Encounter* then unsettles recognition and subsumption – a metaphysical violence.[42] It is not about making legal rules quantitatively more numerous in order to respond to the multiplicity, differences and ubiquity of life. Rather, it is about the primacy of that which is thought about – the fact situation. Real thought lies in the Encounter's primacy. Primacy is therefore understood as rejecting recognition, resisting the privileging and centricity of the rule, and elevating the fact situation being thought about in all its complexity. This complexity is revealed in the variegated past, both in the conditions of the sedimented past and the internal difference of *durée.* The 'thing' that is thought about – the fact situation – ceases to be an identifiable instance of the rule, but in its ubiquity and complexity, exceeds the rule.

The Encounter renders the creative and transformative impulses of CLJ possible. It is a moment which forces the courts to think beyond the strictures of the rigid rules (like the anticipatory logic of subsumptive theories of judgement). It is that which 'shocks the law and initiates the uncovering of a problem that will establish the facts of the situation'.[43] The Encounter can be more accurately described not as a 'particularisation' of the rule but as a 'singularity'[44] – in effect, a unique case. If adjudication is subsumptive, cases can only be, following the cases recognition, considered as 'interior' to the rule, limiting the capacity for legal rules, as sensed, to change. The subsumption theory therefore cannot deal with the Encounter in which the 'concept of the transcendental delimits the frame for every possible experience and event before it occurs and defines if not what occurs, then at least what can- or cannot- occur'.[45] Normative aspirations for adjudication as a radical and transformative practice must therefore afford the *primacy* of the Encounter that forces rules to *change their form* in response to cases which are always different and unique. This is what is meant by rules being *senseless. They do not sense or anticipate the facts of the case but rather allow the difference and contingency emergent in the facts – and different types of pasts – to dictate the integrity of the rule.* The primacy of the Encounter engages the variegated pasts which reveal the difference, contingency and complexity of the legal event and subject. This is instead of the legal event and subject being conceptualised as an already anticipated or presumed instantiation of the legal rule. *Thus, legal form is contingent on the primacy of the Encounter which enables the engagement of variegated pasts in CLJ.* This will therefore have a knock-on effect on what legal futures are produced by the legal form, given that it operates not as a rigid rule that anticipates the fact situation but as one that, in affording the primacy of the Encounter, operates as a standard that produces an unclear, but potentially transformative future (more on this later).

The final part of the CLJ process is what Lefebvre refers to as the Problem.[46] This is a device which attempts to create rights to improve a situation and is a specific puzzle of a case that confronts the legal rule towards a resolution.[47] Specifically in CLJ, the legal form responds to real Problems that the judge articulates. For example, if confronted with a civil disobedience case, would the judge directing the jury articulate the problem about the case in terms of our overall fidelity and obligation to the law therewith in, say, punishing criminal damage or trespassing, or would she instead reckon with the goals of the dissenters and activists as responding to the sedimented past of climate breakdown and war? Might the stating of a problem acknowledge structural violence and inequalities that render a person a defendant in a trial? The Problem states that 'life proceeds according to the posing of singular problems with correspondingly singular situations'.[48] Indeed, 'they are the transcendental condition of creative adjudication'.[49] The stating of the Problem guides how the form of legal rule(s) is constructed and whether the Encounter is afforded primacy to subsequently construct the legal event and subject through the production of variegated pasts. How a Problem is stated therefore holds the key for the primacy of the Encounter; whether the variegated pasts are engaged; and, more fundamentally, the transformative and creative potential of the legal decision. This will all become clearer in the following case studies of legal decisions that tend towards CLJ.

Producing untimely futures and the potential for radical social change

What this also means, therefore, is that if the engagement of the variegated pasts alters the form of the legal rule by giving new content to the legal norm, this will also determine the production of futures in CLJ. Predictable and anticipatable futures emergent from a legal rule that only engages the spatial past (i.e. a contained and agential legal subject that is responsible for pouring petrol on her husband) are *relinquished* when incorporating either the enduring or sedimented pasts in judicial fact determination (i.e. the enduring past of battered woman syndrome produced the new outcome of manslaughter rather than murder and establishing a new defence for homicide). Rather than following a teleological trajectory that linearly threads the spatial past and sensed legal rule of a legal decision towards a knowable future outcome, CLJ engages the variegated past to produce futures which are untimely. It is within the production of these untimely and unpredictable futures that the potential for social transformation is possible. Once again,

Kathryn McNeilly is instructive on this. Drawing on Elizabeth's Grosz's work, untimely futures have the productive potential to imagine and create radically new futures that are not tethered to the lineal teleology of the past and present. Grosz writes how 'the implications and effects of conceiving a temporality in which the future remains virtual and beyond the control of the present'[50] rejects a graduated temporality wherein the future is largely defined by the strictures of the present. Indeed, she invests in 'a concept of a temporality not under the domination or privilege of the present, that is, a temporality directed to a future that is unattainable and unknowable in the present'.[51]

McNeilly astutely observes the fruits of these radical open futures in the work of Drucilla Cornell and Judith Butler. In Cornell, Grosz observes how a feminist teleology limits the possibilities of unpredictable futures which are central to social transformation, submitting instead to a 'future that we cannot foresee or understand'.[52] Similarly, unknowability for Butler offers possibilities beyond our current understandings of gender. Indeed:

> In opening terms to unsettlement and uncertain futures through ongoing reiteration, a wider future-focused democratic politics can be stimulated which facilitates social change by being open to new forms, shapes or directions for social life. This vision of politics always looking to the future, debating its shape and form in an ongoing way, is a particularly useful element of Butler's work.[53]

CLJ is not committed to producing sensed rules and, thus, predictable futures. If the *form* of the legal norm is not a rigid rule that anticipates facts as if they are inhered in the rule- which would produce a certain future decision- but instead a *standard-like* legal norm which is provided new content emergent from the variegated past, the outcome is likely not going to be predictable. Variegated pasts will reveal a radical singularity in its rendering of the facts, not comparable with other cases, and it is thus likely to produce untimely futures. Herein lies the possibility for social transformation. Teleological futures, however, privilege the present and the spatial past, eliding difference and situatedness that is inhered in the liberal legal subject. This produces a future which is known and follows on from the spatial past (i.e. the willed actor that does X will be convicted of Y). However, the variegated past introduces difference which complicates notions of legal responsibility (i.e. is its knowable that the constituted actor that does X will be responsible for Y?)

Specifically for CLJ, unpredictable futures emerge from the legal form as senseless, which provides the possibility of new content for legal norms. This new content, or new facts, emerges from the variegated pasts in which the courts have to confront not just mental and physiological conditions – the enduring pasts – but social structures or structural violence – the sedimented past. Recognition and acknowledgement of these pre-existing conditions opens up the possibility of social transformation. For example, recognition of socio-economic models of governance, what Susan Marks calls 'background conditions, enabling frameworks and overarching systems',[54] or Naomi Klein refers to as 'planned misery',[55] may compel judges and juries to reconsider the legal event of an alleged theft or purported criminal damage. This will become more apparent in the ensuing chapter, but within the limitations of knowable or teleological futures, the potential for transformation is limited as these structures of violence and mental and physiological conditions are ignored. ALJ, which ignores sedimented and enduring pasts though its production of the spatial past, means that it institutionally reproduces the sedimented (structural violence) and enduring pasts (mental and physiological conditions) by its very ignorance of them.

Conclusion

The adjudicative temporalities of CLJ imbue[56] features of *durée*, effective history and untimely futures and their concomitant effect on subject and event formation. In doing so, these adjudicative temporalities produce radically altered constructions of legal subjects that are contingent, situated and constituted by either mental, physiological conditions or social structures. The inclusion of the enduring and sedimented pasts – collectively, the variegated past – reveals potentially exculpatory facts that emerge in these different productions of legal times. Importantly, however, these variegated pasts do not simply reveal themselves over the course of trial courts. This requires the articulation of the legal problem that engages the primacy of these variegated pasts or elevating the Encounter in adjudication. As this happens, it provides the legal norm with new content garnered from the variegated past, thus simultaneously altering the legal norms form. Indeed, legal form is contingent on the primacy of the Encounter which enables the engagement of variegated pasts in CLJ. These forms, in engaging these non-spatial, variegated pasts, produce futures that are not knowable. As Karin Van Marle writes in her characterisation of legal judgement as 'slowness and delay', 'memory, of course, like imagination is a construction and in this sense the traditional concepts of linear and chronological time are disrupted'.[57] Whereas spatial pasts in ALJ follow the linear, teleological progression of time to produce knowable futures, CLJ disrupts that teleology, in its incorporation of variegated pasts, to produce a potentially new imagery, an unknown and unanticipated future- and the possibility for radical social transformation. Notably, however, all of this – the Problem, the Encounter, the changing of the form of the rule, the engagement of the variegated pasts and its production of the legal event and subject – happens contemporaneously, as part of an interrelated whole, as we shall see in the following chapter, rather than a chronological process by the judge and jury. Indeed, this can't be easily separated into a simple judicial inventory.

In ALJ, at least in theory, one observes that these types of pasts, enduring and sedimented, are not produced for the sake of producing particular types of legal subjects and events that are conducive to theories of responsibility, judicial analytical convenience and clarity. CLJ, in its pursuit of redeeming that complexity, also recognises what is missed out in the determination of fact. The next chapter attempts to tether these abstractions to the case law and institutional practice.

Notes

1 Karin Van Marle, 'Law's Time, Particularity and Slowness' (2003) 19 South African Journal on Human Rights 242.
2 Elizabeth Grosz, *Time Travels: Feminism, Nature, Power* (Duke University Press 2005) 2.
3 Brad Sherman, 'Hermeneutics in Law' (1988) 51 Modern Law Review 386–402.
4 See also Francis Joseph Mootz, 'Hermeneutics and Law' in Niall Keane and Chris Law (eds), *The Blackwell Companion to Hermeneutics* (Wiley & Sons 2016) 595–603; Brad Sherman, 'Hermeneutics in Law' (1988) 51 Modern Law Review 386; William N Eskridge Jr. 'Gadamer/ Statutory Interpretation' (1990) 3832 Yale Law School Faculty Scholarship Series 609; George Wright, 'On a General Theory of Interpretation: The Betti-Gadamer Dispute in Legal Hermeneutics' (1987) 32,1 American Journal of Jurisprudence 191.
5 Steven L Winter, 'Indeterminacy and Incommensurability in Constitutional Law' (1990) 78 California Law Review 1486.
6 Karl Marx, *A Critique of Political Economy* (George Allen & Unwin Ltd 1928).
7 Georgia Warnke, *Hermeneutics, Tradition and Reason* (Polity Press 1987) 3.
8 Johan Galtung, 'Violence, Peace, and Peace Research' (1969) 6,3 Journal of Peace Research 167–191.
9 Hans-Georg Gadamer, *Truth and Method* (Joel Weinheimer and Donald G Marshall trs, 2nd edn, Continuum Publishing Group 2004) 362–369.
10 William N Eskridge Jr, 'Gadamer/ Statutory Interpretation' (1990) 3832 Yale Law School Faculty Scholarship Series 623.
11 This could be used to explain a case such as *R v. R* [1991] 3 WLR 767 (in which the matrimonial exception to rape was reversed without legislation) with Lord Keith's comments being particularly illuminating:

> It may be taken that the proposition was generally regarded as an accurate statement of the common law of England. The common law is, however, capable of evolving in the light of changing social, economic and cultural developments. Hale's proposition reflected the state of affairs in these respects at the time it was enunciated. Since then the status of women, and particularly of married women, has changed out of all recognition in various ways which are very familiar and upon which it is unnecessary to go into detail... In modern times any reasonable person must regard that conception as quite unacceptable.

12 Habermas and Gadamer engaged in a fruitful debate, in which the former accused the later of inherent conservativism, which Gadamer refuted. For a succinct summary of these arguments see also William N Eskridge Jr, 'Gadamer/ Statutory Interpretation' (1990) 3832 Yale Law School Faculty Scholarship Series 630.

13 Of course, the relationship between legal text, subject and judgement occurs in various feminist, postcolonial, queer projects, and, though not conscious of temporal analyses, it does seek to approach histories and legal subjectivity in adjudication in a manner which echoes the approach in this book. See also Rosemary Hunter, Clare McGlynn and Erika Rackley (eds), *Feminist Legal Judgements: From Theory to Practice* (Bloomsbury 2010); Eve Darian-Smith and Peter Fitzpatrick (eds), *Laws of the Postcolonial* (University of Michigan Press 1999); Martha Fineman, Jack Jackson and Adam Romero, *Feminist and Queer Legal Theory: Intimate Encounters, Uncomfortable Conversations* (Ashgate 2009).
14 Alexandre Lefebvre, *The Image of Law: Deleuze, Bergson, Spinoza* (Stanford University Press 2008) 102.
15 Elizabeth Grosz, 'Bergson, Deleuze and the Becoming of Unbecoming' (2005) 11,2 Parallax 4.
16 Gilles Deleuze, *Bergsonism* (Hugh Tomlinson and Barbara Habberjam trs, Zone Books 1991) 99.
17 Alexandre Lefebvre, *The Image of Law: Deleuze, Bergson, Spinoza* (Stanford University Press 2008) 94.
18 See also Mark S Muldoon, 'Henri Bergson and Postmodernism' (1990) 34,2 Philosophy Today 184.
19 A similar point is made by Renisa Mawani. See also 'The Times of Law' (2015) 40,1 Law & Social Inquiry 255.
20 Suzanne Guerlac, *Thinking in Time: An Introduction to Henri Bergson* (Cornell University Press 2006) 147.
21 For a parallel with Gadamer, his analogy of 'play' in aesthetic understanding is illustrative. Hans-Georg Gadamer, *Truth and Method* (Joel Weinheimer and Donald G Marshall trs, 2nd edn, Continuum Publishing Group 2004) 101.
22 Henri Bergson, *Matter and Memory* (Nancy Margaret Paul and W Scott Palmer trs, Digireads.com Publishing 2010) 88.
23 Karl Marx, *The 18th Brumaire of Louis Bonaparte* (Mondial 2005 (Originally published in 1852)).
24 Steven L Winter, 'Indeterminacy and Incommensurability in Constitutional Law' (1990) 78 California Law Review 1488.
25 Rosemary Coombe, 'Same as It Ever Was: Rethinking the Politics of Legal Interpretation' (1989) 34 McGill Law Journal 603.
26 Lord Scarman, *The Brixton Disorders 10–12 April 1981 Report* Command 8932.
27 Alan Norrie, *Crime, Reason and History: A Critical Introduction to Criminal Law* (CUP 2011) 137–140.
28 Robert Sullivan, 'Is Criminal Law Possible?' (2002) 22 Oxford Journal of Legal Studies 750–751.
29 Johan Galtung, 'Violence, Peace, and Peace Research' (1969) 6,3 Journal of Peace Research 168.
30 Iris Marion Young, *Responsibility for Justice* (OUP 2011).
31 Iris Marion Young, 'Five Theses of Oppression' in Lisa Heldke and Peg O'Connor (eds), *Oppression, Privilege, & Resistance* (McGraw Hill Humanities) 37–63.
32 Susan Marks, 'Human Rights and Root Causes' (2011) 74,1 Modern Law Review 72.
33 Antonio Gramsci, *Prison Notebooks* (1929–1935).
34 For an overview, see also Sharon Hays, 'Structure and Agency and the Sticky Problem of Culture' (1994) 12,1 Sociological Theory 57–72; For a more detailed overview, see also Mike O'Donnell (eds), *Structure and Agency* (Sage Publications 2010).

35 As was mentioned at the start of the book, it's worth stressing again that while the focus has been on criminal law, it is hoped that the uses of this analysis stretch beyond this field.
36 William Lucy, *Law's Judgement* (Bloomsbury Press 2017) 7.
37 Williams Wilson, *Criminal Law: Doctrine and Theory* (Pearson Education 2003) 99.
38 See also Mark Kelman, 'Interpretive Construction in the Substantive Criminal Law' (1981) 33,4 Stanford Law Review 593.
39 See also Duncan Kennedy, 'Form and Substance in Private Law Adjudication' (1976) 89 Harvard Law Review 1685; Pierre Schlag, 'Rules and Standards' (1985) 33 University of California Law Review 379.
40 Alexandre Lefebvre, *The Image of Law: Deleuze, Bergson, Spinoza* (Stanford University Press 2008).
41 Gilles Deleuze, *Difference and Repetition* (Paul Patton trans, Columbia University Press 1994 (Originally published in 1968)) 68–69.
42 Alexandre Lefebvre, *The Image of Law: Deleuze, Bergson, Spinoza* (Stanford University Press 2008) 73.
43 Alexandre Lefebvre, *The Image of Law: Deleuze, Bergson, Spinoza* (Stanford University Press 2008) 237.
44 Karin Van Marle, 'Law's Time, Particularity and Slowness' (2003) 19 South African Journal on Human Rights 241.
45 Alexandre Lefebvre, *The Image of Law: Deleuze, Bergson, Spinoza* (Stanford University Press 2008) 71.
46 Alexandre Lefebvre, *The Image of Law: Deleuze, Bergson, Spinoza* (Stanford University Press 2008) 85.
47 This he borrows from Spinoza. See also Alexandre Lefebvre, *The Image of Law: Deleuze, Bergson, Spinoza* (Stanford University Press 2008) 197–259.
48 Alexandre Lefebvre, *The Image of Law: Deleuze, Bergson, Spinoza* (Stanford University Press 2008) 96.
49 Alexandre Lefebvre, *The Image of Law: Deleuze, Bergson, Spinoza* (Stanford University Press 2008) 213.
50 Elizabeth Grosz, *Time Travels: Feminism, Nature, Power* (Duke University Press 2005) 1.
51 Elizabeth Grosz, *Time Travels: Feminism, Nature, Power* (Duke University Press 2005) 1.
52 Kathryn McNeilly, 'Are Rights Out of Time? International Human Rights Law, Temporality, and Radical Social Change' (2018) 824 Social and Legal Studies 8.
53 Kathryn McNeilly, 'Are Rights Out of Time? International Human Rights Law, Temporality, and Radical Social Change' (2018) 825 Social and Legal Studies 9.
54 Susan Marks, 'Human Rights and Root Causes' (2011) 74,1 Modern Law Review 72.
55 Noami Klein, *The Shock Doctrine: The Rise of Disaster Capitalism* (Henry Holt and Company 2010).
56 A potential difficulty alluded to earlier requires circumventing the problem of capturing *durée* (experiential time) in a discursive endeavour such as adjudication. Earlier, it was explained how Bergson distinguishes between the *Immediate Consciousness* (IC) and the *Reflective Consciousness* (RC). Real time as *durée* exists in the IC and is characterised by the unmediated sensations of the consciousness that are accumulating and interpenetrative, varying by quality rather than by degree. The past 'states' melt into the moving present and cannot be considered separated from it. Memory and Perception are entangled in a dynamic and reciprocal relationship in which the entirety of the past is always

immanent to the present. RC however is a static representation of this pure, unmediated consciousness. For example, the discursive element of human sociality spatialises and thus represents the IC. Adjudication, as that which is both *ex post factum* and discursive, therefore would necessarily operate within the RC. ALJ is an example of spatialising reality under (legal) concepts and rules to produce representative phenomena. However, adjudication, whether ALJ or CLJ, will surely always be spatial? How can a form of adjudication produce durational temporalities?

> What would a return to the immediate mean? To detach oneself from space without leaving extension. Here Bergson returns to the problem of language. And could not immediate consciousness find its own justification and proof in itself, if one could establish that these difficulties, these contradictions, these problems arise primarily from the symbolic figuration that covers them over, a figuration that we have come to identify with reality itself and whose thickness can only be pierced by an exceptional, intense effort?
>
> (Guerlac 2006, 158)

In this argument, a 'return' to the IC requires CLJ's creative embrace of some of the central features of Bergson's *durée* (and Gadamer's effective history).

57 Karin Van Marle, 'Law's Time, Particularity and Slowness' (2003) 19 South African Journal on Human Rights 242.

Chapter 5

Adjudicative temporalities and judicial fact construction

A case law analysis

Introduction

It is worth restating once again the claim of the centrality of time to adjudication that this book makes. This is not a discussion of law in time but time in law – specifically, the juridical production of time in adjudication. It has been argued that adjudicative temporality structures fact construction, event and subject formation, legal form and responsibility ascription in criminal law. Adjudicative temporalities, therefore, are not epiphenomenal, nor are they a curious and novel retrospective re-framing of how judicial fact construction operates. It hastens our attention to not only the erstwhile silence of legal temporalities, but their indeterminacies and thus the larger implications of the politics of legal judgement. Given these general silences, this chapter embarks upon a creative reading of case law to illustrate the ways in which adjudicative temporalities determine fact construction in decisions that tend towards either ALJ or CLJ. Recall some of the methodological limitations – that triers of fact will not officially record the case in law reports, the general acceptance of these facts in subsequent appeals to the higher courts and the fairly brief summation of facts in the headnotes of the law report. However, as well as trying to supplement appeal judgements with transcripts of trial courts, much can also be read in the silences of the law report. Finally, as has been apparent throughout, the focus has been primarily on criminal law doctrine, the reasons of which have been briefly explained elsewhere.

This final chapter will begin with a brief restatement of the antipodal ends of the spectrum of judgement, ALJ and CLJ, describing their temporalities and how their temporalities shape their construction of facts. The next section will then focus upon two key case studies that demonstrate the claims of this book. The first will be a detailed exegesis of the *Ahluwalia* litigation, before looking at the legal defence of 'lawful excuse' in civil disobedience cases. Distinctions between the outcomes and subsequent successes (or not) of the cases are explained through their differential adjudicative temporalities, which reveals a site of the politics of legal judgement that would otherwise be invisibilised.

Restatement

Let us begin with briefly describing the features of ALJ and CLJ, respectively. ALJ 'judges us (i) not in all our particularity but as identical abstract beings; (ii) by reference to general and objective standards equally applicable to all such beings; (iii) the application of these standards being mitigated only by a limited range of exculpatory claims'.[1] ALJ is productive of a spatial temporality which imbues features of uniformity, divisibility, juxtaposition and simultaneity. This allows reality to be chronologised, the process of distinguishing, selecting and placing adjacent to one another, states into a sequence that are presumed to be causally related, what Kelman and Nousiainen otherwise refer to as time frames. Crucially, it is time frames that are responsible for event construction in adjudication. The subjectivities that ALJ produces therefore, the liberal legal subject (or 'presumed identity'), is one that is contained within the time-framed legal event, born and reborn at each moment and producing the mythological deracinated and agential subject of law. This latter point is particularly important in the case of broadening, which describes the process in which legal judgement adopts a broader time frame but still maintains a legal subject which is contained within the legal event with an overarching temporality of repetitive new beginnings (to borrow an earlier phrase from Sarah Keenan). As ALJ produces spatial pasts which contain legal subjects within the legal event, it will likely produce predictable outcomes or, in other words, knowable futures. This is entirely consistent with a legal form which is sensed such that it anticipates the facts which it determines relevant for adjudication.

CLJ, however, is 'tempered not just with mercy but also by knowledge: not only of the conduct in question and its context, but knowledge of our character...in all our particularity...we are not strangers but intimates, with a history'.[2] This type of legal judgement is productive of Bergsonian (*durée*), Gadamerian (effective history) and Groszian (untimely futures) temporalities. The former two largely imbue characteristics of interconnectedness, in which the past and present are resistant to division. In *durée*, time is qualitative, as each present moment is constituted by an accumulating past. Effective history situates the present within the tradition and entirety of the past. As for the latter, Grosz's neo-Bergsonian untimely futures are unlike the lineal teleology of knowable futures, instead privileging unknown and unpredictable futures above the present. CLJ therefore produces variegated pasts, one which is enduring, like *durée*, and the other which is sedimented, drawn from the features of Gadamer's effective history. One may liken enduring pasts to mental and physiological conditions that are attributed to the legal subject, which pre-exist the legal event when it was happening. Sedimented pasts refer to social structures, such as the configuration of socio-economic milieus, that precede and constitute the subject. The legal subject in CLJ is therefore contingent, situated and constituted as a product of historical and social processes. The engagement of the variegated past, however, is only possible in CLJ, with the primacy of the Encounter which does not see the fact situation as an instantiation of the legal rule but elevates it to a level of primacy in determining the content of the legal rule. Thus the legal form of the rule is contingent on the primacy of the Encounter which enables the engagement of variegated pasts. The primacy of the Encounter, in turn, is dependent upon how the courts pose the Problem in adjudication, which is understood as the framing of the issue that ultimately seeks to establish rights for the litigant. Finally, because the legal form is contingent on the variegated past, CLJ produces futures which are not deterministic, but untimely. It is this that reveals the transformative potential in CLJ. Table 5.1 attempts to summarise these distinctions.

This chapter will primarily look at a series of defences in criminal law cases. Defences are typically examples of a limited range of exculpatory claims that litigants can make but still presume the construction of the liberal legal subject (unless that is absolutely compromised by 'defects of reason'). Thus, it does not recognise exculpatory claims on the basis of facts, revealed in particular types of pasts that constitute contingent

Table 5.1 Comparing the features of ALJ and CLJ

	Abstract Legal Judgement (ALJ)	*Concrete Legal Judgement (CLJ)*
Temporalities	Spatial	*Durée*/effective history
Types of Pasts	Spatial/'time frames' (either narrow or broad)	Variegated (spatial, enduring and sedimented)
Types of Futures	Teleological	Untimely
Legal Subjectivities	Liberal legal subject which is contained within the time frame of the legal event and is born and reborn at each moment	Contingent, situated subject of law that is constituted by both enduring and/or sedimented pasts
The Encounter	Fact situation is mere instantiation of legal rule(s)	Fact situation is elevated and provides new content for legal rule(s)
The Problem	States the problem in a manner which does not engage the variegated past	Identifies specific problems based on the concrete case that provides new content for the legal rule(s) with recognition of the variegated past
Legal Form	Rule-like/sensed	Standard-like/senseless

legal subjects. To quote Lucy once again, 'when accepting exculpatory claims, the law rarely delves into the particularities of the defendant's context or character as reinforced by something else: such exculpatory claims are usually only valid if reasonable. Reasonableness requirements are the principal means by which the law treats those before it as abstract beings rather than the beings they actually are'.[3] However, what the following cases illustrate is not that defences mitigate responsibility but the temporalities and thus pasts that give new content to the legal norms.

The first case will revisit *R v. Ahluwalia*,[4] where Battered Woman Syndrome as a pre-existing mental condition was newly considered under the partial defence of diminished responsibility to homicide. This case is explanatorily illuminating as the two defences of provocation and diminished responsibility that were used illustrate tendencies towards ALJ and CLJ, respectively (though the difference was not on the success of different defences but on different temporalities, the latter of which gave new content to the legal norm of diminished responsibility). Following this exegesis, the chapter will compare and contrast popular civil disobedience cases that sought to engage the defence of Lawful Excuse. The subsequent differences in the determination of facts are symptomatic of different adjudicative temporalities at play, which ultimately meant that the allocation of responsibility had similarly changed.

To be clear, what this means is that in cases where defences are not pleaded, alternate temporalities can be deployed, but the likelihood is diminished, given that there will be less expenditure of judicial effort to mitigate responsibility. This is not to say that other types of pasts do not exist. It merely means that they are even more invisibilised. Indeed, in the absence of any discussion about defences or mitigation, it forecloses the possibilities of a decision tending towards CLJ. Finally, part of determining what pasts and futures are produced, how the Problem is stated, whether the primacy of the Encounter is afforded and what the legal form looks like necessitates a creative reading of the case law.

R v. Ahluwalia – a case of 'temporal stretching'

On the evening of the 9 May 1989, Kiranjit Ahluwalia poured petrol on her husband and set him alight whilst he was asleep. Badly burnt, he survived for only a few days before passing away. Ahluwalia was promptly charged with murder under s.2 (1) *Homicide Act 1957*. At the trial, she said that she did not have the requisite *mens rea* for murder, claiming she only wanted to inflict some pain and that the conduct was partially justified on the basis of provocation.[5] This was rejected by the trial court, but Ahluwalia appealed on the grounds, first, that the trial judge's direction to the jury on applying *Duffy*[6] in the provocation defence was incorrect and, second, that the defence of diminished responsibility, not disclosed at trial, was open to the appellant. The case was held on the former grounds, but the judge allowed the appeal on the basis of diminished responsibility. At the re-trial, the crown accepted her plea of diminished responsibility for manslaughter, for which she was sentenced for a time in prison that she had already served.

What was particularly interesting about Lord Taylor CJ determination of the facts of the case in the appeal was the detailed rendering of the back-story of the appellant. This is especially determinative in ascertianing how the facts of the case were in any way incorporative of just spatial or also enduring and sedimented past and how, if at all, ascriptions of responsibility were altered. One of the key differences between the trial hearing and the appeal was that Ahluwalia was clearly a victim of sustained domestic violence – something that was omitted from the trial given.

Ahluwalia is important for the fact that the case history, at trial and appeal, demonstrated divergent tendencies towards both ALJ and CLJ. The portion of the analysis that deals with the failed provocation defence is an example of ALJ. It is problematic for the reasons that it seemed to produce spatial pasts and adopted a narrow time frame that both resulted in the failure of the provocation defence and elided the enduring past of her being a victim of sustained domestic violence. Therefore, the limitations of ALJ's spatial temporality can be demonstrated with the invocation and resultant failure of the provocation defence, where a brief reference is made to an analogous case which did adopt a broader time frame, and the general elision of the enduring past. All this will be juxtaposed to the operation of Battered Woman Syndrome as a type for diminished responsibility through the appellate court's engagement of the enduring past, thus illustrating a tendency towards CLJ, which was successful in incorporating this history of violence into the construction of the legal event and subject, altering the ascription of responsibility.

To begin with, the old provocation defence upon which this case was decided needs to be examined. The first limb of the defence – *sudden and temporary loss of self-control* – was given its classic exposition in *Duffy*[7] as conduct 'which would cause in any reasonable person and actually causes in the accused, a sudden and temporary loss of self-control'. Now recall, first, that this book diverts from an exclusive focus on rule-centric correspondence theories that argue laws correspond to facts 'out there'. Instead, which facts are deemed relevant is, in large part, determined by adjudicative temporalities and not the rule *per se*. We are more interested in the facts that give content to these rules and how adjudicative temporalities produce these facts. Second, though relatedly, the form of the rule is largely contingent on the temporalities (and the pasts and futures) produced by legal judgement. Here, the defence failed because there was a lapse of time between the most recent provocation and Ahluwalia's act of setting her husband on fire, which appeared to undermine 'an essential ingredient of the defence'.[8] In effect, the courts swung towards ALJ by adopting a narrow time frame. Indeed, a longer lapse of time or a broader time frame, that would have given different content to this limb of the rule, had also been rejected in the earlier case of *R v. Thornton.*[9] A broad time frame was often considered as a 'cooling off' period, in which the defendant is assumed to have regained level-headedness, which thus invalidated the defence. The appellant, however, articulated the possibility, based on expert evidence, 'that women who have been subjected frequently over a period to violent treatment may react to the final act or words by what he calls a slow-burn reaction rather than an immediate loss of self-control'. Though this was rejected, Lord Taylor CJ in the appeal did not eliminate the possibility that a latent period between the provocation and the transgression may be successful in future litigation and encouraged the courts instead to adopt a piecemeal approach.[10] However, one can unearth the indeterminacy of the legal production of times if we contrast this with the case of *R v. Baillie (John Dickie).*[11] In that case, a man, who upon hearing that his son had been threatened by a drug dealer, then set off for the drug dealer's house, was able to successfully argue to the courts that a lapse of time – adopting a broader time frame – amounted to a sudden and temporary loss of self-control. The appeal judge in that case, Lord Henry J, thought that refusing to accept a slow-burn reaction – in other words, a broader time frame – was harsh. Indeed, he said of the judge in the trial hearing that 'it seems to us that that approach is too austere an approach'.[12]

The second limb – reasonable person – can be understood to be operative within the spatial past and therefore appearing only within the spatial past-legal event. As far as both the trial judge and jury and appeal judge were concerned, Ahluwalia was contained within the narrow time-framed legal event, born and reborn at each moment, with all her enduring or sedimented histories elided. Indeed, this was evidenced by the refusal of the trial judge to accept the appellant's argument that the trial judge was incorrect when directing the jury on determining the reasonable 'person limb' by excluding her being a battered woman as a relevant characteristic. Interestingly, the appeal judge summarily rejected this *on the provocation ground*: though, not on the basis that it could not be admitted as a characteristic of the reasonable person but rather on the basis that there had been no evidence to this effect before the trial judge and jury. So, this was a procedural issue rather than one that was rejected on substantive grounds.

The judicial construction of the legal event that gave content to the two limbs of the provocation defence in this particular case is an example of tending towards ALJ. It can explain the reticence of the court in accepting the 'slow-burn' rationale (i.e. a broad time frame) and why the reasonable person, despite apparently being destabilised by seemingly engaging the variegated past (history of violent conduct against the appellant), still returned a negative verdict on this defence. Provocation can be considered an *instant* – antecedent to the *mens rea* – that broadens the time frame of the legal event. Affirming the 'slow-burn' approach ('that women who have been subjected frequently over a period to violent treatment may react to the final act or words by what he calls a slow-burn reaction rather than an immediate loss of self-control') would allow for the adoption of an even broader time frame (which has been accepted in other cases).[13] The judge's dismissal of the slow-burn is effectively the production and adoption of a narrow time frame, as is entirely consonant with ALJ.[14] Efforts towards broadening the time frame of the legal event (or incorporating variegated pasts) are met with caution and are eventually resisted. Indeed, it could be argued that this demonstrates a general principle in criminal law doctrine against remoteness that maintains the predilection towards proximity,[15] with the slow-burn operative as a kind of *novus actus interveniens*. On the basis of this limb, it constructs Ahluwalia as a legal subject contained in this narrow time-framed legal event, and thus devoid of her idiosyncrasies emergent in the variegated past.

What was particularly interesting about the trial judge's direction on the reasonable man limb is that he directed the jury to consider the whole history of the marriage. This appears to sound like an attempt to engage the variegated past, which would have had the possible effect of releasing the legal subject from the boundaries of the narrow time-framed legal event. However, despite the jury being directed to the variegated past in which the defendant committed the act for the purposes of this limb,[16] they still returned a negative verdict on the basis of provocation. This can be explained due to the *absence of the primacy of the Encounter* (symptomatic of tending towards ALJ). In other words, though the trial jury accepted that there had been a history of violence against the defendant, this was not considered a condition, or sedimented, past in which to locate and contextualise the killing (on this specific ground), which would have produced a contingent and situated legal subject.[17] Indeed, its exclusion from the facts of the case were neither explained nor meaningfully acknowledged. Engaging the history of violence as a type of sedimented past and incorporating this into the judicial summation of facts would require affording the primacy of the Encounter. Without the primacy of the Encounter, the dominance of spatial temporality prevails and the history of violence is not meaningfully acknowledged. This gives the content of the common law rule of provocation such that its legal form is sensed, producing a legally certain and therefore knowable future. Thus the legal subject stays 'trapped' within the narrow time-framed legal event where the adoption of broader time frames or the variegated pasts are elided. The absence of the primacy of the Encounter as that which fails to recognise the variegated past (the history of violence as the sedimented past) is tacitly alluded to when Lord Taylor CJ says:

> True, there was much evidence that the appellant had suffered grievous ill-treatment; but nothing to suggest that the effect of it was to make

> her a different person from the ordinary run of [woman] or to show that she was marked off or distinguished from the ordinary [woman] of the community.[18]

This can be read as meaning 'yes there are variegated pasts, specifically the enduring past of battered woman syndrome in which the killing took place but, within the way in which we have given content to the defence of provocation, the variegated past won't be meaningfully acknowledge as unsettling the presumed reasonable persons'. Both limbs work to contain Ahluwalia: the first by adopting a narrow time frame for what constitutes sudden and temporary loss of self-control (with suggestions of broadening met with resistance operant within the spatial past), and the second, the ignorance of the Encounter which would have meaningfully engaged the variegated past. Indeed, without the primacy of the Encounter to situate Ahluwalia's actions through the engagement of the variegated past, she only appears within a narrowly time-framed event, and as such, the decision resembles tending towards ALJ. In addition, the judgement lacks a stating of the Problem[19] pertaining to this particular defence, and so it cannot 'guide' the re-construction of the legal rule of provocation to allow for the slow-burn approach via a broader time frame or the engagement of the variegated past. In effect, the case, on the basis of which the provocation defence is sensed, is seen merely as a particularisation of the rule rather than in its concrete singularity. As far as the jury is concerned, the legal event began when a woman gathered the materials to eventually kill her husband. Those are the salient facts.

To strengthen this reading of *Ahluwalia*, it is worth also contrasting this with the provocation defence used in *Hill*,[20] a case that was granted leave to appeal upon referral by the Criminal Cases Review Commission. After an evening of drinking, the appellant left the pub with the victim and went back to the victim's house. At some point, the appellant had strangled the victim to death. He claimed that he had fallen asleep and awoke to see the victim fumbling with the appellant's zip with the intention of sexual activity. The first grounds of the appeal were that there was fresh evidence[21] that the appellant had suffered childhood sexual abuse, which may have provided acquittal for murder on the grounds of provocation. The second ground was that scientific advancements could be used to demonstrate that the appellant was suffering from diminished responsibility. Both counts were rejected, the former on the basis that the appellant had ample opportunities to disclose the history of sexual abuse and the latter in that the evidence from the MRI did not indicate impaired reason and thus diminished responsibility.

The fresh evidence of a history of sexual abuse against the defendant in which he was 'assailed by a flashback to the similar conduct of the foster father'[22] is interesting. The courts cited independent evidence that corroborated this claim, which may have provided the basis for the variegated past in which to situate the particular sensitivity of the appellant to the provocation and thus the gravity of it. Had it been considered at the hearing of first instance, this may have altered both the structure of the legal event and subject, and, potentially, the consequent ascription of responsibility which the appellate court ended up agreeing with (though, of course, not in these specific terms). The appellant's history of childhood sexual abuse, on the second limb of the provocation of reasonableness, engages the variegated past, which the court referred to as an 'oppressive history'.[23] Recalling the judge in *Ahluwalia*, he similarly entertained the possibility of a legal subject constituted by their variegated past, but instead took the option to see the case as a particularity of the rule rather than in its radical singularity.

Provocation in the case of *Ahluwalia* is problematic for the reason that it seems to meaningfully ignore the history of domestic violence against the appellant woman who had suffered innumerably. Provocation *could* have been interpreted as a *senseless rule*, in a manner that did consider the history of violence as meaningful (engaging the variegated past and enabling a 'situated reasonable persons') or the 'slow-burn' approach as appropriate (adopting a broad time frame as seemed to be the case in *Baillie*),[24] thus tending towards CLJ. In other words, though both limbs on their face appear to adopt narrow time frames, they *could* have been read to adopt broader ones or engage the sedimented past. Thus, the 'newly sensed-provocation' rule would have created a caveat for 'slow-burners' who had been victims of a sustained history of domestic violence. The provocation defence therefore, as interpreted in this case, despite the possibilities for change in future litigation,[25] makes out as if the appellant only appears within the confines of the event and as if the history of violence had not even happened. While the defence of provocation has now been replaced with the loss of control defence in ss.54 and 55 *Coroners and Justice Act 2009*,[26] this has provided an example of both the operative role of adjudicative temporalities and the resultant assignation on criminal responsibility.

The trial judgement, however, can be contrasted with the foregrounding of Battered Woman Syndrome as a new category of diminished responsibility in the appeal. Lord Taylor CJ began his judgement 'on May 9, 1989, the appellant, after enduring many years of violence and humiliation from her husband'. Almost immediately, it appears to engage the variegated past, situating the defendant's transgression within the enduring past which pre-exists the spatial past of the narrow time-framed legal event (i.e. the pouring and setting alight of the petrol over her husband as it was happen*ing*). Tellingly, he describes this past that constituted the appellant as 'enduring'.[27] Thus, it is not a mere instant of time (such as a provocation) which may warrant the adoption of a broad time frame but the production and engagement of a qualitatively different type of past. This fact is past not by virtue of the positioning of the legal case *ex post factum* but was also past when the event in question was happening. It was and continues to be.

As a result of the introspection into this tortured past of violence, the legal event is augmented, not merely by moving to a moment antecedent to the *mens rea* but with a perennial and enduring past. These include being hit over the head with a telephone eight years prior, then two years later in 1983, being pushed whilst pregnant and attempting suicide in 1986.[28] Battered Woman Syndrome is not a moment prior to the transgression – *it pre-exists it*. Unlike in the failed provocation defence that tended towards ALJ, Ahluwalia's appearance in the process of event construction is not delayed and contained in a narrow time as was the case in the hearing of first instance. It pre-exists the pouring of petrol on her husband. This is also an indication of the Encounter's primacy in which the courts demonstrate openness to facts that are revealed in the variegated pasts. Thus, the form of the legal rule of diminished responsibility is senseless. Specifically, 'what judges do, therefore, is provide a sense for the rule, which is to say that a judgment creates a rule insofar as it connects together the old form (tradition, the rule) and a new content (the reasons provided for the rule)'.[29] Prior to the case, Diminished Responsibility did not recognise Battered Woman Syndrome. Thus, the new content of the rule is derived from engaging the variegated pasts; altering the form of the legal norm; and, in the process, producing an untimely future – a new defence in which women who are the victims of sustained domestic violence can argue that they are not legally culpable for murder of their spouses. CLJ's temporalities, therefore, can explain how different event and subjects are constructed in legal judgement in such a way as to both potentially mitigate responsibility as well as produce transformative outcomes (a new defence).

James Boyle's comment regarding the battered woman syndrome is interesting and worth quoting at length:

> Think of the battered spouse defence. You have a woman who is in a marriage which is extremely abusive, she has been beaten for five years, she has been repeatedly threatened, her husband has shot her in the leg on one occasion. Finally, when he's asleep, she grabs up a knife and stabs him. The standard notion of legal self-defence, given our stripped-down subject, sees no self-defence here. How can there be? The husband is asleep. There is no immediate threat in the brief time horizon of our genderless, contracting subject. But the battered spouse's defence lengthens the time horizon of the subject and makes the subject exist through time. The lawyers and scholars who created this defence argued that the time-horizon for self-defence in this case was five years not five-minutes. Now what is that but a broadening, a temporal stretching, if you will, of the legal subject? Yet at the same time that they are using the traditional genre of legal arguments about the subject and self-defence, these advocates are also calling that genre into question- the apparently fixed

> world of free will and its limited exceptions around which criminal law is constructed.[30]

Though Boyle may not be deploying the exact terms and distinctions that are used in this book (spatial, enduring and sedimented past), the sentiment is very much the same. The 'time horizon' which he mentions is related not to the event but to that of the person and is analogous to the horizon espoused by Gadamer, which necessarily situates the natural persons. 'Temporal stretching' can therefore be taken to mean the engagement of the variegated pasts and the resultant enrichment of the legal event. The 'stripped-down subject' who is 'our genderless, contracting subject' is akin to the liberal legal subject that is contained within a legal event, born and reborn at each moment.

The production of and engagement with the variegated past reveals facts which may potentially mitigate her responsibility. This overcomes the problematic shortcomings of the provocation defence used in a way characteristic of ALJ, by generally ignoring this history of violence (accepting that provocation *could* have been interpreted in a manner of CLJ). Indeed, this also appears to settle the difficulty of a legal event being constructed *ab aeterno.* Mere stretching of the spatial past goes against the intuitive tendencies of criminal legal systems general antipathy towards constructions that undermine proximity. Instead, diminished responsibility in this case introduces an altogether qualitatively different past that enriches the legal event, without the legal event beginning *ab aeterno.*

The more discerning may have noticed an expediency in using these examples to illustrate the claims of this book. The old common law rule of provocation, as well as the legal authorities expounding the rule, contains references to time, tenses or time periods: 'sudden and temporary', 'slow-burn' and so forth. There may be a claim, therefore, that the assertions I make only really refer to laws which have such references. There are two rebuttals to this. The first is that even when laws do contain references to time, this does not preclude law and adjudication's ability to interpret and construct these times in the way they see fit and that is not analogous to clock or calendrical time. Indeed, even with the old law of provocation, one sees in several cases how the legal authorities interpret it to adopt narrow time frames[31] and broad time frames.[32] References to 'clock-time' or 'calendrical time' are no less immune from the hegemony of juridical production of temporalities in the interpretation of those time provisions in laws. The second rebuttal is that seemingly non-temporal provisions of law can be interpreted in ways contingent on productions of time. This was evidenced in the 'reasonable man' limb of the defence and is now the focus on a series of cases which contain a mix of laws with and without explicit temporal references.

R v. Hill & Hall and R v. Saibene – civil disobedience as responding to the sedimented past

The following cases illustrate perhaps a starker and more controversial, but no less illuminating, example of different adjudicative temporalities and their rendering of legal subjectivities and events – one of attempted civil disobedience in which the appellants were convicted, and another of direct action civil disobedience which resulted in over 100,000 pounds of damage – and which was lawfully excused.

Within the 'Western canon', civil disobedience was popularised by Henry David Thoreau in his seminal essay *Resistance to Civil Government*[33] and has since been meticulously examined by theologians, political scientists, lawyers and sociologists. It has provided the modus operandi for social movements, from Mohandas Gandhi's Salt March, Martin Luther King Jr's bus boycotts in Montgomery, Alabama to Rosa Parks and Claudette Colvin's resistance of refusal to segregation laws. While often responding to the egregious policies formulated and instigated by persons or institutions, the commonalities of civil disobedience is that it often presses against an enduring structural injustice that pre-existed the event of their civil disobedience but continues to persist. Gandhi sought to expel Britain's violent imperial rule, while King, Colvin and Parks pushed back against the institutional capture of white supremacy.

Like most concepts, however, with some positing descriptive accounts of civil disobedience and others outlining normative claims, it lacks semantic consensus. Many liberal philosophers, for example, underwrite their reflections of civil disobedience with an overall fidelity to the law, requiring dissenters to accept the consequences of their actions. Indeed, the 1960s Committee of 100 accepted arrest in their anti-war civil disobedience, as have numerous climate breakdown activists after them, including, most recently, groups like UK Black Lives Matter[34] and Extinction Rebellion.[35] Some additionally state that civil disobedience requires the absence of violence. Responding to this, Howard Zinn stated that to abstain from violence would be to ignore the pathologically violent nature of a system, what others have referred to as structural violence[36] or oppression,[37] which will always produce choices of means which will be inescapably violent in the transition to a more egalitarian world.[38] Importantly, common to all streams of thought is its distinguishability from other forms of criminal activity and coercive political action by virtue of its moral defensibility.

Ironically in a case that perhaps substantially limited the legal viability of civil disobedience (perhaps an oxymoron), Lord Hoffman stated that:

> Civil disobedience on conscientious grounds has a long and honourable history in this country. People who break the law to affirm their belief in the injustice of a law or government action are sometimes vindicated

> by history in this country. The suffragettes are an example which comes immediately to mind. It is the mark of a civilised community that it can accommodate protests and demonstrations of this kind.[39]

Defendants vary as to whether they plead guilty or not guilty,[40] largely depending on whether they perceive the act to be criminal or they see its execution as necessary, given the gravity of the purported injustice they seek to address. Many defendants also use the courtroom as a forum in which to bring greater press attention to the structural injustice they see as pressing, a recent example being the Stansted 15,[41] who were charged with an offence ostensibly created for countering terrorism in their efforts to stop a UK Home Office-chartered deportation flight from removing undocumented migrants, many to places where they faced real threats to their lives. For those who pled guilty, the defences that have typically been used include lawful excuse, prevention of crime as per s.3 of the *Criminal Law Act 1967*, defence of other people, necessity or duress and *Article 10 of the ECHR*. Aggravated trespass under the *Criminal Justice and Public Order Act 1994* tends to be the main charge for most activists engaging in civil disobedience which involve entering premises, typical of campaigners such as *Plane Stupid*.[42] Interestingly, this charge requires the courts to scrutinise the business activities which are the target of such civil disobedience to determine whether they are 'lawful activities.[43] If a business, for example, is suspected of engaging in a criminal offence that is 'integral to the core activity', it may be considered unlawful for the purposes of CJPOA 1994.[44] Civil disobedience therefore compels courts to look beyond a specific transgression and to particular conditions that have seemingly warranted such conduct. It is for such reasons that they stimulate the interest of this chapter.

This section's focus is much narrower, centring primarily upon civil disobedience cases which use the defence of lawful excuse. This has successfully been used in a few cases to mitigate alleged criminal responsibility pursuant to s.5(2) of the *Criminal Damage Act 1971*. The famous 'Kingsnorth 6' case,[45] in which six Greenpeace activists were able to occupy a smokestack of a power station and paint the words 'Gordon' on the side, argued that they were trying to prevent damage to property caused by carbon dioxide emissions produced by the power plant. It was the first time that such an argument had been used as part of a lawful excuse defence and, with the help of expert witnesses that testified to the environmental damage that the power plant had *already caused*, the six were exonerated. Lawful excuse was also successfully used in the North Irish case of *R v. McCann and others*,[46] in which a group or protestors entered an arms company in Derry, causing tens of thousands of pounds worth of damage. The protestors sought to rely on lawful excuse, saying that the action was executed to defend property belonging to people in southern Lebanon, which was being destroyed by Israeli war jets that had had parts supplied to it by the arms company.

However, for the purposes of analysis, the principal focus will be a 2011 Crown Court case *R v. Saibene and others.*[47] This will be juxtaposed with an identical case heard some 20 years prior, *R v. Hill* and *R v. Hall*[48] (hereafter *Hill and Hall*), which, unlike *Saibene*, unsuccessfully argued lawful excuse. It is claimed that the different outcomes may be explained by the different adjudicative temporalities used to determine the material facts of the case which gave content to the legal rules.

6.21 R v. Hill and Hall

The case of *Hill & Hall* involved two appellants who were charged under s.3 of *the Criminal Damage Act 1971*[49] after having been found with a hacksaw, with the intention of using it to saw through part of a fence of the US Naval Facility at Brawdy, Wales. They justified their attempt under s.5 lawful excuse.[50] In order to satisfy the statutory defence that the damage amounts to protection,[51] the courts have to establish what the defendants' honestly held belief was (it is immaterial whether this is a *justified belief*): that the property was in immediate need of protection and that the means adopted were reasonable with regard to all circumstances. The wording of the legislation appeared to suggest that this was an entirely subjective test:

> If he destroyed or damaged or threatened to destroy or damage the property in question or, in the case of a charge of an offence under section 3 above, intended to use or cause or permit the use of something to destroy or damage it, in order to protect property belonging to himself or another or a right or interest in property which was or which he *believed* to be vested in himself or another… …and at the time of the act or acts alleged to constitute the offence he *believed*—(i)that the property, right or interest was in immediate need of protection; and (ii)that the means of protection adopted or proposed to be adopted were or would be reasonable having regard to all the circumstances.[52]

The cases were factually identical, and so the appellate judge dealt with the evidence provided by Ms Valerie Hill. Her reasoning for the damage against the naval base was that her attempt was an effort to force the UK to abandon its nuclear weapons programmes and prevent the destruction to their property and their neighbours. The trial judge directed the jury to convict on the grounds, first, of the absence of a causative relationship between the act and the alleged protection of their property and their neighbours such that the act could not objectively be seen as a protective act, and, second, that she could not be said to have believed that the property was in need of immediate protection. An application to appeal against the judgement was brought on the basis that these were both entirely subjective tests, and was thus a *question of fact* that should have been left to the jury such that the judge was wrong to direct the jury to convict.

In the appeal, Lord Lane CJ paraphrased what constituted Ms Valerie Hill's description of the threats and thus her belief that she was protecting property belonging to another:

> This particular base was to monitor the movements of Soviet submarines, that in the event of hostilities breaking out between the United States and the Soviets, or the Soviets and ourselves [UK], the base would be subject of a nuclear strike with devastation in the area...the Soviets might select the site at Brawdy as a target for a sudden nuclear strike...that if enough people took a hacksaw blade and did as she intended to do, namely cut a strand of the perimeter wire, the Americans might come to the conclusion that it was no longer possible to maintain the safety and integrity of their base.[53]

Accepting that this was her belief, the judge moved on to the test of 'whether the defendants' actions on the facts believed by them could constitute protection, was a matter of law' rather than what appeared to be subjective. This test followed *R v. Hunt*[54] where the appellant set fire to a guest room in an old people's home so as to summon the attention of others to a defective fire alarm system. The trial jury and the Court of Appeal in *Hunt* both ruled it was for the judge to decide whether the facts, as believed by the defendant, constituted protection of property.

Holding up the 'objective test', Lord Lane CJ quoted and affirmed what the trial judge in *Hill and Hall* had said, citing that 'the causative relationship between the acts which she intended to perform and the alleged protection was so tenuous, so nebulous, that the acts could not be said to be done to protect viewed objectively'.[55] On the immediacy element, the judge's reading of the defendants' established belief was similarly critical. At the trial stage, when probed about the immediacy of the threat, Ms Valerie Hill replied:

> I see the international situation as being constantly changing and sometimes far more threatening than others, and when we play with nuclear weapons, when we play the nuclear game, there is always the possibility at any time...that somebody will press the button and a bomb will fall... perhaps I can make an analogy...my husband is an epileptic; he suffers from epilepsy. This does not mean every minute of every day I go round thinking Ian is going to have a fit, but it is something that is kept in mind at all times as a possibility, and I would say this is an analogy really as to how I feel about Brawdy. I don't expect a nuclear bomb to fall today, or tomorrow, but there is always that possibility that it is going to happen.[56]

Based upon what the defendants had outlined as their objectives, it could not be said (controversially) as a matter of law that their actions amounted to protection of property belonging to another. This was on the bases that the proposed action was too remote from the defendants' eventual aim[57] (i.e. that it was too remote into the future, requiring the adoption of a 'broader time frame' and was thus indeterminate) and it also lacked immediacy[58] (i.e. in effect, reifying a narrow time frame). The application was refused.

Therefore, *Hill and Hall* stipulated that, contrary to what one may understand as the natural meanings of the statutory defence, the role of the court was to first, determine the belief that the defendant was protecting property belonging to another and to second, interpret that belief objectively as to whether it constituted protection of property. The task here is to understand the ways in which the legal event and subject have been structured; what they tell us about the legal temporalities produced; and what problems, if any, they may reveal.

This case was a decision which was characteristic of ALJ. In establishing causation between the attempted criminal act and the immediacy of the threat, the beliefs of the risks that were attributed to Ms Hill were entirely speculative and thus indeterminable.[59] By speculative, it is meant that the responses that Ms Hill gave to the trial judge were predicated on future projections which were entirely hypothetical and did not follow the lineal teleology of ALJ of certainty and predictability. Nothing in her evidence (or indeed in the judgement) attempted to engage the variegated past, such as evidence of previous attacks or threats that would suggest the likelihood of an attack, or other pre-existing physiological or mental factors which may have shaped her intent to commit criminal damage. Instead, the arguments were anchored in speculations, what we may call untimely futures. Of course, 'threats' are often established on indeterminate forecasts, but their likelihood can be reified by information from the past, however constructed. One example of this, in which a particular type of past helped to interpret the future, specifically through the adoption of a broad time frame, was demonstrated in the case of *Bolton v. Stone*.[60] The courts had to decide if the defendant was negligent for conduct that was not reasonably foreseeable, that is, hitting a cricket ball out of the ground which struck the plaintiff. Admittedly, unlike in *Hill and Hall*, this referred to a breach that was future *ex ante* but had manifested *ex post*. In determining the foreseeability of a risk rather than focussing on the relation between the breach of a duty of care and the harm, the determination of foreseeability was premised upon evidential history. Lord Normand stated that 'the evidence about the infrequency of hits out of the ground is directed to the period since 1910, and is sufficient basis for a judgment on the degree of risk and on the duty resting on the defendants'.[61] This was also echoed in the statements of Lord Oaksey[62] and Lord Reid.[63]

Forecasts, which are common in legal rules ('foreseeability', 'likelihood', 'immediacy') that are not rooted in any type of past, whether spatial (specifically broader time frames), enduring or sedimented, render the construction of the legal subject in such a way that would make it more challenging in satisfying the test of the defence. Given this, they defendants would ultimately be culpable. Ms Hill only appears from the instant of the attempt, and as such, the difficulty of the defence lies in the absence of situating the appellants within their constitutive pasts and subsequently introspecting into those pasts. In other words, it lacks a constituting horizon in which to situate the defendants and in which to understand their intended criminal damage. The judgement, including the beliefs of the appellants, is exclusively speculative and entirely divorced from the production of and introspection into the variegated past. There is nothing against which to determine the viability between the causal relation and the intended act and the threat.

Unlike in *Ahluwalia* where the appeal made reference to the variegated past, it is more difficult in these conjoined cases to make any normative assessment of what elisions are made in ALJ's fact determination. Therefore, one can only speculate. The future remains uncertain, which is a riposte to ALJ. However, generally speaking the variegated past which seeks to overcome some of the problems inherent within the spatial past, was altogether elided in the current case. This is itself problematic for the judges would be none the wiser as to what an enriched construction of the legal event and subject may have revealed (and whether it would have subsequently effected apportioning responsibility).

In *Hill and Hall*, production of and introspection into the variegated past which suggested the likelihood of attacks, such as previous and similar incidences of attacks or threats of attacks on American naval bases, *may* have strengthened the relationship between the exclusively speculative threats in the appellant's submissions and the intended action, not on causative grounds but situating the intended act of criminal damage within the constitutive horizon of previous belligerence. Otherwise, for the purposes of ALJ, Ms Valerie Hill emerges only from the point of approaching the naval base. Nothing of the variegated past is engaged, whether relating to enduring features of the defendant or sedimented conditions that speak to the belligerence and thus likelihood of an attack. In other words, speculation undermines the teleological futures produced by ALJ.

Another indication that this was decided in the manner of ALJ related to the 'objective' reading of the defendant's speculative state of mind. The legal clock, as it were, only started when Ms Hill took a hacksaw and approached the naval facility at Bawdy.[64] It is only these facts which give content to the legal rule, foreclosing the possibility of difference, contingency and situatedness. This is, in effect, undermining the primacy of the Encounter in which the facts emergent in the engagement of the different types of past would determine the form of the legal rule rather than the rule anticipating the facts of the legal event.

Lawful excuse in the incumbent example, unlike a defence of provocation, does not pertain to a point in time that precedes the intentional element; rather, it is rooted in forecasts. This is not to say that laws should not proscribe certain conduct that seeks to prevent future wrongdoing (though that can be wrought with problems)[65]; rather, an interpretation of a defence focussed exclusively on speculations may lead to certain difficulties, if not supplemented by a determination of facts that are rooted in whatever typologies of constructed pasts to determine its likelihood (as in the 'Kinsgnorth 6' case).[66] For the purposes of this book's argument, it is woefully abstract in its rendering of the legal subject which appears only from the commencement of the event. Determining the speculative threat, whether it eventually manifests or not, needs to be rooted in certain types of pasts which *Hill and Hall* simply did not do. As such, the defence is interpreted in a manner symptomatic of ALJ, and it is for these reasons, it is claimed, that the jury convicts. The following case, however, could be said to overcome this limitation by rooting the relation between the act and its causal relation to an immediate threat in the variegated past.

Though a Crown Court ruling, *R v. Saibene and others* proved to be an especially controversial decision, not least as it attracted opprobrium from the Office for Judicial Complaints, following accusations of judicial bias from the presiding judge, His Honour Bathurst-Norman J. Indeed, it was seen as a political judgement.[67] However, in keeping with the non-reporting of lower court judgements, scholarly commentary has been scant, limited primarily to the academic blogosphere.[68] A full summing-up of this judgement, however, was printed in the popular press.[69]

The defendants in the case, all from Bristol, were Ornella Saibene, Elijah Smith, Robert Nicholls, Tom Woodhead and Harvey Tadman.[70] After having exhausted all 'democratic means',[71] on 17 January 2009 they broke into the premises of an American defence company, EDO MBM (hereafter EDO), located in Moulsecoombe, Brighton. Engaging in what they referred to as a 'citizens' decommissioning', the defendant's threw filing cabinets and computers out of the factory windows causing damage in the region of £180,000. The purported criminal damage was justified as a last resort in response to the 2008–2009 war in the besieged Gaza Strip, *Operation: Cast Lead*. EDO was targeted as it had provided component parts for Israeli F-16 jets that were central to a military campaign that resulted in nearly 1,400 Palestinian deaths and around 5 deaths of Israel security forces.[72] All seven defendants were charged with conspiracy to commit criminal damage but said they had a lawful excuse and that the decommissioning was a necessity. To focus on the comparisons with the *Hill and Hall* case, the focus will only be upon the lawful excuse defence. The defendants in this case were successful. The claim of this book is that this can be explained as an example of

CLJ and its production and engagement of the variegated past which, it is argued, convinced the jury to acquit.

In CLJ, the construction of the legal subject(s) and legal event is enriched by the production of and introspection into the variegated past. It is claimed that with an enriched retrospective narrative, this may change ascriptions of responsibility. Further, CLJ requires the primacy of the Encounter to stimulate this process. The legal rules, in this case that of criminal damage and the defence of lawful excuse, are considered as *senseless* or malleable, as guided by the Problem, and given new content from the variegated past. This, in effect, creates the possibility of new futures in which radical direct action in the service of averting greater threats can be facilitated by the courts.

The similarities to the *Hill and Hall* case are notable. Both included acts (or at least intended acts) of civil disobedience and purported to protect property belonging to another. Specifically in the case of *Saibene*, this was to undermine efforts of the Israel Defence Forces' ability to damage property in the Gaza Strip by effectively disrupting the supply chain. With the former case however, as that which tended towards ALJ, the construction of the legal event was structured by spatial pasts that were divisible from other pasts (either broader time frames or the variegated pasts). As such, there was nothing that could enrich the determination of judicial facts, specifically the incorporation of enduring or sedimented pasts to locate the intention to commit criminal damage that may have persuaded the judge and jury in their assessment of the intended act of criminal damage at Brawdy. Contrastingly, however, the different outcome arrived at in the *Saibene* litigation is an example of CLJ, which the following illustrates.

Reading the judicial summary, there is initially a broad time frame adopted by the Crown Court that revealed that there was prior agreement carried out in accordance with the intentions of the group which resulted in the commission of the offence that constitutes the conspiracy requirement. This is the first distinction from the *Hill and Hall* litigation: the adoption of a broader time frame to construct the legal event. However, the broadening of the legal event is still only operant within the spatial past, containing the several legal subjects that are born and reborn at each moment. The adoption, therefore, of the broader time frame doesn't appear to mitigate any responsibility but instead revealed another element in the commissioning of the act. How the case emerges as significantly different from the previous case, however, was in its engagement of the variegated past.

To re-iterate, for lawful excuse to be successfully invoked, the defendants must have an honestly held belief that the property in the Gaza strip was in immediate need of protection (immaterial as to whether it is justified) and that the defendants' action were reasonable in protection of that property. The cases can be distinguished on the basis of the primacy of the Encounter and the stating of the Problem. Recall that 'an Encounter shocks the law and initiates the uncovering of a problem that will establish the facts of the situation'.[73] What is shocked is the prefiguring or anticipation of the facts through the spatial past as if they were already inhered in the legal rule. What 'shocks', therefore, is the elevation of the variegated past that attempts to locate the damage caused at the arms factory within a different typology of past that would otherwise be elided by ALJ's temporalities. This gives new content to the legal rule too. However, to engage the variegated past requires a particular stating of the Problem. Remember that the Problem explains differentiation within the law and fundamentally provides the parameters in which to establish the facts of a case[74]; in other words, the types of pasts that are engaged and promulgated in judicial fact determination. The Problem guides the legal rule of lawful excuse in its pragmatic application. Because of the singularity of the case, afforded through the primacy of the Encounter, the judicial crafting of the Problem is similarly unique.

The very engagement and incorporation of the variegated past into the court's determination of what happened comes from the Encounter and, in the eyes of some detractors, its ambitious and ultimately controversial stating of the Problem by the judge. If, for example, his Honour Bathurst-Norman J were to have stated the Problem merely as maintaining a general fidelity to the law or the sanctity of private property rights, then it could be argued that he would have not needed to have directed the jury towards the variegated past in the way that his summing-up strongly seemed to suggest. This would have been an open-and-shut case, where the agential legal subject, contained within a typically (though not always) narrow time-framed legal event, would have been held culpable. The judge, instead, framed the Problem as one of international crime prevention (and thus protection of property in the Gaza strip). Indeed, the judge stated that 'in this case, the purpose of the defendants in damaging MBM's property has to be to prevent the destruction by the Israeli Air Force of property in Gaza'.[75] The summing-up also went further on to state that all other non-direct action means had been exhausted. In effect, the Problem was about how to protect the welfare of others and the prevention of war crimes rather than *just* the property rights of an international arms manufacturer.[76] Had this been constructed using a narrow time frame (and thus within the spatial past) in which the defendants appear only within the confines of said legal event, it would simply not have been able to 'solve the Problem' stated by the judge. In other words, if the facts revealed in the commission of the offence were only focussed on, it would naturally have ignored any reference to the conditions revealed in the variegated past. What the judge necessarily required to solve the unique Problem as stated was engagement of the variegated past, specifically the sedimented past. By contrast, if the Problem were stated simply as protecting commercial property (or ensuring national security or a competitive market in the sales of arms etc.), the facts contained within the narrow spatial past would have sufficed.

The form of the legal rule of lawful excuse defence was *senseless*. In other words, it was operative more as a standard, given the new content from incorporating the sedimented past. The legal subject and legal event differed from the aforementioned case for the simple reason that it situated the civil disobedience within its sedimented past or 'background conditions, enabling frameworks and overarching systems'.[77] The judge spent ample amount in his summing-up, describing what that sedimented past was and how it clearly had a role in his direction to the jury. In an effort to encourage them to 'look at the evidence coldly and dispassionately', he stated:

> I am going to start with the background relating to Israel and Palestine and to the evidence which points to the war crimes being committed by Israel in Gaza...[UNSC]resolutions condemning Israel on no less than forty occasions...the barrier, and the judgment of the International Court holding it illegal and to stop building settlements in the West Bank are simply ignored...so with that broad picture in mind let me concentrate on Gaza...It is surrounded by a fence. That fence is patrolled by Israeli tanks, planes fly overhead...Israel decides what goes in and out...[they] impose a land, air and sea blockade...the Dahiyah doctrine, namely that Israel would apply disproportionate force and cause great damage and destruction to any village...Israel's attack on Gaza involved the use of disproportionate force...in three minutes 40 seconds, 250 Gazans were killed on the first day...the Al-Quds hospital was bombed. Hospitals, ambulance depots, mosques, United Nations compound, industrial and agricultural sites, the sewage and the electricity power plants were all targeted and damaged or destroyed.[78]

As is the case with typologies of pasts underwritten by Bergsonian and Gadamerian temporalities, it identifies conditions that pre-existed the criminal damage whilst it was happen*ing*. In other words, these facts were not merely past by virtue of adjudication's positioning *ex post facutm*. Instead, they are analogous to the third form of the variegated past, the sedimented past, that provides what Norrie called the 'deeper causes' in an effort to enrich the legal event.

The requirements of lawful excuse for the protection of property require that the defendants believe that the property was in need of immediate protection and that the force was reasonable. Assuming that the variegated past had not been engaged (or like *Hill and Hall*, the attempted justification had been exclusively predicated upon speculative futures), there would be nothing to substantiate that property in the Gaza Strip was in need of protection-and therefore for the jury to consider in its determination of responsibility. This may seem obvious, but it speaks to a broader question about what is effectively missed out in the court's rendering of the legal event more generally. In determining whether it was 'reasonable' would mean something completely different, had it only been considered within the confines of the narrow time-framed legal event. This would have only included the preceding agreements that constituted conspiracy and the destruction of the arms factory. 'Immediacy' and 'reasonableness' take on new *sense* – or are given new factual content – when situated within the context of the variegated past. To smash up an arms factory that results in £180,000+ worth of damage for the sake of it (which would have been the case had the variegated past not been engaged) or centred exclusively on a forecast with no allusions to any types of past (as was the case in *Hill and Hall*) would seem unreasonable. However, within the context of the military attacks by the Israeli Defence Forces in Gaza, the purported criminal act is interpreted differently. In constructing this enriched legal event, it is not enough to direct the jury to the conspiracy. The context of the war in Gaza is a necessary component of that retrospective narrative, one that incorporates the variegated pasts and revealed to the jury that which changed their ascription of responsibility. Indeed, even *immediacy* takes on a radically different meaning when situated with the variegated past. It is not understood in the narrow time frame sense but as a response to a pre-existing threat emergent in the sedimented past. It also reifies the causal relation between the damage and the harm it sought to prevent, because it is anchored in a determinable past (rather than an exclusively speculative, non-actualised future as in *Hill and Hall*). The judge engaged this past and thought it necessary, in an effort to solve the Problem stated, to direct the jury accordingly.

Accordingly, the courts in *Saibene* produced an untimely future, one which diverged from the lineal teleology of a knowable outcome which would have been the case had the spatial pasts been adopted. In this, one observes the possibility of the lower courts exercising a transformative role through facilitating collective and militant direct action. It seems to challenge the reproduction of social harms and international crimes through the possibility of radical reform enacted by disrupting supply chains – and one which the courts can facilitate.

Saibene, therefore, is a decision that tends towards CLJ, capturing the central features of *durée* and effective history, an interpenetrative past and present, an accumulating past, a time that is qualitative and ontological. It disrupts the 'chronologisation of the past' (the process of distinguishing, selecting and placing adjacent to one another, states into a sequence that are presumed to be causally related) and instead tries to gather, to use Bathurst-Norman's J words, a 'broad picture' of what happened. The enrichment of the legal event, locating the legal subjects within these variegated pasts, pushes the judge and jury to observe whether their normative assessment of legal responsibility alters. It is for these reasons – the productive work of the adjudicative temporality of CLJ – that the defence was successful (Table 5.2).

Table 5.2 Comparing Lawful Excuse on ALJ and CLJ

	R v. Hill and Hall	*R v. Saibene et al.*
Rule	Defence of lawful excuse	Defence of lawful excuse
Problem	No problem stated	International crime prevention (and thus protection of property in the Gaza strip)
Primacy of Encounter	✗	✓
Pasts	Spatial past	Variegated past, specifically the sedimented past
Outcome	Unsuccessful	Successful
Type of Adjudication	ALJ	CLJ

Conclusion

It is important to understand the way in which legal decisions that tend towards CLJ proceed. Such an adjudicative procedure is characterised by a multi-faceted and coterminous relationship between the Problem, the primacy of the Encounter, temporalities and legal form. In other words, they do not proceed in a linear and chronological fashion – in which one follows the other; rather, this chapter has attempted to illustrate how these processes occur contemporaneously. For example, the primacy of the Encounter requires recognition that variegated pasts exist which concurrently recognises the form of the legal rule as senseless. This is an important point as it explains, in part, the obfuscation and undertheorisation of law and time and partly why few references are made to temporality. Further, it explains how the component parts of subject and event formation (the variegated pasts, etc.) are framed as the outcome of temporalities. One observes, therefore, continuities in what Kelman refers to as the unconscious interpretive constructs.

The creative readings of the cases in the lower courts have arguably been adventurous in their interpretive takes. The central claim is that subject and event formation in legal judgement are conditioned by juridically produced temporalities. If that is accepted, other constructions of the legal subject and event require examining what adjudicative temporalities produce them. This chapter observes resonances with other subject formations in the works of Gadamer, Bergson and Grosz (who draws much on the work of Bergson).

Emergent in the variegated pasts are *potentially* exculpatory claims. Theories of causation in criminal law tend to reject, for example, socio-economic background, which partly connects with some elements of the variegated past, as exculpatory. CLJ attempts to illustrate how such elisions are possible and what is 'lost' in those elisions. Indeed, those elisions, a temporal construction, are what produce the agential, liberal legal subject, presumed in criminal law. Relatedly, these elisions show how adjudication can acquiesce in the social reproduction of structures of violence or oppression through their very elision in its rendering of the legal event and subject formation. Adjudication chooses to accept these 'normalised conditions', as Norrie refers to them, by their very elision in event formation. Finally, while this chapter may not convince many about the merits of CLJ, it will hopefully unravel how these questions around fact construction are questions of time, specifically legal time, and how power in the rendering of subject and event formation is enacted through temporal governance.

Notes

1 William Lucy, 'Abstraction and Equality' (2006) 62,1 Current Legal Problems 23.
2 William Lucy, 'Abstraction and Equality' (2006) 62,1 Current Legal Problems 22.
3 William Lucy, *Law's Judgement* (Bloomsbury Press 2017) 7.
4 [1993] 96 Cr. App. R. 31.
5 This has since been amended by the Coroners and Justice Act 2009 and will be dealt with below. As a general rule, the courts have said that most of the case law relating to the old provocation defence is to be disregarded.
6 *R v Duffy* [1949] 1 AER 932.
7 *R v Duffy* [1949] 1 AER 932.
8 *R v. Ahluwalia* [1993] 96 Cr. App. R. 31 [138].
9 [1992] 1 ALL E.R. 306.
10 This is important for the reason that even a defence which appears on the face to adopt narrow time frames ('sudden and temporary loss of self-control') can be tailored (i.e. as a standard rather than a sensed rule) in such a way as to produce a broader event, for example, the 'slow-burn' approach. This was demonstrated in the Court of Appeal case *R v. Baillie (John Dickie)* [1995] 2 Cr. App. R. 31, where the trial judge was criticised for taking too austere an approach to the 'sudden and temporary loss of control' limb.
11 *R v. Baillie (John Dickie)* [1995] 2 Cr. App. R.
12 *R v. Baillie (John Dickie)* [1995] 2 Cr. App. R [37].
13 *R v. Baillie (John Dickie)* [1995] 2 Cr. App. R. 31.
14 The tension (indeterminacy) between the 'cooling off' and 'slow-burn' approaches was mentioned as a problem in the Law Commission's consultation paper of reforming provocation. See also 'Murder, Manslaughter, and Infanticide; Proposals for Reform of the Law' (2008) CP19/08 Ministry of Justice, 8 <http://webarchive.nationalarchives.gov.uk/20110218135832/http:/justice.gov.uk/consultations/docs/murder-manslaughter-infanticide-consultation.pdf>
15 Lindsay Farmer, 'Time and Space in Criminal Law' (2010) 13,2 New Criminal Law Review: An International and Interdisciplinary Journal 343.
16 As with the note above, the reasonable man could potentially be understood in a context which situates him, but in the current case, it fails to situate the 'reasonable man' due to the absence of the primacy of the Encounter.
17 Lord Taylor CJ did imply that if the right sort of evidence was brought before the trial judge, it may be considered as part of the characteristics of the reasonable person provided they were permanent. This, in effect, is a type of 'situated reasonable person' possible by constructing the legal subject *qua* reasonable

person with a variegated past rather than merely contained within the narrow time frame of the legal event. One problem perhaps is the requirement that the trait be permanent.

18 *R v. Ahluwalia* [1993] 96 Cr. App. R. 31 [141].

19 Incidentally, an extract in a popular criminal law text book which looks at BWS cases says that 'such cases must be considered in the light of the social background and in particular the problem of domestic violence'. This appears to state both the Problem and engages the variegated past. See also Jonathan Herring, *Criminal Law: Text, Cases, and Materials* (OUP 2014) 308.

20 *R v. Hill* [2008] EWCA Crim 2.

21 Which may be admitted pursuant to s.23 *Criminal Appeal Act 1968*.

22 *R v. Hill* [2008] EWCA Crim 2 [13].

23 *R v. Hill* [2008] EWCA Crim 2 [21].

24 *R v. Baillie (John Dickie)* [1995] 2 Cr. App. R.

25 For a further critique of the case, see also Rohit Sanghvi and Donald Nicolson, 'Battered Women and Provocation: The Implications of R v. Ahluwalia' (1993) Criminal Law Review 728.

26 The general limitations of *Ahluwalia* ruling pertain to trumping analytical convenience over concreteness, the former of which is concomitant with spatial temporality. However, the more specific injustices of this case appear to be that, though we are aware of the history of domestic abuse that the appellant faced, the now old law tactlessly ignored it; this is the principle limitation of a decision that tends towards ALJ and its sensed use of the old provocation defence.

The law of provocation has since been replaced by the Loss of Self-Control defence that sought to, it appears, respond to the problems of the 'cooling off period' that previously undermined the defence in many domestic violence cases (See also 'Murder, Manslaughter, and Infanticide; proposals for reform of the law' (2008) CP19/08 Ministry of Justice, 8) whilst also ameliorating 'crimes of passion' (s.55(6)(c); though sexual infidelity is generally proscribed, for various reasons the courts have hesitated to read it literally as it often may provide the context in which the qualifying trigger makes sense under the provisions of ss. 55(3) and (4). See also *R v Clinton* [2012] EWCA Crim 2 [61]; Jonathan Herring, *Criminal Law: Text, Cases, and Materials* (OUP 2014) 248–249) (predominately by male defendants) and maintaining the proscription on revenge killings (*R v. Ibrams & Gregory* (1982) 74 Cr. App. R. 15). In addition, it sought to limit the range of provocative acts that were justifiable for killing.

Under the latest legislative changes, s.54(1) stipulates that a person who kills or is party to a killing will instead be convicted of manslaughter where (a) loss of self-control exists; (b) that loss of self-control had a qualifying trigger; and (c) a person of the defendant's sex and age with a normal degree of tolerance and self-restraint, and in the circumstances of the defendant might have reacted in the same way to them (Section 54(5) says that if 'sufficient evidence' is adduced, the jury must assume that the defence has been successfully satisfied unless the prosecution proves otherwise beyond reasonable doubt.)

Part (a) Loss of self-control requires (perhaps surprisingly) that the defendant has the *mens rea* of at least grievous bodily harm. Therefore, it involves the combination of a defendant who knows what they are doing but with severely impaired powers that would otherwise stop themselves. The loss of self-control requirement need not be 'sudden and temporary' (the courts have sometimes referred to 'cumulative provocation/impact', as in the case of *R v. Dawes*, which also can relate not just to the lapse of time but to the circumstances of the qualifying trigger in assessing whether a person of a normal degree of tolerance and self-restraint would have done what the defendant had) as per *R v. Duffy*. Indeed, this was outlined by Lord Judge CJ when he said 'provided there was a loss of control, it does not matter whether the loss was sudden or not. A reaction to circumstances of extreme gravity may be delayed' (*R v. Dawes* [2013] EWCA Crim 322). Thus, broader time frames appear to be enabled, albeit within the spatial past.

Part (b) Qualifying trigger is detailed in s.55(3) and (4). It may occur where the defendant's loss of self-control is attributable to his *fear of violence* from his victim against him or another identified person, *or* where the qualifying trigger is a thing said or done (or both) which constitutes circumstances of an extremely grave character *and* causes the defendant to have a justifiable sense of being seriously wronged (both decided objectively by the courts). The statute is not clear as to what constitutes circumstances of such a grave character, though small day-to-day mishaps (or even the ending of a relationship) cannot be seen as satisfying such requirements.

Part (c) sets out the requirements for a normal degree of self-restraint and tolerance to be decided by the jury, and this limb aims to counter the problem of defendants who had low tolerance thresholds but could previously rely upon the old defence. For example, if a defendant was racist and had received news that their child was marrying someone who was Bangladeshi, it could not be said that they were seriously wronged under the new law nor would 'normally tolerable people' kill in such an instance. The reference to *self-restraint* is an expectation that people ought to demonstrate control in the face of insults, jibes or other provocations (save for these exceptions) (Note that the defence only requires that they show that a person of a normal degree of tolerance and self-restraint *might* have reacted in the manner they did and if they are uncertain, the defence should be admitted). It also focusses on the characteristics of the defendant's age and sex as potentially mitigating. Thus, these characteristics will change the expectation of self-restraint and tolerance among men and women, adults and children. Section 54(3) also states that '"the circumstances of D[defendant]" is a reference to all of D's circumstances other than those whose only relevance to D's conduct is that they bear on D's general capacity for tolerance or self-restraint'. Though this appears to be a strict test that focusses on behaviour, (1)(c) and (3) allow for a level of context. For example, determining whether a person of a normal degree of tolerance and self-restraint will respond to a qualifying trigger *could be* contingent on whether that qualifying trigger brought back painful memories of a troubling past, as was entertained in the case in *R v. Hill.*

There have been no analogous cases to *Ahluwalia* that have tried to invoke the recent defence, so one can only speculate, based on the application of its various limbs in other non-analogous cases, whether it may overcome the limitations of the old provocation defence when decided in a manner of adjudication as cognition. There seems to be a suggestion that the 'boiling over' principle has been accommodated into the law and was re-enforced by Lord Judge CJ in *R v. Dawes* [2013] WLR(D) 130. Ahluwalia would certainly have been able to demonstrate that she was facing circumstances of a grave character, a justifiable sense of being seriously wronged and clearly she had a fear of serious violence from her husband. Therefore, establishing the presence of a qualifying trigger would not have been an issue. The difficulty arises in establishing whether she lost self-control, as it seems, in the *narrow time frame* presumed by s.54(1)(c) that she was acting calmly and deliberately. Would a person of her age, gender and circumstances *but* with a normal degree of tolerance and self-restraint have acted as she did? In other words, does s.54(1)(c) *contain* the appellant in the same manner that Lord Taylor did in discussing the reasonable limb in the provocation defence (despite discussing the history of violence *sans* the primacy of the Encounter)? Perhaps the *R v. Hill* case, had the evidence been admitted, *may* have been enlightening in this respect. However, though speculating, it seems as though Kiranjit Ahluwalia's defence under the new law would most likely have failed, and for these reasons, it appears to succumb to the problematic limitations of ignoring the history of violence to situate the appellant, and normalising ALJ as a conventional form of judgement. However, this is only speculation and there is nothing to preclude the possibility of such a case tending towards CLJ, which afforded primacy of the Encounter, changing the form of the new rule to engage the variegated pasts.

27 This is not to suggest that a literal reading be adopted as a methodological approach.

28 *R v. Ahluwalia* [1993] 96 Cr. App. R. 31 [135].

29 Alexandre Lefebvre, *The Image of Law: Deleuze, Bergson, Spinoza* (Stanford University Press 2008) 102.

30 James Boyle, 'Is Subjectivity Possible? The Postmodern Subject in Legal Theory' (1991) 62 University of Colorado Review 522.

31 *R v. Ahluwalia* [1993] 96 Cr. App. R. 31.

32 *R v. Baillie (John Dickie)* [1995] 2 Cr. App. R.

33 Henry David Thoreau, *Resistance to Civil Government* (YogeBooks 2008).

34 Matthew Weaver and Jamie Grierson, 'Black Lives Matter Stop Flights at London City Airport', *The Guardian* 6th September 2016 <https://www.theguardian.com/uk-news/2016/sep/06/black-lives-matter-protesters-occupy-london-city-airport-runway> accessed 10 September 2017.

35 Bruno Rinvolucri, Irene Baqué, Christopher Cherry, Adam Sich and Katie Lamborn, "We Can't Get Arrested Quick Enough': Life inside Extinction Rebellion', *The Guardian* 22nd November 2018 <https://www.theguardian.com/world/video/2018/nov/22/we-cant-get-arrested-quick-enough-life-inside-extinction-rebellion-video?CMP=share_btn_tw> accessed 20th November 2018.

36 Johan Galtung, 'Violence, Peace, and Peace Research' (1969) 6,3 Journal of Peace Research 167–191.

37 Iris Marion Young, 'Five Theses of Oppression' in Lisa Heldke and Peg O'Connor (eds), *Oppression, Privilege, & Resistance* (McGraw Hill Humanities 2004) 37–63.

38 Howard Zinn, Disobedience and Democracy: Nine Fallacies on Law and Order (South End Press edition 2002) 39–41.

39 *R v. Jones* (Margaret) [2006] UKHL 16.

40 A Jury may acquit 'according to conscience'- Bushell Case (1670) 124 E.R. 1006.

41 Luke de Noronha and Tanzil Chowdhury, 'The Stanstead 15 and the Terror of Law', *Verso Blog* 12 December 2018 <https://www.versobooks.com/blogs/4171-the-stansted-15-and-the-terror-of-law> accessed 13 December 2018.

42 BBC News 'Heathrow Protestors Arrested after Block Tunnel', *BBC News* 26 November 2015 <https://www.bbc.co.uk/news/uk-england-london-34930769> accessed 27 November 2015.

43 Tom Wainwright et al., *The Protest Handbook* (Bloomsbury Professional 2012) 114–115.

44 Richardson v. DPP [2012] UKSC 8.

45 See also Richard Harvey, 'Climate Change in the Courtroom' (2010) 54, Socialist Lawyer 20–25.

46 [2008] NICA 52.

47 *R v. Saibene and* other (Crown Court 2011) This is an unreported case however, the analysis is based upon a full summing-up 'Judge Bathurst-Norman: The Full Summing Up' (*The Jewish Chronicle*, 15 July 2010) <https://www.thejc.com/judge-bathurst-norman-the-full-summing-up-1.16888> accessed 9th January 2015.
48 *R v. Hill and Hall* (1989) 89 Cr App Rep 74.
49 'A person who has anything in his custody or under his control intending without lawful excuse to use it or cause or permit another to use it... (a)to destroy or damage any property belonging to some other person... shall be guilty of an offence.'
50 '(2)A person charged with an offence to which this section applies, shall, whether or not he would be treated for the purposes of this Act as having a lawful excuse apart from this sub-section, be treated for those purposes as having a lawful excuse:

> (a)if at the time of the act or acts alleged to constitute the offence he believed that the person or persons whom he believed to be entitled to consent to the destruction of or damage to the property in question had so consented, or would have so consented to it if he or they had known of the destruction or damage and its circumstances; or
>
> (b)if he destroyed or damaged or threatened to destroy or damage the property in question or, in the case of a charge of an offence under section 3 above, intended to use or cause or permit the use of something to destroy or damage it, in order to protect property belonging to himself or another or a right or interest in property which was or which he believed to be vested in himself or another, and at the time of the act or acts alleged to constitute the offence he believed—
>
> (i)that the property, right or interest was in immediate need of protection; and
>
> (ii)that the means of protection adopted or proposed to be adopted were or would be reasonable having regard to all the circumstances.
>
> (3)For the purposes of this section it is immaterial whether a belief is justified or not if it is honestly held.

51 This is one of two ways to establish lawful excuse, with the other being consent.
52 [emphasis added].
53 *R v. Hill and Hall* (1989) 89 Cr App Rep 74 [76].
54 *R v. Hunt* [1987] AC 352.
55 *R v. Hunt* [1987] AC 352 [77]. The appellate court agreed with the decision in the case of *Ashford & Smith* (unreported) – which followed the court in *Hunt* (1978) in which the appellant set fire to a guest room in an old people's home to draw attention to the defective fire alarm system – that the first limb of s.5(2)(b) of the defendant's belief was a subjective test and that the second limb (despite contestations from the advocate) of determining the causal relation and immediacy of the speculative act was an objective test.
56 *R v. Hill and Hall* (1989) 89 Cr App Rep 74.
57 *R v. Hill and Hall* (1989) 89 Cr App Rep 74.
58 *R v. Hill and Hall* (1989) 89 Cr App Rep 74.
59 Interestingly, in the unreported case of 'The Kingsnorth 6' which successfully invoked the lawful excuse defence, expert advice testified that there was an immediate need to protect property endangered by rising sea levels rather than a speculative future threat; see also Richard Harvey, 'Climate Change in the Courtroom' (2010) 54 Socialist Lawyer 20–25.
60 *Bolton v. Stone* [1951] A.C. 850.

61 *Bolton v. Stone* [1951] A.C. 850 [862].
62 *Bolton v. Stone* [1951] A.C. 850 [863].
63 *Bolton v. Stone* [1951] A.C. 850 [864].
64 The difference between the spatial past and the variegated past is not analogous to objective and subjective. The Spatial past allows for arbitrariness in delineating legal events, as has been outlined elsewhere, and the variegated pasts posit that the natural persons are both constituted and constituting, and thus adjudicative analysis should encapsulate this (rather than the idea of radical subjectivity).
65 Lindsay Farmer, 'Time and Space in Criminal Law' (2010) 13,2 New Criminal Law Review: An International and Interdisciplinary Journal 343.
66 Interestingly, in the unreported case of 'The Kingsnorth 6' which successfully invoked the lawful excuse defence, expert advice testified that there was an immediate need to protect property endangered by rising sea levels rather than a speculative future threat; see also Richard Harvey, 'Climate Change in the Courtroom' (2010) 54 Socialist Lawyer 20–25.
67 The case was unreported and so the analysis is based on the judge's full summing-up; 'Judge Bathurst-Norman: The Full Summing Up' (*The Jewish Chronicle*, 15 July 2010) <https://www.thejc.com/judge-bathurst-norman-the-full-summing-up-1.16888> accessed 9th January 2015. After having contacted the Lewes Crown court, a full transcript was estimated at around £40,000. The full summing-up judgement however adequately outlines the law and facts.
68 Adam Wagner '"Hell on Earth" Gaza acquittal a Miscarriage of Justice?' (*UK Human Rights Blog*, 6 August 2010) <http://ukhumanrightsblog.com/2010/07/16/hell-on-earth-gaza-acquittal-a-miscarriges-of-justice/) accessed 21 September 2011; Joshua Rozenberg, 'No Hell on Earth for Bathurst Norman' (*Standpoint Blogs*, 6 August 201) <http://www.standpointmag.co.uk/node/3273> accessed 21 September 2011.
69 The case was unreported and so the analysis is based on the judge's full summing-up; 'Judge Bathurst-Norman: The Full Summing Up' (*The Jewish Chronicle*, 15 July 2010) <https://www.thejc.com/judge-bathurst-norman-the-full-summing-up-1.16888> accessed 9 January 2015. After having contacted the Lewes Crown court, a full transcript was estimated at around £40,000. The full summing-up judgement however adequately outlines the law and facts.
70 Christopher Osmond and Simon Levin were also among the defendants but did not enter the premises. Instead, they acted as watch posts.
71 This was described by local Green MP, Caroline Lucas as a form of 'non-violent direct action'. See also Bibi van der Zee and Rob Evans, 'Jury Clears Activists Who Broke into Brighton Arms Factory', *The Guardian* 30th <https://www.theguardian.com/world/2010/jun/30/activists-arms-factory-acquitted> accessed 17 May 2018.
72 B'Tselem, 'Fatalities during Operation Cast Lead' <https://www.btselem.org/statistics/fatalities/during-cast-lead/by-date-of-event>; The Palestinian Centre for Human Rights puts the figure slightly higher. See also Press Release: Confirmed figures reveal the true extent of the destruction inflicted upon the Gaza Strip; Israel's offensive resulted in 1,417 dead, including 926 civilians, 255 police officers, and 236 fighters', 12 March 2009 <https://web.archive.org/web/20090612193512/http://www.pchrgaza.org/files/PressR/English/2008/36-2009.html> accessed 10 January 2010.
73 Alexandre Lefebvre, *The Image of Law: Deleuze, Bergson, Spinoza* (Stanford University Press 2008) 237.
74 Alexandre Lefebvre, *The Image of Law: Deleuze, Bergson, Spinoza* (Stanford University Press 2008) 216.

75 *R v. Saibene and* other (Crown Court 2011) This is an unreported case however, the analysis is based upon a full summing-up 'Judge Bathurst-Norman: The Full Summing Up' (*The Jewish Chronicle*, 15 July 2010) <https://www.thejc.com/judge-bathurst-norman-the-full-summing-up-1.16888> accessed 9th January 2015; Grander claims citing threats to political virtues were also expressed that

> democracy would not exist unless there were reporters and members of the public who were prepared to stand up for what they believed to be right, and sometimes, as in the case of the suffragettes, even to go to prison for their beliefs.

76 ibid 9.
77 Susan Marks, 'Human Rights and Root Causes' (2011) 74,1 Modern Law Review 72.
78 *R.v. Saibene and* other (Crown Court 2011) This is an unreported case however, the analysis is based upon a full summing-up 'Judge Bathurst-Norman: The Full Summing Up' (*The Jewish Chronicle*, 15 July 2010) <https://www.thejc.com/judge-bathurst-norman-the-full-summing-up-1.16888> accessed 9th January 2015.

Concluding remarks

Adjudication can be thought of as the point at which the task of reconstructing the past and imagining the future converge – what we might call 'the present'. The task of this book has been to reflect on how adjudication attempts to determine the past and imagine the future, how they are produced and what, if anything, they may tell us about the transformative potential of legal praxis.

In explaining 'how past and futures are produced', the book of course first has to commit the sin of 'anti-modernity'. That is, not only (if at all) does the law exist *in* (Platonic) *time*, but that law *produces* time. Such is the foundational claim of the nascent 'temporal turn' in socio-legal studies, legal anthropology and jurisprudence. After this, the book sets sail from two departure points. The first, drawing on legal realist and critical legal studies insights, has sought to reject an overly rule-centric correspondence theory of fact construction in adjudication, what has been referred to as the subsumption thesis elsewhere. Indeed, it was Lord Bingham who stated that 'in deciding facts, the judge knows no authority, no historical enquiry and (save on expert issues) no process of ratiocination will help him. He is dependant, for better or worse, on his own judgment'.[1] However, it would be credulous to dispose entirely of the legal rule and its role in fact determination. Clearly it has some bearing. All this book claims is that the form of legal rules is in fact contingent on adjudicative temporalities. The second of the departure points is from Nousiainen and Kelman's work that claims time frames determine fact construction. It is through this that the book begins to explore what underpins 'time framing' and whether alternative adjudicative temporalities are perhaps resistant to this dividing or chronologising of reality into fragmented temporal units. Finally, if adjudicative temporalities are multiple, then in the absence of some meta-criteria determining which is preferable, indeterminacy and 'law as politics' rear their heads. The politics of judgement thus becomes a question of time.

This leads us on to the 'what question' of the features and textures of those pasts and futures. ALJ and CLJ, productive of antonymous temporalities, produce different pasts and futures. In the former, one observes pasts which imbue features of space – divisible, uniform, juxtaposed and simultaneous – that lend themselves to chronologising. This is the process of distinguishing, selecting and placing adjacent to one another states into a sequence that are presumed to be causally related. This underwrites what Nousiainen and Kelman refer to as time framing. ALJ also produces knowable futures which follow the lineal teleology of certainty. The future is not perceived as unknown and thus as a horizon of possibility and change, but something that needs to be controlled and 'certain-ised'. CLJ, however, produces pasts that are variegated. The multiplicity of these pasts is persistent and ever present. The Enduring past signals a past which is ever accumulating and resistant to division. The Sedimented past is one of background conditions, overarching structures. The futures of CLJ are conversely 'untimely'. CLJ sees value not in certainty but in possibility, in change. It privileges not the present's hegemony over the future, but the dominance of a future in dictating the present.

Finally, it is in these untimely futures that we observe the possibility for radical social change. These pasts and futures are central to how adjudication structures its event and subject formation in legal judgement, which has a corollary effect on rights and responsibilities. ALJ claims that the construction of the deracinated liberal legal subject, what is typically understood as the reasonable man, is a temporal construction. CLJ argues that a contingent, constituted and situated legal subject reveals the complexity of this so-called fully agential subject of law. It is in CLJ – with its attendant construction of the variegated past – that one observes exculpatory possibilities. In ALJ, we observe the elision of those possibilities. Indeed, if the variegated pasts include structures of violence or oppression, we see ALJ reproducing those structures through its very ignorance of them. CLJ, *as a minimum*, hastens their visibility. We might liken the difference between ALJ and CLJ to what Robert Cox, in his reflections on theorising in international relations, as the difference between 'problem-solving' and 'critique'. Observing that 'theory is always for someone and for some purposes',[2] he writes how problem-solving theory 'takes the world as it finds it, with the prevailing social and power relationships and the institutions into which they are organised, as the given framework for action.'[3] ALJ's focus on the spatial past – and, by implication, its's elision of the sedimented past – is clearly an example of adjudication as problem solving 'which, intended or unintended, sustain the existing order'.[4] Contrastingly, Cox describes critique as 'directed towards an appraisal of the very framework for action… which problem-solving necessarily accepts as it parameters'.[5] CLJ, in its inclusion of the variegated past, meaningfully recognises these social structures and, through such inclusion, opens up the possibility or disrupting them rather than reproducing them. Indeed, CLJ as critique is 'a guide to strategic action for bringing about an alternative order'.[6]

Practicalities, determinism and the dissolution of responsibility

In *On the Uses and Disadvantages of History for Life,*[7] Nietzsche derides the 'idolatry of the factual', where, as Eric Posner writes, 'every event in history is seen as a link in an inexorable chain of causes and effects-a view that excludes the possibility of human freedom or creativity'.[8] Such an understanding renders a determinist view of history (and the future) in which all events seem to be causally related in hyperextended and filipendulous lines of connectivity, where inferences on the basis of proximity dissolve – anathema to modern criminal law doctrine. Indeed, it speaks to the merits of ALJ, which uses time frames (and a predilection towards narrow time frames) to prevent the absurdity of legal events beginning *ab aeterno.* One can read this along with Bergson in order to illustrate a potential tension of the book that contrasts with Bergson's theory of creativity and my interpretation of his work that recognises the *constraints* on agency. The brain and consciousness, according to Bergson, ought to invite separate intellectual treatment, observing the intrusion of science as relegating humans to the level of automatons, undermining the central axiom of his life's work which was creativity. *Durée* as the stream of consciousness, therefore, is a site of freedom. This seems to be at odds with the construction of a legal subject that is constituted by their pasts of whatever their shape. CLJ appears to use *durée*, along with Gadamer's effective history, to render a subject of law that is extant and indivisible from its socio-economic ecology, where the future is in fact limited by the over-bearing weight of the pasts' ability to direct the subject of law.

However CLJ, rather than trying to exploit Bergson's *durée,* in fact uses it to presage greater freedom through the transformation of that socio-economic milieu. *Durée* and effective history enable CLJ to visibilise that which is invisible and that which renders agency as circumstantial and contingent. It is in the process of visibilisation, this process of demystification, that CLJ uses these theories of time to potentially re-shape the organisation of society by recognising those limitations, by enabling law and adjudication to facilitate the ways in which subjects are trying to change it and the ways in which laws and legal systems may stymie that aim.

Whether we accept that response, there is another issue at hand: the spectre of nihilism and the dissolution of responsibility in criminal law doctrine. If the variegated pasts bring with them potentially exculpatory value, is their necessary incorporation or meaningful recognition the death knell of criminal responsibility? This is felt more acutely when we think of serious crimes, by either the state as well as individuals. A good example that ought to invite reflection upon the merits of CLJ is the case of *R v. A (No 2),*[9] in which a defendant charged with rape argued on human rights grounds that the complainant had to divulge her sexual history to the court, something which was no longer generally required under s.41 *Youth Criminal Justice and Evidence Act 1999*. Ignoring for the moment the volumes of literature that convincingly undermine any inference between consent and sexual history, would the engagement of the variegated past or the adoption of a broader time frame have included this into the construction of the legal event (as the House of Lords decided)? These issues acutely bring home the difficulties latent in CLJ.

An important qualifier, however, is that these variegated pasts (and broader time frames) are *potentially* exculpatory. CLJ does not seek to dissolve the doctrine of responsibility but merely to illuminate the presumptions upon which *conventional* doctrines of responsibility are predicated and to explain how this presumption is one which is a juridico-temporal formation. The responsible legal subject – the liberal legal subject – is a temporal construction which necessarily elides its contingency and construction by wider social forces. It can also unearth other potential exculpatory conditions not recognised by law, which could have certain normative weight but which are only otherwise emergent in these pasts produced CLJ. William Lucy puts this as follows.

> Almost as trite is the observation that some things the law's 'progress' from barbarism is marked by greater permissiveness and flexibility in its recognition of excusing conditions. The salient point, for current purposes, is that far fewer exculpatory claims are currently legally recognised than would be if the defendants were judged by reference to all the detail of their context and particular attributes. If each defendant's conduct was judged not just against the law's general standards, but also fine-grained assessment of her particular capacities on this particular occasion, in these precise circumstances, then the grounds for excusing her conduct would multiply.[10]

It must be forthrightly stated, however, that determinism is not the consequence of the variegated past given its potentially exculpatory qualities. Quite the opposite. It opens up the possibilities of new futures by making visible, in the construction of the legal event and legal subject, that which compromises the agency of the individual.

There are also other practical obstacles whose detailed rehearsal is not much needed as they are obvious. The complexity that bursts forth from CLJ is clear: one is of scale, and the other is of method. On *scale*, what do we actually include as part of the legal event and legal subject? Indeed, to the liberal legal imagination, there would be clear counter-intuitive opposition in including what Norrie refers to when discussing the Scarman report as 'poor social environment, racial discrimination, police harassment'[11] – let alone grander narratives, such as the modes of production and the attendant gendered structures of violence. These would be particularly at odds with our strong causally proximate intuitions, not because they are too remote but because they engage a qualitatively different type of past. The other issue is of *method.* How do we discern what is relevant? What can we say has an impact upon the responsibility (or lack thereof) of the legal subject? These questions may seem unintelligible, but it is not entirely alien to the roles of expert witnesses and assessors in trials, despite the limits of what they are invited to contribute to judicial proceedings, nor is the increasing use of social science research of the family courts, which provide the openings for this kind of analysis.[12] Indeed, the Kingsnorth 6 Case, referred to earlier, used experts to determine the legal claims of the defendants. And then there is also the problem of the workability of such judicial craft in jurisdictions that favour formalism over pragmatism. Clearly CLJ is an example requiring a radical form of judicial pragmatism. Finally, while CLJ may seem at times fantastical, the paucity of this kind of judgement should not be a deterrence. Indeed, 'there are also laws in most legal systems which attempt to take account of the context or character or particularity of a specific class of claimants or defendants, but these, too, are often regarded as exceptional, as concessions to equity or mercy or some allegedly non-legalistic virtue'.[13]

Despite these issues, it is important to remember that the variegated pasts always exists and because they exist, it requires a wilful effort in ALJ to ignore this. The aim of CLJ has been that, given this book's general rejection of a correspondence theory of adjudication, courts ought to acknowledge the *presence* of the variegated past. Whether that ought to impinge upon how courts direct juries, given the focus on criminal law, in responsibility attribution is another matter for the reasons stated above. A decision in which they do not meaningfully recognise these requires acknowledging another issue. If temporalities are responsible for fact construction in adjudication, and conventional types of legal judgement, such as ALJ, render legal events and subjects in a particular way, this means that the operation of conventional types of legal judgement *make a political decision to necessarily cut out certain facts for the purposes of analytical prudence and to prop up a very particular doctrine of responsibility.* If there is any contribution this book makes, it is this.

The absence of legal temporalities, modernity and CLJ as a site of radical social change

Part of the extirpation of times contingency is, in part, to do with Modernity. As Barbara Adam puts it, the consequence of modernity is that time and space are seen as objective and thus external to human experience, and as such, have come to be taken for granted.[14] Indeed, Modernity has been described not only as a 'chronologically distinct span of historical time, marked out by epochal changes in the structure of European societies'[15] but also as imbuing a kind of temporality of its own, 'in which time ticks away with perfect uniformity; in which space is devoid of gods, goddesses, and other nonhuman agents; and in which history unfolds with no help from providence, destiny, or apocalypse'.[16] Lindsay Farmer writes, 'we should note that the disappearance of concepts of time and space in the modern law...is only an instance of the more general disappearance of these concepts in modernity. There has been a move towards the general, the objective, and the context independent'.[17] We can therefore locate the general invisibalisation and undertheorisation of legal temporalities within the larger network of Modernity's attempts to, as Mawani refers to it as, exteriorise time. This exteriorisation of time, however, can obfuscate how the liberal legal subject, ahistoric, deracinated and a product of modernity,[18] is not created 'out of time' but is actively produced by it.

In some respects, even when it is recognised that law is not merely (if at all) in time but that time is in law, ALJ imbues the features of Modernity as temporality. The spatial pasts are like divisible, juxtaposable units of time. This is echoed by Manuel Castells that 'in the modern world in particular, time is conceived of in spatial terms: it is continuous and measurable, divided into spaces that can be filled, it can be vacant or unoccupied, and it is taken to imply limits or deadlines'.[19] Further, the futures follow the lineal teleology of predicable futures, much like the natural sciences. Indeed, 'Modernity, it is said, arose, first, as the temporality of modern science'.[20] This results in a process of abstraction, to the detriment of the concrete and singular, in which we may find the seeds for radical social transformation.

So what of CLJ as a form of transformative adjudication? Lindsay Farmer frames Kelman's 'arational' account of criminal law adjudication as 'processes of selecting from all potentially available facts, which excluded certain possible arguments and favoured a particular ideological view of the criminal law'.[21] The political implications of ALJ and CLJ, particularly in the absence of preference for either, are clear. To recall CLJ may be described as 'tempered not just with mercy but also by knowledge: not only of the conduct in question and its context, but knowledge of our character...in all our particularity...we are not strangers but intimates, with a history'.[22] What CLJ attempts to do is to explain how adjudicative temporalities incorporate 'context', 'particularity' and 'history' into the construction of the legal event and legal subject through its engagement of the variegated past, predicated upon Gadamerian and Bergsonian temporalities.

Socially constructed contexts necessarily precede any given individual and one is unavoidably situated in already existing social practices and conditions that form the grounds and horizons of our world. Adjudication therefore ought to incorporate or at least meaningfully acknowledge these grounds and horizons, especially as they may change the normative assessment of legal responsibility. CLJ hastens the asking of these very questions. By engaging the variegated past that is immediate, exists in its entirety and in which the legal subject is constituted, the court's job becomes not just weaving a tapestry of causal relations – to chronologise – but enriching that very tapestry with conditions to augment our legal prudence. This is where the transformative potential lies. CLJ begins with the exploration of social structures that prefigure the legal subject which are otherwise normalised (though their elisions and ignorance) in ALJ. Indeed, as Iris Marion Young writes, 'we cannot eliminate this structural oppression by getting rid of the rulers or making some new laws, because oppressions are systematically reproduced in major economic, political, and cultural institutions'.[23] The same can be said of ALJ, which knowingly or otherwise reproduces them. Do structures of violence explain the role of young Black men in the Brixton Riots and their (entirely legitimate) animosity toward the police, as Lord Scarman alluded? If so, ought that not to be incorporated into adjudication's articulation of the legal subject and event in any matter it adjudicates over such litigant?

The 'particularly' of the legal subject, the 'history' and the 'context' may be likened to Karin Van Marle's legal strategy of slowness and delay, which she describes as follows:

> With a material recollection goes a greater openness towards the particular and that this is necessarily associated with slowness- it takes more time to reflect on and be attentive to material circumstances than to merely follow or apply a rule, or consider and issues in a linear chronological, abstract and mostly predictable manner.[24]
>
> An attitude of slowness and attentiveness when approaching life and when interpreting and negotiating the past, present and future is open to the various traces that occur and reoccur...in following an approach of slowness to law and legal interpretation, an openness for traces and for other ways of remembering, imagining and justifying could come to the fore.[25]

It may seem obvious that making these kinds of complex determinations that CLJ would warrant (scale and method) would be slow, but this is not a moot point. Van Marle attributes this kind of strategy to a transformative type of legal judgement. Reflecting on different typologies of archaeological temporality, material time 'goes to a greater openness towards the particular and that this is necessarily associated with slowness – it takes more time to reflect on and be attentive to material circumstances that to merely follow or apply a rule, or consider an issue in a linear chronological, abstract and mostly predictable manner'.[26]

Young rightly critiques:

> The social ontology underlying many contemporary theories of justice is methodologically individualist or atomist. It presumes that the individual is ontologically prior to the social. This individualistic social ontology usually goes together with a normative conception of the self

> as independent. The authentic self is autonomous, unified, free, and self-made, standing apart from history and affiliations, choosing its life plan entirely for itself.[27]

In its rendering of the legal event and legal subject, this book has argued that these are all fundamentally questions of adjudicative temporality. CLJ recognises that the legal subject is one which constitutes and is constituted by is socio-economic ecology. This book has attempted to articulate how that might be represented (or not) in adjudication and how that claim is fundamentally a question of time. In addition, to conceptualise, to envisage the type of radically oriented adjudication that CLJ sets out, argues that untimely futures are crucial in visbilising certain types of past. This is reminiscent of Drucillia Cornell's paradox,[28] which is summed up well again by Van Marle: 'because we employ our past experiences when we imagine and our imagination when we remember, the paradox of imagining the past and remembering the future is created'.[29] Indeed, upon reflection- and contradicted the opening sentences of these concluding remarks- this is the paradox of all legal judgement. Rejecting an instrumentalist conception of law and rather a 'constitutive theory',[30] one may be able to imagine adjudication as a sight for radical, social transformation, predicated on a deeper, complex reading of legally produced variegated pasts which can open up all kinds of possibilities for a future that is not yet imagined.

Notes

1 Tom Bingham, *The Business of Judging: Selected Essays and Speeches* (OUP 2011) 3.
2 Robert Cox, 'Social Forces, States, and World Orders: Beyond International Relations Theory' (1986) 10 Millennium 128.
3 Robert Cox, 'Social Forces, States, and World Orders: Beyond International Relations Theory' (1986) 10 Millennium 128–130.
4 Robert Cox, 'Social Forces, States, and World Orders: Beyond International Relations Theory' (1986) 10 Millennium 128–130.
5 Robert Cox, 'Social Forces, States, and World Orders: Beyond International Relations Theory' (1986) 10 Millennium 128–130.
6 Robert Cox, 'Social Forces, States, and World Orders: Beyond International Relations Theory' (1986) 10 Millennium 128–130.
7 Friedrich Nietzsche, *On the Uses and Disadvantages of History for Life, in Friedrich Nietzsche, Untimely Meditations* (Hollingdale trs, CUP 1983) 57.
8 Eric Posner, 'Past-Dependency, Pragmatism, and Critique of History in Adjudication and Legal Scholarship' (2000) 7 University of Chicago Law Review 573.
9 [2001] UKHL 25; [2002] 1 AC 45.
10 William Lucy, *Law's Judgement* (Bloomsbury Press 2017) 7.
11 Alan Norrie, *Crime, Reason and History: A Critical Introduction to Criminal Law* (CUP 2011) 137–140.
12 Laura Robertson and Karen Broadhurst, 'Introducing Social Science Evidence in Family Court Decision-Making and Adjudication: Evidence from England and Wales' (2019) 33,2 International Journal of Law, Policy and the Family 181–203.

13 William Lucy, *Law's Judgement* (Bloomsbury Press 2017) 7.
14 Barbara Adam, *Time and Social Theory* (Polity Press 1990) 104–126.
15 Peter Osbone, *The Politics of Time: Modernity and the Avant-Garde* (Verso 1995) 1.
16 William Reddy, 'THE Eurasian Origins of Empty Time and Space: Modernity and Temporality Reconsidered' (2016) 55 History and Theory 325–356.
17 Lindsay Farmer, 'Time and Space in Criminal Law' (2010) 13,2 New Criminal Law Review: An International and Interdisciplinary Journal 342.
18 Chris Thornhill, 'Critical Theory and Legal Theory - A Genealogical Study' (2004) 15,1 King's Law Journal, Thornhill 24.
19 Manuel Castells, *The Information Age: Economy, Society and Culture: The Power of Identity* (Wiley & Sons 2011) 441.
20 William Reddy, 'THE Eurasian Origins of Empty Time and Space: Modernity and Temporality Reconsidered' (2016) 55 History and Theory 326.
21 Lindsay Farmer, 'Time and Space in Criminal Law' (2010) 13,2 New Criminal Law Review: An International and Interdisciplinary Journal 340.
22 William Lucy, 'Abstraction and Equality' (2009) 62,1 Current Legal Problems 22.
23 Iris Marion Young, 'Five Theses of Oppression' in Lisa Heldke and Peg O'Connor (eds), *Oppression, Privilege, & Resistance* (McGraw Hill Humanities) 37–63.
24 Karin Van Marle, 'Law's Time, Particularity and Slowness' (2003) 19 South African Journal on Human Rights 247.
25 Karin Van Marle, 'Law's Time, Particularity and Slowness' (2003) 19 South African Journal on Human Rights 255.
26 Karin Van Marle, 'Law's Time, Particularity and Slowness' (2003) 19 South African Journal on Human Rights 247.
27 Iris Marion Young, 'Five Theses of Oppression' in Lisa Heldke and Peg O'Connor (eds), *Oppression, Privilege, & Resistance* (McGraw Hill Humanities) 37–63.
28 Drucillia Cornell, *Transformations* (1993) 23–44.
29 Karin Van Marle, 'Law's Time, Particularity and Slowness' (2003) 19 South African Journal on Human Rights 241.
30 Karl Klare, 'Law-Making as Praxis' (1979) 40 Telos 123–135.

Index

Note: **Bold** page numbers refer to tables and page numbers followed by "n" denote endnotes.